JOURNAL FOR THE STUDY OF THE OLD TESTAMENT SUPPLEMENT SERIES

64

Editors
David J A Clines
Philip R Davies

JSOT Press
Sheffield

TO SEE AND NOT PERCEIVE

Isaiah 6.9-10 in Early Jewish and Christian Interpretation

Craig A. Evans

Journal for the Study of the Old Testament
Supplement Series 64

For my wife Ginny
and daughters Carrie Lynn and Jill Anne

BS
1515.2
. E90
1989

Copyright © 1989 Sheffield Academic Press

Published by JSOT Press
JSOT Press is an imprint of
Sheffield Academic Press Ltd
The University of Sheffield
343 Fulwood Road
Sheffield S10 3BP
England

Typeset by Sheffield Academic Press
and
printed in Great Britain
by Billing & Sons Ltd
Worcester

British Library Cataloguing in Publication Data

Evans, Craig A.
    To see and not perceive : Isaiah 6. 9 - 10 in early
    Jewish and Christian interpretation.
    1. Bible. O.T. Isaiah - Expositions
    I. Title
    224'.106

ISBN 1-85075-172-2

KRAUSS LIBRARY
LUTHERAN SCHOOL OF THEOLOGY AT CHICAGO
1100 EAST 55th STREET
CHICAGO, ILLINOIS - 60615

CONTENTS

PREFACE

The present work represents a complete revision of the author's doctoral dissertation written under the direction of the late Professor William H. Brownlee of Claremont Graduate School. Although the problem of obduracy in the Old Testament has been addressed by Franz Hesse, *Das Verstockungsproblem im Alten Testament* (1955), and the problem of Isa. 6.9-10 in the Synoptic Gospels by Joachim Gnilka, *Die Verstockung Israels: Jesajas 6.9-10 in der Theologie der Synoptiker* (1961), there has been no study to date that systematically examines the history of interpretation of Isa. 6.9-10, probably the single most important obduracy text in the Bible, from its origin to its later interpretation in the post-biblical period. Because of the provocative nature of this text, its presence in both Testaments, its differing interpretation and application among Jews and Christians, and its possible significance for understanding the hermeneutics of monotheism, such a study is called for. It is the author's hope that this work will provide some answers and at the same time raise new questions that will lead to further progress in this area of inquiry.

I wish to express my thanks to the faculties of Claremont Graduate School and the School of Theology at Claremont. Among these good people I wish especially to thank Professor James A. Sanders who, although not my advisor, read several drafts of this study and provided encouragement, inspiration, and invaluable advice. A word of thanks is also due Richard A. Wiebe, Reference Librarian at Trinity Western University, for preparing the indices to this volume. Finally, I wish to record my deepest appreciation to my wife and daughters who with patience and good humour tolerated the long hours and inconvenience required in preparing this book.

Craig A. Evans
Trinity Western University
Langley, British Columbia
Canada

Spring 1988

ABBREVIATIONS

AB	Anchor Bible
AJSL	*American Journal of Semitic Languages and Literature*
AnBib	Analecta Biblica
ANET	*Ancient Near Eastern Texts*, edited by J.B. Pritchard
ASTI	*Annual of the Swedish Theological Institute*
ATD	Das Alte Testament Deutsch
AUM	Andrews University Monographs
AUSS	*Andrews University Seminary Studies*
BASOR	*Bulletin of the American Schools of Oriental Research*
BBB	Bonner biblische Beiträge
BDB	*Hebrew and English Lexicon of the Old Testament*, edited by F. Brown, S.R. Driver, and C.A. Briggs
BeO	*Bibbia e oriente*
BETL	Bibliotheca ephemeridum theologicarum lovaniensium
BH	*Biblia Hebraica*, edited by R. Kittel
Bib	*Biblica*
BKAT	Biblischer Kommentar: Altes Testament
BM	*Beth Miqra* (בת מקרא)
BT	*The Bible Translator*
BTB	*Biblical Theology Bulletin*
BZ	*Biblische Zeitschrift*
BZAW	Beihefte zur *Zeitschrift für die alttestamentliche Wissenschaft*
CBQ	*Catholic Biblical Quarterly*
CBQMS	*Catholic Biblical Quarterly* Monograph Series
DBSup	*Dictionnaire de la Bible, Supplément*
EKKNT	Evangelisch-katholischer Kommentar zum Neuen Testament
EtB	Études Bibliques
EvT	*Evangelische Theologie*
ExpTim	*Expository Times*
FC	Fathers of the Church
GCS	Griechische christliche Schriftsteller

GNS	Good News Studies
GTS	Gettysburg Theological Studies
HBT	*Horizons in Biblical Theology*
HNTC	Harper New Testament Commentary
HTS	Harvard Theological Studies
HUCA	*Hebrew Union College Annual*
ICC	International Critical Commentary
IDB	*Interpreter's Dictionary of the Bible*
IDBSup	*Interpreter's Dictionary of the Bible, Supplement*
IEJ	*Israel Exploration Journal*
IJT	*Indian Journal of Theology*
Int	*Interpretation*
ISBE	*International Standard Bible Encyclopedia*, revised edition
JBL	*Journal of Biblical Literature*
JJS	*Journal of Jewish Studies*
JMUEOS	*Journal of the Manchester University Egyptian and Oriental Society*
JNES	*Journal of Near Eastern Studies*
JQR	*Jewish Quarterly Review*
JR	*Journal of Religion*
JSJ	*Journal for the Study of Judaism in the Persian, Hellenistic, and Roman Period*
JSNT	*Journal for the Study of the New Testament*
JSOT	*Journal for the Study of the Old Testament*
JSOTSup	*Journal for the Study of the Old Testament* Supplement Series
JSS	*Journal of Semitic Studies*
JTS	*Journal of Theological Studies*
LCL	Loeb Classical Library
LSJ	Liddell-Scott-Jones, *Greek-English Lexicon*
LXX	Septuagint
MT	Masoretic Text
NCB	New Century Bible Commentary
NEB	New English Bible
NHL	Nag Hammadi Library
NIC	New International Commentary
NIGTC	New International Greek Testament Commentary
NovT	*Novum Testamentum*

NovTSup	*Novum Testamentum* Supplements
NTS	*New Testament Studies*
Numen	*Numen: International Review for the History of Religions*
OTL	Old Testament Library
OTS	*Oudtestamentische Studien*
PTS	Patristische Texte und Studien
RB	*Revue biblique*
repr.	reprinted
RestQ	*Restoration Quarterly*
RevQ	*Revue de Qumran*
RGG	*Die Religion in Geschichte und Gegenwart*
RHPR	*Revue d'Histoire et de Philosophie religieuses*
RSV	Revised Standard Version
RTR	*Reformed Theological Review*
SANT	Studien zum Alten und Neuen Testament
SBL	Society of Biblical Literature
SBLDS	Society of Biblical Literature Dissertation Series
SBLMS	Society of Biblical Literature Monograph Series
SBT	Studies in Biblical Theology
ScEccl	*Sciences ecclésiastiques*
SFEG	Schriften der finnischen exegetischen Gesellschaft
SJT	*Scottish Journal of Theology*
SPB	Studia postbiblica
ST	*Studia Theologica*
Str-B	H. Strack and P. Billerbeck, *Kommentar zum Neuen Testament*
SWJT	*Southwest Journal of Theology*
TDNT	*Theological Dictionary of the New Testament*, edited by G. Kittel and G. Friedrich
THKNT	Theologischer Handkommentar zum Neuen Testament
TLZ	*Theologische Literaturzeitung*
TrinJ	*Trinity Journal*
TS	*Theological Studies*
TSJTSA	Theological Studies of the Jewish Theological Seminary of America
TU	Texte und Untersuchungen zur Geschichte der altchristlichen Literatur

TynBul	*Tyndale Bulletin*
TZ	*Theologische Zeitschrift*
UCOP	University of Cambridge Oriental Publications
USQR	*Union Seminary Quarterly Review*
UUÅ	Uppsala Universitets Årsskrift
VC	*Vigiliae Christianae*
VT	*Vetus Testamentum*
VTSup	Vetus Testamentum Supplements
WBC	Word Biblical Commentary
ZAW	*Zeitschrift für die alttestamentliche Wissenschaft*
ZNW	*Zeitschrift für die neutestamentliche Wissenschaft*
ZTK	*Zeitschrift für Theologie und Kirche*

INTRODUCTION

The Problem
In his vision of the enthroned and exalted Lord, one of the best
known passages of the Old Testament, Isaiah the prophet is told to
tell his people 'to see and not perceive', and thus harden their hearts,
'lest they repent' (Isa. 6.9-10). Most who read this passage are
perplexed. To be sure, we may have found the hardening of
Pharaoh's heart a trifle unfair, but there is something about
deliberately rendering the people of God obdurate that is particularly
disturbing. Then we turn to the New Testament and discover,
according to Mark's Gospel, that Jesus speaks parables for the same
reason: lest 'outsiders' repent and be forgiven. It all seems so strange
that it is no wonder that interpreters (ancient and modern) have from
time to time suggested that Isaiah, Jesus, or both have been
misquoted or misunderstood. The present work analyzes this
problematic text and the theology out of which it arises and to which
it contributes. However, the study is not limited to a particular point
in time, but rather it is concerned with the variety of interpretations
and applications to which this powerful text has given rise during the
period of time that saw the growth and recognition of that
compilation of writings we now call the Bible.

The Method
With the relatively recent recognition of midrashic interpretation in
early Jewish and Christian times,[1] there is increasing evidence, if the
burgeoning bibliography in this field tells us anything, that scholars
regard this new area of study (often called 'comparative midrash') as
highly profitable for exegesis of biblical literature.[2] Rather than being
limited by the traditional view that 'midrash' is a rabbinic literary
form (e.g., the midrashim, or 'commentaries' on portions of the
Bible), it has become widely recognized that midrash is an exegetical

method which was practiced in wider Jewish and primitive Christian circles.[3] Underlying midrash was the conviction that authoritative traditions (i.e., 'scripture' at either the canonical or pre-canonical stages) have enduring meaning for the community of faith and that these traditions address themselves to, and elucidate, the community's historical experience. Committed to this hermeneutic, the community searches (*darash*) the scriptures with the conviction that an interpretation (*midrash*) will be found that will give meaning to its experience. Because historical situations change and because scripture was more or less stabilized as sacred text, the challenge of the midrashist was to unpack from scripture meaning that was relevant to the needs of the contemporary community. Consequently, the basic purpose of midrash, as well as most methods of exegesis, was to update authoritative traditions or, as G. Vermes has put it, 'to fuse Scripture with life'.[4]

Another important and related factor is the new appreciation of haggadah, that is, that aspect of midrashic interpretation concerned with elucidating biblical contents not concerned with legal matters. Whereas halachic exegesis engaged in the effort to update the laws of Torah so that virtually every contingency in Jewish life might be met, haggadic exegesis was concerned to draw out theological significance from, and to explain difficulties in, the narrative portions of Torah, the Prophets, and the Writings. Haggadic exegesis is that area of midrash in which the community is able to find itself in scripture and to learn more about itself from scripture.[5] The community's experiences are found in scripture and, at the same time, scripture explains more fully to the community its experiences. It is this aspect of midrashic exegesis that appears so often in both Testaments and is of such great importance for biblical interpretation.

Since midrash is now being viewed more as method rather than genre (though the rabbinic *midrashim* certainly constitute a distinctive literary genre), new attention has been given to its appearance in the Old Testament as well as in the New Testament.[6] But of particular importance is the emergence of comparative midrash for New Testament study. Rather than only asking questions pertaining to the verbal accuracy of Old Testament quotations in the New Testament (questions often concerned with harmonization[7]), questions are raised pertaining to the resignification and applications of the text in question. Alterations in a given text do not always point to faulty memory or confusion between similar texts, though at times they may, but often they point to thoughtful and deliberate exegesis; and we should assume that this exegesis to a certain extent mirrors the experience of the community out of which it arose. The studies of Peder Borgen, Wayne Meeks, David Hay, Jane Schaberg, Klyne Snodgrass, and Mary Callaway are among the finest examples of this method of study.[8]

New Testament comparative midrash means looking beyond the appearance of formal quotations and verbal allusions[9] and looking for similar structure and theology, particularly for cases in which the New Testament writer has modeled larger portions of his writing after extended passages and particular themes found in the Old Testament.[10] Ultimately, the goal of comparative midrash is to discover how the older traditions have been interpreted and applied in the newer contexts.[11]

The Task
The present study is a study in comparative midrash. The focus will be upon a particular text (Isa. 6.9-10), and it will be studied in as many historical contexts, or stages,[12] as possible. Not only is such a study useful, in that it makes a contribution to our understanding of the variety of theological perspectives in early Jewish and Christian history, but it contributes to our understanding of canonical hermeneutics as well. However, in mentioning 'canon' I hasten to add that this study does not intend to enter the dialogue currently being developed by J.A. Sanders[13] and B.S. Childs,[14] among others,[15] although the study does reflect the methodology advocated by the former. It is out of a conviction that the canonical process itself is of much hermeneutical and historical value that this study is undertaken (though I am not sure that I can agree with Sanders that the very processs is itself 'canonical'[16]). Although it is a highly specialized study, its results have implications for this wider theological concern. Finally, this work hopes to shed some light on the meaning of an important text within its various New Testament contexts, an aspect which alone should justify it.

The procedure of the book is simple enough. The *terminus a quo* is the eighth-century prophet Isaiah who uttered the original words of Isa. 6.9-10. The *terminus ad quem* is the respective usages of this prophetic text in rabbinic and patristic literature. Isa. 6.9-10 is a text that is particularly suitable for a comparative study, for it has given various believing communities theological explanations of major significance in times of disaster, turmoil, rejection, and self-doubt.

This book is interested in a particular text and the hermeneutic to which it gives expression. But it is not intended to be a study of the motif of obduracy,[17] though Isa. 6.9-10 is certainly a major witness to that tradition. The prophetic motif of obduracy is but a manifestation of a more fundamental theological issue, that of affirming the sovereignty of God in the face of religious apostasy, political disaster, or rejection and ostracism. I am not primarily interested in either Isaiah the prophet or Isaiah the book. Rather, I am interested in the text of Isa. 6.9-10 because in a certain sense it epitomizes the struggle to monotheize, that is, to explain all of existence in terms of God and his sovereign will. I believe that Isa. 6.9-10 is perhaps one of the most important prophetic witnesses to the monotheistic hermeneutic, the hermeneutic that lies at the very heart of the canon.

Chapter 1

ISAIAH 6.9-10 IN THE CONTEXT OF ISAIAH

Introduction

Isa. 6.9-10 has an interesting history of textual transmission and interpretation. An analysis of this history will prove to be a major factor in the study of the function of Isa. 6.9-10 in Judaism and early Christianity. This chapter is primarily concerned with a meaning of this passage in Isaiah (the prophet and the book), although the text's relationship to the Old Testament in general will be taken into consideration. It is divided into four major parts: (A) the text of Isa. 6.9-10 in the MT; (B) Isa. 6.9-10 in the context of the prophet Isaiah; (C) Isa. 6.9-10 in the context of the book of Isaiah; and (D) Isa. 6.9-10 and related obduracy texts of the Old Testament.

A. *The Text of Isaiah 6.9-10 in the Masoretic Text*[1]

We begin with a grammatical analysis of the MT. For the moment it is assumed to be the original, although its pointing will become a matter of debate later in the study.[2] The text of the MT is as follows:

9	ויאמר לך ואמרת לעם הזה
	שמעו שמוע ואל־תבינו
	וראו ראו ואל־תדעו
10	השמן לב־העם הזה
	ואזניו הכבר
	ועיניו השע
	פן־יראה בעיניו
	ובאזניו ישמע
	ולבבו יבין
	ושב ורפא לו

9 And he said, 'Go, and say to this people:
"Hear and hear, but do not understand;[3]
See and see, but do not perceive".
10 Make the heart of this people fat,
and their[4] ears heavy,
and shut their eyes;
lest they[5] see with their eyes,
and hear with their ears,
and understand with their hearts,[6]
and turn and be healed'. (RSV)

There are several important grammatical, textual, and exegetical observations to be made. (1) The expression, 'this people' (in contrast to 'my people', cf. Isa. 40.1) connotes a sense of contempt.[7] This negative connotation is intrinsic to the entire passage, and is expressed elsewhere in Isaiah (8.6, 11-12; 28.14; 29.13).

(2) Both 'hear' and 'see' are imperatives followed by their respective infinitive absolute forms, a construction that usually connotes emphasis or continual action.[8] It has from time to time been suggested that the text is descriptive rather than imperatival.[9] This suggestion, however, is conjectural and sometimes assumes that the descriptive reading found in the Targum and much of the rabbinic literature reflects the original Hebrew text. If such a reading had been in the Hebrew (or at least understood to be the proper meaning of the consonantal text), it seems odd that later scribes would alter (or point) the text from descriptive to imperative. As will be shown below, the scribal tendency was the reverse. This type of saying may very well have been proverbial, as seen in Demosthenes, *Contra Aristogenes* 1: 'so that the proverb results, "Seeing they do not see, hearing they do not hear"'.[10] A similar proverb is found in Aeschelus, *Prometheus Bound* § 446: 'Seeing, they saw in vain; and hearing, they did not understand'.

(3) Both 'don't understand' and 'don't perceive' are in form qal imperfects and doubtlessly have imperatival force,[11] as the prohibitive particle אל would indicate. These verbs are meant to convey sarcasm and underscore the total refusal of the people to listen to the prophet's message.

(4) The verbs 'make fat' (or 'make dull'), 'make heavy', and 'smear over' are hiphil imperatives. To recognize the causative force of these hiphils is important for the interpretation of this passage.[12] It could

be argued that the passive voice of the verb that translates השמן in the LXX is a reflection of the presence of hophals in the Hebrew text rather than hiphils, as the Masoretes have pointed the radicals. In fact, A. Cohen has suggested that these three words may not be verbs at all, but 'adjectives describing the sick condition (in terms of physical defects) of the people'.[13] But again, as discussed with reference to v. 9 above, it is difficult to understand why scribes would have altered hophals or adjectives to hiphil imperatives. It is very probable that the hiphils represent the original meaning of the text.

(5) The verbs 'see', 'hear', and 'understand' are qal imperfects (third masculine singular, agreeing with the singular 'people' [עם], but in the RSV they are translated *ad sensum* as plurals). With the conjunctive lest (פן) they have the purposive meaning, 'so that they should not see',[14] etc.

(6) The subject of the clause, 'and be healed' (ורפא לו), is likely 'the people', the subject of the previous verbs (rather than God, i.e. 'God should heal them'). Therefore, it should be translated, 'and they [lit. 'it'] be healed'.[15]

In summary, it would seem that Isa. 6.9-10 means that it is God's intention to render his people obdurate through the proclamation of his prophet. The purpose of this obduracy, it would appear, is either to render judgment certain, as is implied in vv. 11-13, or perhaps to make it more fully deserved. It is possible that both ideas are in view. How such a message as vv. 9-10 should be understood in the context of Isaiah's theology is the question to which the discussion turns in the next section.

B. *Isaiah 6.9-10 in the Context of the Prophet Isaiah*

1. *Isaiah's Vision*

The prophet declares that he received his vision in the year that King Uzziah died, and that he saw the Lord enthroned and attended by the heavenly court (6.1-4). Isaiah's response was one of fear and recognition that he stands fully culpable before the holy God. He identified himself with his people of 'unclean lips' and was purified by the touch of a coal from the altar (6.5-7). Then a voice called out asking who is to be sent in behalf of the heavenly council, to which Isaiah responded: 'Here am I! Send me' (6.8).[16] It is at this point that the prophet received his fate-laden message: 'Go, and say to this people: "Hear and hear, but do not understand; see and see, but do not perceive". Make the heart of this people fat, and their ears heavy, and shut their eyes; lest they see with their eyes, and hear with their ears, and understand with their hearts, and turn and be healed' (6.9-10). Their fate has been sealed. There is no escape. Isaiah, no doubt out of concern for his countrymen, asked: 'How long, O Lord?' How long must Isaiah proclaim this harsh message and carry out the unhappy task of heightening the spiritual obduracy of God's people?[17] Yahweh's answer was that Isaiah was so to preach until total destruction and exile had taken place (6.11-13).

Some scholars, on literary grounds, have expressed doubt regarding the originality of the whole of vv. 12-13, since they appear to be out of harmony with the preceding text (vv. 1-11).[18] At the turn of the century K. Marti had regarded vv. 12-13 as clearly post-exilic in their setting[19] and more recently O. Kaiser and R. Knierim have observed that the shift from second person to third in vv. 11-12, the change of meter, and the different perspectives all indicate that these verses are secondary.[20] Nevertheless, many scholars see no compelling reason to doubt the authenticity of these verses.[21] In my judgment, the verses are probably not original to Isaiah 6, but do derive from the eighth-century prophet. Even if we should admit to doubt concerning vv. 11-13, it seems on the face of it quite likely that the message of vv. 9-10 anticipated the kind of judgment described in these verses, whenever and by whomever they were appended.

We are also confronted with a textual problem. The last clause of v. 13, 'a holy seed is its stump' (מצבתה זרע קדש), is not represented in the best Greek manuscripts.[22] It is possible that this clause was not present in the original Hebrew, for it is difficult to imagine why it would have been intentionally omitted.[23] However, its omission in the LXX may have been the result of homoiteleuton where, in this case, the scribe jumped from αὐτῆς of v. 13b to 7.1, skipping v. 13c which also ends in αὐτῆς.[24] The main reason, however, that might make one suspect that v. 13c is not original is that it brings into this negative passage a wholly unexpected positive element.[25] Verses 9-10 describe the message of obduracy, while vv. 11-12 describe destruction and exile that will result. Verse 13ab describes further tribulation for the remaining 'tenth',[26] which in itself points to the severity of the judgment, not to consolation.[27] Why in this context the prophet would describe this tenth, a burned 'stump' of a tree,[28] as a 'holy seed' is not easily answered, to say the least. (In 4.3 the survivors who remain in Jerusalem are called 'holy', but in that context the reference is neither unexpected nor out of place.) Thus, the clause could represent some development in remnant theology, in which the remnant is understood as the 'holy seed'.[29] However, even though v. 13c probably represents a later intrusion into the context of Isaiah 6, it may nevertheless derive from the eighth-century prophet.[30] Since the prophet Isaiah apparently anticipated the survival of a restored remnant, as will be argued below, there is nothing about v. 13c that is out of step with the theology of the prophet.

2. *The Perspective of the Call Narrative*

One of the most frequently debated points has to do with the prophet's personal perspective behind the words of ch. 6. Are these words to be taken at face value; that is, did the prophet actually understand that he was to render his people obdurate and impenitent? Although several interpreters have so concluded,[31] others believe that these are the words of later reflection, perhaps even of bitter disappointment after years of preaching to a people that consistently rejected the message.[32] Indeed, at least one interpreter, reacting to the offensiveness of the passage, has argued that Isaiah 6 was not originally addressed to Judah at all, but to the apostate Northern Kingdom.[33] It has even been suggested that ch. 6 was not written by Isaiah, but by a later tradent who was trying to explain the disaster of defeat and exile.[34]

Another point of debate, and one that is closely related to the question of the prophet's perspective, concerns form-critical and chronological issues. Does the vision of ch. 6 represent the prophet's inaugural call to the prophetic vocation, or is this vision something else? Until recently, interpreters have assumed that the vision of Isaiah 6 does constitute the inaugural call of the prophet, even if (re)written later in the prophet's ministry.[35] It is probably for this reason that many find it hard to take the chapter at face value, for it seems inconceivable that God's call of a prophet would consist chiefly and primarily of a message whose intended effect was the promotion of obduracy. It is not, of course, unusual that prophets sometimes are informed at the inauguration of their ministries that they will meet with stubborn resistance. In the case of Ezekiel, God warns the prophet that the people will not listen to him: 'The house of Israel will not listen to you; for they are not willing to listen to me; because all the house of Israel are of a hard forehead and of a stubborn heart' (3.7; cf. 12.2-3). But here there is no hint that the prophet's message in any way contributes to the obduracy of the people. The people are already obdurate.

However, the closest parallels to the Isaianic vision suggest that Isaiah's prophetic vocation at the time of his vision was already established.[36] Knierim and others cite 1 Kgs 22.19 and Amos 9.1, where the prophets Micaiah and Amos, already established in their prophetic vocations, have similar visions.[37] The significant parallels include the following: (1) The beginning statements of the accounts in Kings and Isaiah are nearly identical: 'I saw the Lord sitting on his throne' (1 Kgs 22.19); 'I saw the Lord sitting upon a throne' (Isa. 6.1). Amos is similar: 'I saw the Lord' (9.1). (2) The Lord is attended by heavenly hosts: 'all the host of heaven standing beside him' (1 Kgs 22.19); 'the Lord, God of hosts' (Amos 9.5); 'above him stood the seraphim' (Isa. 6.2) 'the Lord of hosts' (6.3, 5). In all three accounts, the heavenly council has convened. (3) The vision is in a temple: 'standing beside the altar' (Amos 9.1)); 'his train filled the temple' (Isa. 6.1); 'a burning coal . . . from the altar' (6.6). (4) God makes the 'thresholds' shake (Amos 9.1; Isa. 6.4). (5) The Lord asks 'who' will volunteer for service (1 Kgs 22.20; Isa. 6.8). (6) The volunteer is to blind the hearer to the truth. In the case of 1 Kings, Ahab is to be deceived into going into battle (1 Kgs 22.20), while in Isaiah, the prophet is to dull his hearers (Isa. 6.9-10), particularly King Ahaz (as seen in Isaiah 7). (7) The result of the heavenly council, and of the volunteer's commission, is disaster. It means death for Ahab (1 Kgs 22.20), destruction for the northern kingdom (Amos 9.1-6), and destruction for the southern kingdom (Isa. 6.11). In all three traditions, the heavenly council appears to be a council of judgment.

These parallels, as well as the language of Isaiah 6 itself, suggest that Isaiah's was a vision and commission of judgment and not simply a call to the prophetic vocation.[38] If this is the case, then the objection against the view that God would call a prophet to a general ministry of obduracy is in part answered. Isaiah was not called to a ministry of promoting obduracy, but was called to a ministry that approximates the ministries of the other classic prophets. To view the vision and commission of ch. 6 as representative of Isaiah's entire ministry distorts the prophet's total message. Isaiah's total message simply does not reduce to obduracy and doom, for elsewhere the prophet preaches repentance: In 1.16-20, parts of which probably derive from the eighth-century prophet, the people are enjoined to wash themselves, learn to do good, to reason with God, and to be obedient. Despite the blows delivered against them (as described, for example, in 9.8-12) 'the people did not turn to him who smote them, nor seek the Lord of hosts' (9.13 [Heb. v. 12]). The passage implies that repentance was expected, at least in theory. In 30.15 opportunity for repentance and salvation are offered explicitly: 'in returning [i.e. repenting] and rest you shall be saved; in quietness and in trust shall be your strength'. 28.16b also implies that some will have faith: 'He who believes will not be in haste'. Perhaps the best example is found in 31.6: 'Turn to him from whom you have deeply revolted, O people of Israel'.[39] And, of course, the prophet expects his disciples to remain faithful to his vision and preaching (8.16-20). Furthermore, as will be argued below, Isaiah anticipates the emergence of a purified remnant, one that will read his testimony (30.8). Therefore, since in all probability Isaiah 6 does not represent the prophet's inaugural call, and so does not summarize the whole of the prophet's message, there is no need to view the harsh commission of vv. 9-13 with scepticism.

But there is another reason for taking ch. 6 at face value. The obduracy idea is firmly rooted in the sacred tradition itself; it did not originate with Isaiah. G. von Rad has noted that although there is no uniform or consistent concept of obduracy, 'it is certain that from the very first Israel believed the act of deluding or hardening the heart to be prompted by Yahweh, and this is in one way or another the background to Isaiah's saying'.[40] The most obvious examples are those of the hardening of Pharaoh (Exod. 4.21; 7.3; 9.12; 10.20, 27; 11.10). But of more relevance are examples of God promoting obduracy among Israelites. An early example is the story of the sending of the evil spirit which led to upheaval in Shechem (Judg. 9.23), a spirit which on other occasions tormented Saul (1 Sam. 16.14; 18.10; 19.9). In 2 Sam. 17.14 the Lord deceives the counselors of Absalom so that harm would come to the usurper. Similarly, Rehoboam's foolish decision was prompted by God (1 Kgs 12.15). These, von Rad avers, are 'all precursors of this saying of Isaiah'.[40] I believe that he is correct, for there are additional factors that lend

24   *To See and Not Perceive*

support to this conclusion. For example, the concept of the divine council may reflect Babylonian traditions, in which 'King' Marduk announced to his prophet the fate of Babylon for the coming year. Similarly, 'King' Yahweh announced to Isaiah the fate of Judah.[42] Of related significance, A.F. Key has noted that the word that Isaiah was commanded to speak probably carried with it a magical connotation, as did many prophetic oracles.[43] That is to say, the very act of speaking the word effected the anticipated result.[44] It is concluded therefore that Isaiah's vision was not a vision for the purpose of his call into the prophetic vocation, but was a vision and commission of judgment. Isaiah has witnessed the heavenly council convened for purposes of decreeing a final judgment upon Jerusalem. It is is this sense, then, that Isaiah's 'call' in ch. 6 should be understood. His call was a commission to deliver the message of impending judgment. This judgment began with the very message itself, for the message was to act as a catalyst in promoting obduracy, and so guarantee the certainty of judgment.[45] How the obduracy idea is applied in Isaiah's preaching is the concern of the next section.

3. *Isaiah 6.9-10 and Isaiah's Hermeneutic*

To understand Isaiah's hermeneutic, it is necessary to view the message of obduracy in the light of the oracles and actions of the prophet during the two major crises of his ministry: the Syro-Ephraimite war and the Assyrian invasion. The former crisis is reflected in chs. 7–8, the latter in chs. 28–31. An important theme that runs throughout these chapters is Isaiah's interpretation and application of Davidic/Jerusalem traditions. In his usage of and reference to Israel's sacred tradition (i.e., the torah story, which at that time would have included traditions of conquest under Joshua, and consolidation and expansion under David and Solomon[46]), Isaiah is quite distinctive. Unlike the other canonical Prophets, Isaiah rarely refers to Mosaic traditions, primarily concentrating, instead, on Davidic traditions.[47] Nevertheless, his usage of these traditions reflects a similar hermeneutic.[48] To what extent and in what manner the obduracy idea is represented in these traditions will shed additional light on the prophet's understanding in 6.9-13.[49]

Isaiah alludes to a variety of Davidic traditions: The house of David is mentioned three times (cf. 7.2, 13; 22.22). There is mention of the 'throne of David' (9.6[7]) and the 'tent of David' (16.5).[50]

There are also what Th.C.Vriezen calls 'hints of events' in the life of David (28.21; 29.1). The warning given to Ahaz in 7.9 alludes to the Davidic covenant of 2 Samuel 7. Finally, in passages which many regard as late, David is called 'my servant' (37.35=2 Kgs 19.34), and Yahweh is referred to as 'the God of David, your father' (38.5=2 Kgs 20.5). There are also traditions pertaining to Jerusalem, which will be shortly taken into consideration.

There is also present in Isaiah a limited amount of temple tradition. It is in the temple, before the altar, that Isaiah receives his vision of God and the heavenly council (cf. 6.1, 6). The temple is called the 'house of Yahweh' (2.2) and the 'house of the God of Jacob' (2.3), which however, provides no guarantee of security, if the cult is practiced apart from justice and mercy (cf. 1.10-17).[51] The 'sanctuary' (מקדש) of 8.14 may also be an allusion to the temple, while it is possible that the stone saying of 28.16-17a may also have originally reflected temple imagery.[52]

A major ingredient in official theology was the Davidic covenant in which it was understood that Yahweh would maintain a descendant of David upon the throne in Jerusalem (cf. 2 Sam 7.9-16; Ps. 89.1-37). Isaiah appealed to these traditions (cf. 9.1-7; 11.1-16; 32.1; 33.17; 37.35), but does not find in them guarantee of the inviolability of either Jerusalem or the monarchy. There are two important ideas that must be recognized in order to understand how Isaiah has interpreted and applied the Davidic/Jerusalem traditions. Both ideas reflect a strongly monotheistic hermeneutic. First, in the description of his commission, Isaiah saw Yahweh seated upon his throne (6.1), a description which alone implies that Yahweh is King, and exclaims, 'my eyes have seen the King' (6.5). (Elsewhere he refers to God as Israel's 'King', see 33.22.) The Davidic covenant must be seen in this light. Ultimately it is God himself who is King. Therefore, with or without a descendant of David upon the throne, Israel has an eternal king. Secondly, Isaiah prophesies that God would some day establish a righteous and faithful king who would sit upon the throne of David, and inaugurate an eternal kingdom (9.1-7 [Heb. 8.23-9.6]; 11.1-5). This king, in sharp contrast to the faithless Ahaz, will meet the condition of faith (7.9; 11.5; cf. Ps. 132.11-12). The faithful king will bear all of the characteristics of his fathers David and Solomon: He will sit on the throne of David and rule over his kingdom (9.7 [Heb. 6]; 11.1; cf. 2 Sam. 7.13). The Spirit of

Yahweh will rest upon him (11.2; cf. 1 Sam. 16.13), giving him
wisdom and understanding (2 Sam. 14.17, 20; cf. 1 Kgs 3.5-9), and
enabling him to rule with justice and righteousness (9.7 [Heb. 6];
11.4-5; cf. 1 Kgs 10.9). In poetic contrast to the obdurate who neither
hear nor see (6.9-10), the righteous king will possess such keen
discernment that his judgment will not rely upon what he sees or
hears (11.3).

Although Isaiah has appealed to the Davidic/Jerusalem traditions,
he has applied to them the same hermeneutic as that applied to the
Mosaic traditions by the other canonical prophets. That is to say, if
God could lead the people out of slavery, he could return them to
slavery and then at a later time deliver them again. Similarly, Isaiah
has prophesied that the same God who has in the past fought in
behalf of the throne of David, may fight against it, in order,
paradoxically, to restore it (cf. 11.1). Moreover, the presence of
prophetic agony is in itself one of the criteria of the hermeneutics of
true prophecy.[53] Several of the oracles in the chapters concerned
with the Syro-Ephraimite and Assyrian crises reveal this hermeneutic
clearly.

The Syro-Ephraimite War. Anti-Assyrian sentiment arose in the
Northern Kingdom, and it soon led to a conspiracy to revolt, after
Pekah murdered Pekiah and assumed the throne in Samaria (737
BCE). Pekah formed an alliance with Rezin, the king of Syria,
persuading Philistia and Edom to join. However, Ahaz king of Judah
refused to participate. This refusal led to war in 734 BCE (the Syro-
Ephraimite war) and to a conspiracy to install one Tabe-el as the new
king of Judah (Isa. 7.6; 2 Kgs 16.5). In panic Ahaz ignored Isaiah's
assurances and warning, and appealed to Tiglath-pileser III (745–727
BCE) for help (2 Kgs 16.7). For this help Ahaz depleted the treasury,
and even stripped the Temple, in order to pay the heavy tribute
demanded of him by the Assyrian king (2 Kgs 16.8). Judah's king
went so far as to install Assyrian cultic furnishings in the Temple (2
Kgs 16.10-18). It is against this background that Isaiah 7–8 is to be
understood.

Isa. 6.1–8.18 is often referred to as Isaiah's 'Report' or 'Testimony'
(or *Denkschrift*) of the action that he took during the Syro-
Ephraimite war.[54] The structure of the prophet's report apparently
revolves around the three symbolic names: Shear-Jashub (7.3),

Immanuel (7.14), and Maher-shalal-hash-baz (8.3).[55] All three, including Immanuel,[56] are the prophet's children, given as 'signs and portents in Israel' (8.18). These three names represent the central features in Isaiah's three encounters with Ahaz and Judah's religious leaders during the Syro–Ephraimite crisis. The response of unbelief in Isaiah's message, illustrated by the symbolic names, should probably be understood as the fulfillment of the commission of Isa. 6.9-10.[57] The allusions to Davidic/Jerusalem traditions are critical and ominous.

Isa. 6.1-5. Although there is no reason to think that Isaiah's vision occurred at an enthronement festival in honour of Jotham, the prophet's description of the enthroned Lord must be viewed against Davidic enthronement traditions.[58] By juxtaposing the announcement of Uzziah's death (v. 1) and his vision of Yahweh, Israel's 'King' (v. 5), the prophet puts the Davidic succession tradition into its proper perspective. With the death of King Uzziah, an era has ended; with Yahweh seated on his throne, a new era has begun.[59] What we have here is a 'contrast in kingships'.[60] The leprous king has died, but the holy King lives on (could the prophet's reference to 'unclean' allude to Uzziah's condition?).[61] Future events will not depend on Uzziah, but on Yahweh. Moreover, the contrast between King Yahweh and the various human kings involved in the Syro-Ephraimite crisis is in itself a critical review of the Davidic monarchy.[62] Furthermore, since Isaiah's vision takes place in the temple,[63] a place of safety and refuge, and a symbol of God's abiding, protecting presence, the word of destruction carries with it a sense of irony. Although built by the Davidic line (1 Kgs 6–8; cf. 2 Sam. 7.13), and viewed as a place of refuge, it is the place where the prophet learns of the impending disaster for the monarchy.

The vision is probably meant to be understood against the unbelief of Ahaz in 7.1-17.[64] We see this in the way that 7.1 recalls 6.1: 'In the year that Uzziah died,' Isaiah was given the message of obduracy. 'In the days of Ahaz the son of Jotham, son of Uzziah',[65] the message is realized. Ahaz's lack of faith in Yahweh will now touch off the chain of events that will lead to the catastrophic destruction described in 6.11-13.

Isa. 7.1-17. In Isaiah's encounter with Ahaz (referred to as the 'house

of David' in v. 2), the centrality and importance of the theme of faith
is underscored, a theme which finds expression in passages to be
considered later (28.16; 30.15; 31.1). But what is important here is
the play on words in the oracle found in v.9: 'If you will not believe
(תַאֲמִינוּ), surely you shall not be established (תֵאָמֵנוּ)'.[66] The play on
words is meant to draw attention to אמן, the very verb used in the
Davidic covenant, as expressed in 2 Sam. 7.16: 'And your house and
your kingdom shall be made sure (וְנֶאְמַן) for ever before me; your
throne shall be established for ever'.[67] Isaiah is saying that unbelief
nullifies the Davidic covenant—at least so far as Ahaz is concerned
(see the similar conditional promise of Ps. 132.11-12). In contrast to
the counsel of the false prophets, who give their blessings and
assurances to Ahaz's plan to appeal to Assyria for help, Isaiah warns
that a lack of faith in God will bring about his downfall, not the two
kings conspiring against him.[68]

    The Davidic covenant figures elsewhere in Isaiah, with 1.21-26, a
passage that contains Isaiah's theology *in nuce*, perhaps representing
the most significant instance. The reference to the 'city' (surely
Jerusalem, cf. Isa. 1.1; 2.1) is significant because the promises of 2
Samuel were eventually applied to the 'Holy City' in royal
theology.[69] In vv. 21 and 26 Jerusalem is called קִרְיָה נֶאֱמָנָה, thus
forming an *inclusio*. The RSV translates, 'the faithful city',[70] but the
niphal of אמן often connotes the sense of being 'supported' or
'established'. Because of the references to 'righteousness' and 'justice'
in these verses, the niphal of אמן may in this case be understood, as in
the RSV, as one more moral attribute. It is likely in this instance,
however, that the passage alludes to נֶאְמַן in 2 Sam. 7.16. This is
probable for two reasons: (1) The expressions, 'as at the first' and 'as
at the beginning' (v. 26a), allude to the golden age of the monarchy
under David and Solomon[71] (and not to the time of the judges).[72]
This golden age has its beginning in the Davidic covenant of 2
Samuel. (2) The cycle of sin–punishment–restoration characterizes
both passages. In 2 Sam. 7.14-15 David is warned that his
descendants will be punished if they sin. But restoration always
follows (v. 15a: '. . . but I will not take away my steadfast love from
him. . . '). Similarly in Isa. 1.21-26: the 'established city' harbors
rebels and murderers, but after she has been purged, she will once
again be a city of righteousness.

    Whereas Isaiah apparently based his hope of Jerusalem's eventual
restoration on the Davidic covenant, he refused to interpret this

covenant as narrowly as Ahaz and the official theologians did.[73] He found in it no guarantee that judgment in the time of Ahaz would be averted.

Isa. 7.10-17. In the Immanuel passage Ahaz is rebuked for refusing to ask for a sign from his God: 'Hear then, O house of David! Is it too little for you to weary men, that you weary my God also?' (v. 13). The king's refusal to ask for a sign reveals his lack of faith, and this lack of faith will bring disaster upon the 'house of David'. It is important that whereas the prophet told Ahaz to ask a sign of 'your God' (v. 11), a manner of speaking that recalls Davidic tradition (see 1 Kgs 1.47), in his answer he refers to 'my God'. The shift in the pronoun probably implies God's withdrawl from the king (see 1 Sam. 15.26-30).[74] The Immanuel sign (vv. 14-17), itself probably an allusion to Davidic traditions,[75] seems to mean that in destroying Judah's two present enemies (Syria and Ephraim; see also 8.1-4), God will prove that he is truly with his people, but because Ahaz has sought Assyria's protection, and not God's, God will also bring destruction (through Assyria; see also 8.5-8). Thus 'God with us' seems to be a two-edged sign: God is with his people for salvation, and he is with his people in judgment.[76] Depending upon one's disposition toward God, the sign of Immanuel either threatens or reassures.[77]

Isa. 8.11-15. In 8.4-8 the Lord tells Isaiah that the king of Assyria will conquer Samaria and Syria, and then 'sweep on into Judah'. Following a brief oracle to the Gentiles, the prophet announces disaster for both houses of Israel:

> For the Lord spoke thus to me with his strong hand upon me, and warned me not to walk in the way[78] of this people, saying: 'Do not call conspiracy all that this people call conspiracy, and do not fear what they fear, nor be in dread. But the Lord of hosts, him you shall regard as holy; let him be your fear, and let him be your dread. And he will become a sanctuary, and a stone of offense, and a rock of stumbling to both houses of Israel, a trap and a snare to the inhabitants of Jerusalem. And many shall stumble thereon; they shall fall and be broken; they shall be snared and taken' (8.11-15, RSV).

The prophet is turned away from walking in the way of 'this people' (cf. 6.9, 10; 8.6; 28.11, 14; 29.13, 14) and is told not to call 'conspiracy' what the people call conspiracy.[79] The word translated 'conspiracy' (קֶשֶׁר) can also be translated as 'alliance' or 'treason'. The root meaning of the cognate verb is 'to bind' (cf. BDB), and both noun and verb may denote either the political sense of alliance or conspiracy (cf. 1 Kgs 16.20; 2 Kgs 11.14; 2 Chr. 23.13; etc.) or the religious sense of strict adherence (cf. Deut. 6.8; 11.18; Prov. 3.3; 6.21; etc.).[80] Isaiah and his disciples are not to regard the policy of (political and religious) separation from Assyria as 'treason', as it was regarded by Ahaz and company. Instead, Isaiah and his disciples are to regard the Lord as 'holy' (i.e. separate) and as their real cause of fear. If Isaiah and his disciples sanctify (קרשׁ) the Lord, he will then become a sanctuary (מקרשׁ)[81] to them, and not a stone of offense and a rock of stumbling, as he has become to the two houses of Israel.

Because Judah fears and dreads the Syro–Ephraimite alliance more than she fears Yahweh, God 'will become. . . a trap (פח) and a snare (מוקש) to the inhabitants of Jerusalem' (v. 14b). 'Trap' and 'snare' recall one of David's imprecations against his enemies: 'Let their own table before them become a trap (פח); let their sacrificial feasts be a snare (מוקש)' (Ps. 69.22 [Heb. 23]). What King David desired to happen to his enemies, Isaiah has implied, Yahweh plans to do to his own people. There are other parallels as well. David implores: 'Save me, O God! For the waters (מים) have come up to my neck. . . I have come into deep waters (מים), and the flood sweeps over (שטף) me' (vv. 1-2 [Heb. 2-3]); and: 'Let not the flood (שבלת מים) sweep over (שטף) me, or the deep swallow me up, or the pit close its mouth over me' (v. 15 [Heb. 16]). Isaiah says in 8.8: 'Because this people have refused the waters of Shiloah that flow gently. . . behold, the Lord is bringing up against them the waters (מים) of the River, mighty and many. . . and it will sweep on into Judah, it will overflow (שטף) and pass on, reaching even to the neck' (compare Isa. 28.15, 17). David also prays that the eyes of his enemies 'be darkened, so that they cannot see' (v. 23 [Heb. 24]), language which recalls Isa. 6.9-10. Collectively these parallels point to deliberate allusion to at least one Davidic Psalm. But because of his hermeneutic, Isaiah sees in these words not the destruction of the enemies of the Davidic kingdom, as David's original request had been (and no doubt as the hope of Isaiah's contemporaries would have been), but of the Davidic kingdom itself.

The Assyrian Crisis. In 734 BCE Assyria invaded the Northern Kingdom. In all likelihood it was Pekah's murder (732 BCE) that prevented Tiglath-Pileser from totally destroying the kingdom, although he did annex most of its territory. That same year Assyria conquered Syria, and Rezin was put to death. Hoshea was allowed to reign over Samaria (732-724 BCE), but soon after the death of the Assyrian king (727 BCE), he revolted against Shalmaneser V (727-722 BCE). Samaria was attacked, and Hoshea was taken prisoner (724 BCE), but the city itself was finally taken in 721 BCE by Shalmaneser's successor Sargon II (722-705 BCE). In keeping with Assyrian policy, what was left of the Northern Kingdom's population was deported (2 Kgs 18.9-12).

Hezekiah (715-687 BCE), perhaps sensing Assyrian decline, began to reverse his father's policies, and pursued, among other things, religious reform (2 Kgs 18.3-7). Shortly after the death of Sargon II, Hezekiah tested the strength of the new king Sennacherib (705-681 BCE), who was occupied by revolts in other parts of his kingdom, by joining a revolt including Tyre, Ashkelon, and Ekron, with promise of aid coming from Egypt. By 701 BCE Sennacherib had subdued Babylon and was then able to begin his drive against the western coalition. One by one members of the coalition either submitted or were conquered. An Egyptian army approached, but was defeated. In Judah one fortified city after another fell to Sennacherib's advancing forces (2 Kgs 18.13).[82] Only Hezekiah's decision to come to terms spared Jerusalem the same fate (2 Kgs 18.14).

Isa. 28.1-13. Perhaps the most important oracle uttered by Isaiah during the Assyrian crisis is to be found in Isaiah 28. This chapter contains the prophet's warning given to Judah (ca. 701 BCE) regarding the covenant that had been made with Assyria. In his earlier testimony (Isaiah 7-8), the prophet had been warned not to regard what the people regarded as קשר. The Syro-Ephraimite alliance had caused Judah to be afraid, when her fear and dread should have been reserved for her God. Now the disastrous consequences of her alliance with Assyria are being experienced. Isaiah had been told that like a river overflowing its banks Assyria would sweep over Judah (8.7-8). Ephraim (i.e. Samaria) and Syria had been conquered (appropriately an oracle of woe for Ephraim precedes Judah's warning [cf. 28.1-4]), and now the Assyrian power has begun its southward drive.

Isaiah mocks the priests and prophets who reel and stagger in drunkenness, and 'err in vision' and 'stumble in giving judgment' (28.7).[83] The contrast between the prophet Isaiah and the false prophets is noteworthy. Both have their respective 'visions', that is to say, both have their respective perceptions of God. Isaiah's vision, however, was of God himself, and rather than being convinced that his God was about to deliver Israel, he saw the wide gulf between God's holiness and Israel's sinfulness.[84] Because of this vision he could not, like the false prophets and official theologians, announce deliverance, but was charged with the message of destruction.[85] The false prophets were incapable of perceiving Isaiah's 'vision' (or what we might call his 'hermeneutic'), for God had not revealed it to them (cf. 29.9-12). For them, Isaiah's terrible message remained a closed book (cf. 29.12). Their spirit, says Isaiah, is not the Spirit of the Lord, but a 'spirit of stupor' (cf. 29.9-10).

In 28.9-10 the prophet wonders who is capable of being taught. Will he[86] give instruction to infants and young children who are still learning the alphabet?[87] No one apparently is capable of understanding the message. But the people will indeed learn the message, as vv. 11-13 declare. If his people will not listen to his true prophets, then the Lord will speak to 'this people' through the language of a foreign people. Though Yahweh has offered rest and repose to his people, they have refused to listen, as Isaiah's original commission anticipated and, apparently, intended (cf. 6.9-10). Therefore, the word of the Lord is to them unintelligible babble in order that they may go ahead in their sin and deceit until they are knocked backwards and are 'broken', 'snared', and 'caught' (v. 13; cf. 8.15).

Isa. 28.14-22. These verses constitute an oracle of warning addressed to Jerusalem. Isaiah rails against the rulers whom he calls 'scoffers' (v. 14), a term which in biblical parlance usually refers to the proud and arrogant (cf. Prov. 21.24; 29.8).[88] These rulers have 'made a covenant with death' and an agreement with Sheol (v. 15). The historical background here is Hezekiah's religious reform (cf. 2 Kgs 18.3-6; 2 Chr. 29.2-31.21) and his alliance with Egypt (cf. 2 Kgs 18.19-25; Isa. 30.1-18; 31.1-9).[89] The prophet calls the alliance a covenant made with מָוֶת which against the background of those times would surely call to mind the pagan deity *Moth*, the god of death.[90] It is possible that the references to death and Sheol are to be understood in the light of Isa. 8.19: 'And when they say to you [Isaiah is speaking to his disciples], "Consult the mediums and the wizards who chirp and mutter", should not a people consult their God? Should they consult the dead in behalf of the living?' Rather than consulting with the Lord, the rulers of Jerusalem have consulted with foreign powers, and possibly with foreign deities and spirits. Because of this, the prophet tells them, they have made lies and falsehood their refuge and shelter in assuming that their unholy alliance will see them through the coming danger. For this reason Yahweh has begun laying a new foundation, a sure foundation which will remain after the false refuge and shelter have been swept away (v. 17).[91] In light of this, the prophet calls for a response of faith: 'He who believes [that God is laying a foundation] will not be in haste [*or* shaken]' (v. 16b). Again the hiphil of אמן appears, which recalls the warning given to Ahaz in 7.9, 'If you do not believe. . .' (The need for faith is emphasized in other oracles concerned with Judah's treaty with Egypt [cf. 30.15; 31.1]). But because Judah places her faith in Egypt, she will be judged. It will be after the purging effects of this judgment that Judah's 'covenant with death will be annulled' (v. 18). The call for faith in God's foundation, as opposed to the foundation that Judah's leaders have laid, may very well be a criticism of temple tradition and the royal building program of Hezekiah's time.[92]

At the conclusion of the oracle, Isaiah cites two episodes from Israel's sacred tradition. It is in his appeal to and interpretation of these traditions that the prophet's hermeneutic of prophetic critique becomes poignantly clear:

> For the Lord will rise up as on Mount Perazim,
>   he will be wroth as in the valley of Gibeon;
> to do his deed—strange is his deed!
>   And to do his work—alien is his work! (28.21).

The reference to 'Mount Perazim' recalls David's victory over the Philistines (2 Sam. 5.17-21; cf. 1 Chr. 14.11-12). Because the Lord 'broke through' the Philistine army, David named the site 'Baal-perazim' (i.e., 'Lord of breaking through'). Here again the prophet Isaiah has cited sacred tradition where God is victorious on the field of battle, but applies it against Judah (i.e., God will again be victorious over his enemy, only this time Judah is his enemy; see Isa. 10.17).

The reference to the 'valley of Gibeon' recalls David's second victory over the Philistines (2 Sam. 5.22-25; cf. 1 Chr. 14.13-16). However, because of certain parallels, it may be that the 'valley of Gibeon'[93] refers to Israel's great victory over the Amorites under the leadership of Joshua (Josh. 10.6-14). It is ironic that Isaiah should cite this particular example, if this is indeed the one that is intended, for it was an alliance with a foreign people that touched off the conflict described in Joshua. Because the Gibeonites deceived the Israelites into making a covenant of peace, Israel was obliged to go to war with the Amorites, led by the king of Jerusalem. It is also noteworthy that in this tradition we are told that God threw down stones (אבן) like hail (ברד) upon the fleeing Amorites (10.11), another detail which may have contributed to Isaiah's metaphor of stone (אבן) and hail (ברד) (28.16, 17). Isaiah wishes the rulers of Judah to understand that their God is still as mighty as ever, but this time his might will be turned against them. The hail of stones that fell upon the Amorites will this time fall upon the Judahites. The oracle concludes at v. 22 with the injunction not to 'scoff' (ליץ), which recalls the earlier epithet 'scoffers' (לצון) in 28.14, and so forms an *inclusio*. The oracle ends on the ominous note: 'For I have heard a decree of destruction from the Lord God of hosts upon the whole land' (28.22). This 'decree of destruction' parallels closely the original decree Isaiah had heard many years earlier when he saw the enthroned Lord (Isaiah 6).

Isa. 29.1-4. The cry of 'woe' picks up the somber mood of chapter 28 (v. 1), especially that of the 'covenant with death' (vv. 15, 18).[94] Where once David encamped against his enemies (29.1), God now encamps against his own people (v. 3). The Judahites can receive no assurances from the traditions of David's capture of Jerusalem (2 Sam. 5.6-9). God is now at war with them. The reverse application of the tradition is plainly evident.

Isa. 29.14. The Lord promises his undiscerning people: 'Behold, I will again do marvelous things with this people, wonderful and marvelous' (v. 14a). We are reminded of the 'strange' and 'alien' work of God in 28.21. The idea here is the same. The 'marvelous' and 'wonderful' things probably refer to the great victories that David and Solomon enjoyed (though it is possible that Israel's entire history, from the exodus on, is in view). However, this time the wondrous acts will involve the destruction of the nation. This is what it will take to sober Judah's drunken leaders (see vv. 9-10).

Isa. 30.17. The hyperbole of this verse, 'a thousand shall flee at the threat of one, at the threat of five you shall flee', recalls Josh. 23.10: 'One man of you puts to flight a thousand, since it is the Lord your God who fights for you, as he promised you'. Davidic tradition may also be echoed: 'Saul has slain his thousands, and David his ten thousands' (1 Sam. 18.7). However, Israel is warned of the reverse in the Song of Moses: 'How should one chase a thousand, and two put ten thousand to flight, unless. . . the Lord had given them up?' (Deut. 32.30; cf. Lev. 26.36; Deut. 28.25; Prov. 28.1).

Isaiah has cited tradition which told of Israel's great victories, but he has seen in them God's power, not Israel's. He has seen in them God's wrath brought against sinners, not God's unqualified support for Israel. Herein lies one of the essential differences between Isaiah and the official theologians of his time. The false prophets erred in vision and stumbled in giving judgment (cf. 28.7), because their hermeneutic was wrong. They appealed to the same traditions, to be sure, but they interpreted them entirely differently. They assumed that God had acted in the past the way that he had because Israel was better than the other nations, because Israel had a special claim upon God that in a certain sense limited his sovereignty (in the sense that he was God of Israel, and not of the nations). They found in these traditions a guarantee of continuity, concluding from them that Yahweh was obligated to Israel to maintain the institutions he had given her and was obligated to protect his own reputation among foreign peoples and deities. If Israel sinned, a brief chastisement would be sufficient, and all would be well. But Isaiah read these traditions quite differently. He found in them evidence of God's absolute holiness (cf. 6.3), a holiness which could not tolerate Israel's sin, nor be placated by self-serving reform. For Israel to be fully restored, God would have to purge the nation. His sovereignty not only permitted this, but required it. The wonders that God performed long ago to create Israel would be worked again to create a new Israel. The person who catches this vision and believes will not be in a frenzy (cf. 28.16b; cf. 7.9). This person will find that the provisions of his God are neither too short nor too narrow (28.20).

He will be able to see in God's destructive acts God's creative acts. For in hurling siege stones into the city, God has begun to lay in Zion a new foundation made of tested stones (28.16).[95] As in 8.14,[96] depending on one's hermeneutic, God was either a stumbling stone, or a new foundation/sanctuary for the Israelites, as they stood by and witnessed the unfolding of events. The person who shares Isaiah's faith and vision will be numbered among the remnant.

4. *Remnant and Restoration in Isaiah*

Before any conclusions regarding Isaiah's vision and commission described in ch. 6 can be drawn, the problem of Isaiah's eschatology must be addressed. Whether Isaiah foresaw future deliverance and restoration for Israel or foresaw only unmitigated doom is important to determine, for these opposing interpretations cast Isaiah 6 into very different perspectives. It has been assumed from the outset of this chapter that Isaiah foresaw restoration and a remnant; it is now time to offer support for this assumption.

The problem of restoration in Isaiah has been examined most recently by J. Jensen.[97] He has argued against G. Fohrer's position that there is no future deliverance foreseen by Isaiah,[98] since the early prophets understood Israel as always facing a decision either for or against God.[99] Jensen summarizes Fohrer's interpretation of Isaiah (and the other early prophets) in terms of 'alternatives (*Entweder-Oder*) which the prophet offers the people, never as successive stages (*Vorher-Nachher*)'.[100] This understanding of Isaiah's eschatology leads Fohrer to eliminate as inauthentic most passages which might be understood as proclaiming future deliverance after the judgment, a practice Jensen judges to be arbitrary.[101] Even so, among those passages which Fohrer is prepared to accept there are several that contain an element of hope in a coming restoration. As perhaps the best example Jensen cites 1.21-26, in which it would appear that Yahweh's judgment is designed to purify the city of Jerusalem. A portion of the passage reads:

> 21 How the faithful city has become a harlot,
>   she that was full of justice!
> Righteousness lodged in her, but now murderers.
>
> 25 I will turn my hand against you and will
>   smelt away your dross as with lye
>   and remove all your alloy.

26 And I will restore your judges as at the first,
    and your counselors as at the beginning.
Afterward you shall be called the city of righteousness,
    the faithful city (RSV).[102]

The idea of this passage is that the once faithful (or 'established'[103]) city, now lacking justice, will some day again be faithful. The act of judgment is described metaphorically as removing the dross, or impurities, from the precious metal. After the cleansing, Jerusalem will be a faithful (or 'established') city 'as at first'.[104] Restoration is clearly in view.

Jensen cites three other passages which give some indication of restoration following judgment: 14.24-26, 17.14, and 28.29.[105] The first passage predicts the removal of the Assyrian 'yoke' from Judah. The second passage promises that God will 'rebuke' the nations which have 'despoiled' and 'plundered' Judah. The final passage concludes with statements that grain is not 'threshed' forever, thus implying that there will be a reprieve. Furthermore, the 'cornerstone' text (28.16-17a), whatever its original context may have been, seems clearly to be an expression of hope in a new future.[106] To these oracles J.W. Whedbee adds 9.1-7 and 11.1-9.[107] If these passages are indeed from the eighth-century prophet, and I think that they are,[108] then the idea of restoration was apparently linked to the hope of the coming of a wise ruler. In any case, it would seem that Jensen's argument is well taken, and that among the oracles of Isaiah there is present the hope of future restoration.[109] As will be seen, this conclusion receives further support in the subsequent discussion concerned with the question of the remnant.

In a recent study G.F. Hasel has argued that the remnant idea is present not only in the oracles of Isaiah's later ministry (as conceded by Vriezen[110]), but may be traced to the very beginning of the prophet's ministry.[111] Hasel divides Isaiah's oracles into three broad categories: early oracles, oracles and narratives during the Syro-Ephraimite crisis, and oracles during the Assyrian crisis.

To the first category Hasel assigns Isaiah 6, the account of the prophet's vision and call. It is likely that the account was written several years after the experience, probably during or shortly after the Syro-Ephraimite crisis (hence its association with Isaiah 7-8, which describes the prophet's activities during this period of time). Hasel finds the idea of remnant implied by Isaiah's personal purification, which set him apart from the people of 'unclean lips' (6.5-7).[112] But the idea is made explicit in the prophet's commission to harden the heart of the people 'until cities lie waste without inhabitant. . . and the Lord removes men far away. . . and. . . a tenth remain. . . ' Hasel finds this reference to the remnant as essentially negative (and hence he sees no reason why vv. 12 and 13 cannot be authentic).[113] Since Hasel also accepts the last three words of v. 13, he finds yet further reference to the remnant, only in this case the reference is positive.[114] The remnant, by virtue of its purge through the Lord's judgment of the nation, will constitute a 'holy seed'. As another example of the remnant in Isaiah's early ministry, Hasel cites 1.24-26.[115] The metaphor employed by the prophet implies the emergence of a remnant: 'The removal of the alloy indicates the preservation of the purest residue'.[116] Finally, Hasel finds the remnant idea expressed in 4.1-3.[117] In v. 1 the image of seven women taking hold of one man implies the remnant; and, of course, the remnant idea is made explicit in vv. 2-3.

The second category consists of the narratives and oracles of Isaiah 7–8. In these chapters Hasel finds ample evidence of the remnant idea.[118] He begins with an analysis of the meaning of Isaiah's son's name, Shear-Jashub (שאר ישוב, 'a remnant will return' or 'repent'). In response to the Syro–Ephraimite conspiracy to remove Ahaz from the throne, Isaiah takes along his son Shear-Jashub and offers counsel to the king (cf. 7.1-8). The question raised by Hasel concerns what Shear-Jashub's name was meant to convey to Ahaz in this context.[119] The name could imply a threat, hope, warning, or an exhortation.[120] In a previous study Hasel has shown that the noun 'remnant' is intended to receive the emphasis, and so Shear-Jashub should be translated 'a *remnant* shall return'.[121] The remnant is not Judah (i.e., as a part of Israel as a whole, for Judah herself is to undergo judgment[122]), but is a remnant of Judah. Hasel notes that the remnant idea as expressed by Isaiah prior to the time of the events described in Isaiah 7–8 was both negative (Isa. 6.9-13b) and positive (Isa. 4.2-3; 6.13c).[123] Consequently, the name Shear-Jashub was meant to convey to Ahaz both threat (in that Judah will be reduced to a remnant) and a promise (in that at least a remnant will be spared). The verbal part of the name is open to a variety of interpretations as well. Hasel notes that whereas a few have suggested that ישוב means either a return home from battle[124] or a return from hiding in terror,[125] most see in it 'religious signification'.[126] Isa. 8.18 would appear to support this interpretation: 'I and the children whom the Lord has given me are signs and portents in Israel from the Lord of hosts who dwells on Mount Zion' (RSV). The historical context into which Isaiah's son finds himself thrust would suggest religious significance be attached to his name. Isaiah confronted Ahaz with the need to have faith in God (cf. 7.9b). The monarch is to ask God for a sign so that he will know that the Lord has truly spoken through his prophet (cf. 7.10-17). Isaiah's purpose was to persuade Ahaz to refrain from making an alliance with Assyria and, instead, to have faith in God.[127] If Ahaz will not put his trust in Yahweh then indeed there will be but a remnant. But what sort of people will make up this remnant? The context points to the disciples of Isaiah who will not 'walk in the way of this people' (8.11), but who fear and sanctify Yahweh (8.13). Isaiah's disciples stand in sharp contrast to Ahaz and his counselors who prefer to place their trust in Assyria, rather than in God (7.9). In Isaiah the need for faith is thematic and recurs in oracles concerned with the later Assyrian crisis (e.g., Isa. 28.16b: 'He who believes will not be in haste'; cf. 30.15).[128]

There are other indications in the narratives and oracles of Isaiah from the period of the Syro–Ephraimite war that suggest that the prophet anticipated the survival of a remnant. One indication is the name of the child Immanuel ('God with us', cf. 8.8). Whoever Immanuel was supposed to have been, the name certainly seems to suggest some kind of future hope for the faithful.[129] Finally, the binding and sealing up of Isaiah's 'testimony' for his disciples anticipates, it would appear, the survival of a remnant who would later appreciate and abide by the prophet's teaching (8.16; and the later passage 30.8).[130]

Hasel also points to several passages derived from Isaiah's later career, which seem to imply the survival of a remnant. The first passage is 28.5-6, but not all scholars accept the oracle as having come from Isaiah.[131] Hasel believes that it does in fact come from the eighth-century prophet, and may reflect the time when Hezekiah decided to join in the revolt against Sargon II in 705 BCE.[132] As such, the oracle would be understood as a warning as well as a reason for hope. Isa. 30.15-17 is another oracle, reflecting the same period, that warns against foreign alliances and military activity. The people will be saved through quietness and trust (v. 15), but in choosing the political option (v. 16), their numbers will be decimated (v. 17). Hasel notes that v. 17 contains a hint that at least a small number will be left 'like a flagpole on the top of a mountain'.[133] Another oracle that describes the remnant is 1.4-9. Hasel believes that this oracle reflects 701 BCE when most of Judah had been overrun by Sennacherib (cf. vv. 8-9).[134] Hasel also includes the controversial passage 10.20-23 as deriving from this period, though he acknowledges the fact that many scholars regard the oracle as post-exilic.[135] He also cites 37.30-32 as a 'prose oracle' from Sennacherib's second invasion of Judah (690/89 BCE).[136] As his last example, Hasel cites 11.10-16, with special attention given to vv. 11 and 16.[137] Hasel admits that many scholars deny its Isaianic authorship, but agrees with other scholars 'who have seen no decisive reason to deny the authenticity of this oracle'.[138] Verses 11 and 16 proclaim a second 'exodus' in which God will gather his people from Assyria and other nations as he had originally gathered them from Egypt. Hasel notes that the idea in the oracle that Judahites would have to be gathered from various nations probably reflects the Assyrian practice of deportation,[139] though it may reflect a general diaspora.

It would seem that Hasel has presented convincing arguments for seeing the remnant motif as running throughout Isaiah's ministry, even if we do not accept every oracle and passage that he has cited as having originated from the eighth-century prophet. This work supports Jensen's contention, as discussed above, that weal and woe are juxtaposed themes in the theology of the prophet Isaiah.[140] Judgment is, as Jensen argues, purificatory; and one of the results of this purifying process is, as Hasel has so thoroughly shown, the creation of a remnant that puts its trust in Yahweh and not in foreign alliances and deities.[141] Therefore, it is concluded that the purpose of the prophet's word of judgment in Isa 6.9-13 was to purge the corrupt nation in order to produce a righteous remnant, or 'holy seed'.[142]

C. *Isaiah 6.9-10 in the Context of the Book of Isaiah*

1. *General Observations concerning Composition and Arrangement*
Recently B.S. Childs has underscored the importance of seeing the Book of Isaiah as a theological unity.[143] According to him, First Isaiah (consisting primarily of the utterances of the pre-exilic

prophet of judgment) loses its theological context, when read apart from Second (the exilic prophet of consolation) and Third Isaiah (post-exilic prophet of promise). Likewise, Second and Third Isaiah are bereft of any historical context, if they are read apart from First Isaiah. The final editor has deliberately excised the original historical context of Second and Third Isaiah, and has placed these oracles into the historical context of the eighth-century prophet.[144] Second and Third Isaiah, in their present canonical context, become the vital second part of the theology of judgment and redemption. Attached to Isaiah's eighth-century oracles of judgment, the word of redemption is now understood as having been announced earlier and more forcefully. At all times Yahweh reigned as King of heaven and earth, and by his word accomplished all that he purposed (cf. 40.8; 55.10-11). Together with First Isaiah, Second and Third Isaiah are telling us that redemption actually began with the judgment of God's people. The editing of these materials is such that a timeless theological theme has been created, as Childs has said: 'Sinful Israel would always be the object of divine terror; repentant Israel would receive his promise of forgiveness'.[145]

Another and somewhat different analysis of the contents of Isaiah has been developed by W.H. Brownlee. Several years ago he put forward a tentative thesis that canonical Isaiah was consciously edited and arranged as a two-colume work consisting of chs. 1–33 (volume I) and chs. 34–66 (volume II).[146] His thesis is supported by the observation of a three-line gap between chs. 33 and 34 of 1QIsaiah[a],[147] and by the older contention of C.C. Torrey that chs. 34–35 should be ascribed to Second Isaiah.[148] It is also supported, Brownlee argues, when it is observed that the Qumran scribe utilized one Isaiah scroll for copying Isaiah 1–33 and another scroll for copying Isaiah 34–66.[149] But the best evidence is to be found in observing the parallelism and balance of the two halves.[150] Like Childs' interpretation, Brownlee believes that the editors of the Isaiah school consciously edited and intercalated materials from First and Second Isaiah.[151] In their present literary form, the two 'volumes' interpret each other,[152] and each presents the dialectic of 'ruin and future blessedness'.[153]

This dialect may have a bearing upon the position of ch. 6. Many scholars have assumed that ch. 6 is where it is, since it was the introductory chapter to an ancient scroll containing the prophet's report (chs. 7–8), and ancient tradents were reluctant to break it up.[154] However, since there is ample evidence of editorial activity elsewhere in Isaiah, including chs. 6–8, such an assumption cannot be held.[155] More promising proposals have been made suggesting that the position of ch. 6 serves literary and theological purposes.[156] In my judgment, chs. 1–5 are meant to be understood as laying the groundwork for the severe message of judgment in ch. 6.[157] God's people are rebellious, unjust, and utterly callous toward their Lord. Therefore, the word of obduracy and destruction is pronounced. Judgment follows rebellion, and chs. 7–12 describe aspects of this judgment, including the effects of the hardening commission itself. But, like ch. 6 itself, which has been given a glimmer of hope by the addition of v. 13c. hope is expressed in the sections that precede (1.26-27; 2.1-4; 4.2-6) and follow (8.9-10; 9.1-7; 10.20-27; 11.1-16; 12.1-6). This editorial activity has indeed resulted in a dialectic of doom and salvation. However, I believe that the major purpose for having ch. 6 preceded by much of the material in chs. 1–5 is to justify the severity of the judgment.

2. *Specific Observations on the Obduracy Motif in Isaiah*
In this section those texts that describe or threaten a condition of obduracy and those texts that promise restoration of the spiritual senses will be examined. These obduracy and restoration texts are an important part of the dialectic of ruin and future blessedness to which the book of Isaiah as a whole gives expression. The purpose of this section is to observe in what ways the Isaianic obduracy motif functions in the canonical form of the book of Isaiah.

Obduracy Texts
Isa. 6.9-10 is certainly not the only obduracy passage in the book of Isaiah. Israel's spiritual ignorance and dullness appear to be thematic in this book and are probably to be understood against the background of early wisdom, as Whedbee and Jensen have argued.[158] This is seen in Isa. 1.3, '. . . but Israel does not know, my people does not understand', and 1.5, 'Why will you still be smitten, that you continue to rebel?', as well as in many other passages.[159] However, there are five specific passages that contribute to this theme significantly.

Isa. 29.9-10. The passage that is most closely related to Isa. 6.9-10 is 29.9-10, an oracle that derives from Isaiah. To the leadership the prophet taunts (RSV):

> 9 Stupefy yourselves and be in a stupor,
>   blind yourselves and be blind!
> Be drunk, but not with wine;
>   stagger, but not with strong drink!
> 10 For the Lord has poured out upon you
>   a spirit of deep sleep,
> and has closed your eyes, the prophets,
>   and covered your heads, the seers (29.9-10).

The prophet taunts the rulers who have disregarded his word of warning,[160] enjoining them to be utterly stupefied with horror at what they will soon see (cf. Jer. 4.9; Hab. 1.5). The verb 'stupefy' (תמה) also occurs in the context of the oracle against Babylon: 'They will look aghast at one another' (Isa. 13.8b, RSV). Isaiah urges them to be drunk (recall 28.1, 3, 7-8), and so to fail to heed his warning. But their drunkenness will not be the result of wine, it will happen because the Lord has poured out upon them a spirit of deep sleep (רוח תרדמה, cf. Gen. 2.21; 15.12), and has closed the eyes of their prophets and has covered the heads of their seers. They will not comprehend because God will blind them to the truth. The obduracy theme is continued in vv. 11-14. To the official theologians and prophets, Isaiah's vision is like a sealed book that no one can read. 'This people' (an epithet that recalls Isa. 6.9-10) worships the Lord with their lips, but not with their hearts, therefore God will again do something marvelous, against which their wisdom will vanish (29.13-14). These oracles rival the severity of that of 6.9-13.[161]

Isa. 42.18-20. The theme of obduracy finds itself expressed in Second Isaiah as well, and in three passages we again come across the familiar metaphors of unseeing eyes and deaf ears. In 42.18-20 we read (RSV):

> Hear, you deaf;
>   and look, you blind, that you may see!
> Who is blind but my servant,
>   or deaf as my messenger whom I send?
> Who is blind as my dedicated one,
>   or blind as the servant of the Lord?

He[162]sees many things, but does not observe them;
    his ears are open, but he does not hear.

שמע and ראה recall the similar verbs of Isa. 6.9-10, especially the imperative form שמעו.[163] Verse 20 also recalls Isa. 6.9-10, but this oracle is not one of judgment, as is rightly noted by C. Westermann,[164] but is an oracle containing a hidden promise. Second Isaiah declares that it is time for Israel to wake up and recognize what God has accomplished in recent times. If only Israel could properly interpret this history, then she could see within it God's salvific work.

Isa. 43.8. Set in the context of a trial oracle (cf. 43.8-15), Isa. 43.8 reads (RSV):

Bring forth the people who are blind,
    yet have eyes,
who are deaf,
    yet have ears.

Westermann has noted the paradox of Yahweh calling forth his 'blind' and 'deaf' witnesses.[165] They are witnesses of his mighty deeds, and yet they have failed to grasp the fact that Yahweh alone is God. The nations are gathered together, and in this universal context Yahweh declares that he himself is God and announces the fall of Babylon (cf. 43.14). Israel, blind to the 'former things' (43.9b), now must come to the realization that Yahweh is still her Creator and Redeemer (cf. 43.14-15).

Isa. 44.18. The third obduracy text from Second Isaiah reads (RSV):

For they know not, nor do they discern;
    for he has shut their eyes, so that they cannot see,
    and their minds, so that they cannot understand.

This text is found in the context of the prophet's taunt leveled against the makers of idols. Similar criticism of the idols themselves appear in Jer. 10.5 ('their idols. . . cannot speak. . . cannot walk'). Inspired by Jeremiah's polemic, Ep. Jer. 8-73 ridicules idolatry at length (see also Wisdom 13-15). The Moses of Deuteronomy predicts that Israel 'will serve gods of wood and stone. . . that neither see, nor hear, nor eat, nor smell' (Deut. 4.28). These sentiments find expression in the Psalter as well (Pss. 115.5-7; 135.16-17). Similar language is also employed in the various instances where God's people are described as obdurate. It is interesting to note that in Isa. 44.18 God is understood as the active cause of the obdurate condition of the heathen.

It is likely that the obduracy passages of Second Isaiah (42.18-20; 43.8; 44.18) reflect 6.9-10. However, whereas First Isaiah proclaims that God has actually promoted obduracy (6.9-10; 29.9-10), Second Isaiah only goes so far as to say that the people are in an obdurate condition. The causative idea is not present. (The single causative passage [44.18] refers not to Israel, but to heathen idol makers.) The absence of the causative idea could suggest a mitigation of the severity of the obduracy motif in Second Isaiah. However, it may be presented the way it is as no more than a logical complement to its presentation in First Isaiah. That is to say, in First Isaiah the prophet declares that God will harden Israel; in Second Isaiah the prophet declares that Israel is indeed in a hardened condition. But, in keeping with what we have observed above about the overall arrangement of the book, Second Isaiah also looks to a time of restoration, when the people of God will once again be perceptive (40.5-28). In the earlier vision, the prophet had been commanded to speak the word of obduracy to the people so that they should not hear (שמע), see (ראה), know (ידע), or understand (בין); but, in contrast, the oracles of ch. 40 are spoken so that they should hear, see, know, and understand (שמע, vv. 21, 28; ראה, vv. 5, 26; ידע, vv. 21, 28; בין, v. 21).[166]

Isa. 63.17. In Third Isaiah there is a description of the people that recalls the language of Isa. 6.9-10. Isa. 59.9-10 reads: 'Therefore justice is far from us. . . we walk in gloom. We grope for the wall like the blind, we grope like those who have no eyes; we stumble at noon as in the twilight. . . '. However, in 63.17 we encounter a text that again suggests that God himself on occasion brings about the condition of obduracy. The text reads (RSV):

> 'O Lord, why dost thou make us err from thy ways and harden our
> heart, so that we fear thee not? Return for the sake of thy servants,
> the tribes of thy inheritance'.

This passage is not a prophetic oracle, but rather it is part of a lament, in which the prophet cries out to the Lord in behalf of his people. But what is interesting for our purposes is that here again we find the idea that it is God who hardens the heart, even the heart of his own people. Westermann has commented: 'However much it perplexes them and challenges their faith, they believe that God can harden his chosen people's heart'. What brings Israel to this conclusion is 'her firm belief, admitting of no qualification, that God is one'.[167]

Restoration Texts
All three of Isaiah's major literary components contain restoration passages. The eyes and ears of the people will once again function (32.3-4; 35.5; 42.7, 16; 49.9; 61.1). The prophet proclaims:

'In that day the deaf shall hear the words of a book,
and out of their gloom and darkness the eyes of the blind shall see'
      (29.18).

'Then the eyes of those who see will not be closed,
and the ears of those who hear will hearken.
The mind of the rash will have good judgment. . . ' (32.3-4).

The lawless will receive instruction:

'And those who err in spirit will come to understanding, and those
      who murmur will accept instruction' (29.24).

All will discern what is right:

'All your sons shall be taught by the Lord. . . In righteousness you
      shall be established' (54.13; cf. 30.21).

It would appear, then, that obduracy in the book of Isaiah is meant to be understood as a condition, brought on variously by arrogance, immorality, idolatry, injustice, and false prophecy, that renders God's people incapable of discerning God's will. This inability leads to judgment and calamity. However, it is also understood to be a condition that God brings about himself, as part of his judgment upon his wayward people. But Isaiah, if not the eighth-century prophet, certainly the canonical book, announces that after the judgment, there is restoration, in which perception returns (attended by righteousness, justice, and trust in God).

D. *Isaiah 6.9-10 and Related Obduracy Texts of the Old Testament*

There is a variety of Old Testament texts that bear a certain theological affinity to Isa. 6.9-10 that are worth examining briefly. This task is done chiefly for the purpose of comparing our Isaiah text against the diversity of similar obduracy texts, and to observe in what ways our Isaiah text is similar or distinctive, and so in what ways it contributes to the Old Testament obduracy motif.[168]

Obduracy Texts

We shall consider a sampling of those texts that describe, predict, or threaten Israelites with a condition of obduracy. Throughout the Pentateuch, Israel is described as having a 'stiff neck' (Exod. 32.9; 33.3, 5; 34.9), an 'uncircumcised heart' (Lev. 26.41; Deut. 10.16), or 'stubbornness' (Deut. 9.6, 13, 27; 10.16; 31.27). Israel, moreover, is warned against 'hardening' her heart against the poor (Deut. 15.7). In the Song of Moses Israel is described as having become 'fat' (Deut. 32.15). Here the same word (שָׁמֵן) as in Isa. 6.10 is used. Moreover, obstinacy characterizes Israel's early history: 'But whenever the judge died, they turned back and behaved worse than their fathers, going after other gods, serving them and bowing down to them; they did not drop any of their practices or their stubborn ways' (Judg. 2.19). According to LXX Num. 16.26, the men who followed Korah were 'hard-hearted'. Saul, Israel's first king, is also characterized as rebellious and stubborn (1 Sam. 15.23). Viewing the exile of the Northern Kingdom in retrospect, the author of Kings states: 'But they would not listen, but were stubborn, as their fathers had been, who did not believe in the Lord their God' (2 Kgs 17.14). Remembering the exile of Judah, Ezra prays: 'But they and our fathers acted presumptuously and stiffened their neck and did not obey thy commandments; they refused to obey, and were not mindful of the wonders which thou didst perform among them; but they stiffened their neck. . . they acted presumptuously. . . and turned a stubborn shoulder and stiffened their neck and would not obey' (Neh. 9.16-17a, 29). As has already been mentioned, the notion that Yahweh was often the cause of obduracy, even against Israel, seems to be understood well enough. In 1 Kgs 22.20-23 a lying spirit is sent to 'entice Ahab' into a foolish act. In Deut. 28.28 Moses warns an Israel prone to wander from the Lord: 'The Lord will smite you with madness and blindness and confusion of mind'. However, on occasion God may soften the heart to do his will. For example, in 2 Chr. 30.8 Hezekiah enjoins his subjects not to be 'stiff-necked' as their fathers had been. The chronicler states that on this occasion 'the hand of God was also upon Judah to give them one heart to do what the king and the princes commanded by the word of the Lord' (2 Chr. 30.12). The obduracy idea receives expression in the hymnic and wisdom literature as well, though here it is frequently in reference to individuals or groups, and not to the whole nation (cf. Pss. 78.8; 81.11-13; 82.5; 95.8; 119.69-70; Prov. 20.12; 28.14; 29.1; Job 9.4; Eccl. 7.17). It is, however, in the prophetic literature that we encounter some of the severest expressions of the obduracy idea, some of which approximate what we found in Isaiah. The following examples are selected for special comment because of their similarity to Isa. 6.9-10.

Jer. 5.21-23. This passage, like Isa. 6.9-10, alludes to the three faculties of eyes, ears, and heart (or mind). It reads as follows (RSV):

> 21 Hear this, O foolish and senseless people,
>   who have eyes, but see not,
>   who have ears, but hear not. . .
>
> 23 But this people has a stubborn and rebellious heart;
>   they have turned aside and gone astray.

The obstinacy of 'this people'[169] is contrasted sharply with the ordained laws of nature. The sea may pound against the sandy beaches, but it is not allowed to pass by (v. 22). In contrast, Yahweh's people have a stubborn and defiant heart (לב סורר ומורה), on account of which even nature's course has been disrupted (vv. 24-25; cf. 4.23-28).[170] In this text it is the people itself which is responsible for its condition of obduracy. It has been suggested, and I think correctly, that this text is a conscious reflection of Isa. 6.9.[171] Elsewhere in Jeremiah, the obduracy idea is expressed. The prophet enjoins his people: 'Circumcise yourselves to the Lord, remove the foreskin of your hearts [LXX 'of your hardened heart'], O men of Judah. . . ' (4.4; cf. 9.26; Deut. 10.16). He castigates them as foolish, stupid, lacking in understanding, having faces 'harder than rock', unrepentant (4.22; 5.3), 'stiff-necked' (7.26; 17.23; 19.15) and 'stubborn' (18.12). They have closed their ears and have scorned the word of God (6.10). For being this way, the Lord will throw stumbling-blocks before them (6.21). Jeremiah's descriptions employ almost all of the language of obduracy. However, it falls short of saying that God himself in any way brought about the condition.

Ezek. 12.2-3a. In Ezek. 12.2-3a we read (RSV):

> Son of man, you dwell in the midst of a rebellious house,
>   who have eyes to see, but see not,
>   who have ears to hear, but hear not;
>   for they are a rebellious house.

It is likely that this text reflects Isa. 6.9-10 and Jer. 5.21.[172] It has been suggested that these verses specifically refer to the messages which the prophet Ezekiel acted out (e.g., the placing of the siegeworks around the brick, 4.1-8; the cooking of food over dung, 4.9-17; the cutting and scattering of the prophet's hair, 5.1-4).[173] Elsewhere in Ezekiel the theme of obduracy is expressed. Since Ezekiel has not been sent to 'a people of foreign speech and a hard language', but to Israel, the prophet's message should be heard (3.6).[174] However, the Lord warns his prophet: 'But the house of Israel will not listen to me; because all the house of Israel are of a hard forehead and of a stubborn heart' (3.7; cf. 2.3-7). In 18.31 the prophet enjoins his people: 'Cast away from you all the transgressions which you have committed against me, and get youselves a new heart and a new spirit!' This injunction implies that their present heart and spirit are insensitive to God. Again, as in the case of Jeremiah above, Ezekiel uses similar language, but does not go so far as to say that the Lord brings about obduracy.[175]

Zech. 7.11-12a. In Zech. 7.11-12a we encounter this scathing prophetic criticism (RSV):

> But they refused to hearken, and turned a stubborn shoulder, and stopped their ears that they might not hear. They made their hearts like adamant lest they should hear the law and the words which the Lord of hosts had sent by his Spirit and through the former prophets.

'Hearken' (קשׁב) means more than merely hearing. It has the idea of acting upon what is heard. Rather than heeding what they have heard, the people 'turn a stubborn shoulder' (יתנו כתף סררת), which recalls the stubborn animal that resists being yoked (cf. Exod. 32.9; Deut. 9.6, 13, 27; 2 Kgs 17.14; Neh. 9.29; etc.).[176] Recalling the language of Isa. 6.10,[177] the people have made their ears 'heavy' (כבד) in order not to hear (שמע). It is interesting to note that the prophet declares that the people have dulled their hearing and hardened their ears[178] in order not to hear *torah* or the inspired words of Yahweh's 'former prophets' (הנביאים הראשנים). Although it is debatable whether or not the parallel direct objects (both are governed by את) 'torah' and 'former prophets' have canonical reference, the prophet Zechariah is making it emphatically clear that the people of God have rejected the word of God. They have hardened themselves against it, so as neither to do it nor even to hear it.

Two other utterances from the prophets are worth mentioning briefly. Mic. 4.12 says: 'But they do not know the thoughts of the Lord, they do not understand his plan. . . ' Hab. 1.5b adds: 'For I am doing a work in your days that you would not believe if told' (quoted in Acts 13.41). These texts describe a nation that is dull in its understanding and completely unprepared for what lies ahead.

Deut. 29.1-3. Although not part of the 'prophets', Deuteronomy does contain elements that reflect the period in which many of the prophets already considered ministered, and so will be examined here. Deuteronomy frequently refers to a 'stubborn' Israel (9.6, 13, 27; 10.16; 31.27), recalling the older traditions of Exodus, and warns that her disobedience will only provoke the Lord into afflicting them with 'madness', 'blindness', and 'confusion' (28.28), a description possibly echoing the maladies of Isa. 29.9, 10, 18. However, our last example under consideration approximates Isa. 6.9-10 more closely. We read in Deut. 29.1-3 (RSV, 29.2-4):

> And Moses summoned all Israel and said to them: 'You have seen all that the Lord did before your eyes in the land of Egypt, to Pharaoh, and to all his servants and to all his land, the great trials which your eyes saw, the signs, and those great wonders; but to this day the Lord has not given you a mind [lit. 'heart'] to understand, or eyes to see, or ears to hear'.

This text bears the closest affinity to Isa. 6.9-10. Because Yahweh has not given the people hearts, eyes, and to ears to understand, the people have failed to grasp the full meaning of their past experiences.

The text must be understood in a seventh-century context and, as such, is to be understood as a commentary on Israel's troubles.[179] It is very possible that it reflects, or may even be dependent upon, the Isaianic hermeneutic of obduracy.

This important text seeks to explain human unreceptivity to divine revelation. Ultimately such understanding could be had only if the Lord provided a mind (or 'heart') of understanding (compare 30.6). Without such a disposition, wonders and signs cannot be perceived correctly, as in the case of Pharoah and, unfortunately, as in the subsequent history of Israel. Isa. 6.9-10 represents the other side of the same coin in that obduracy may also be explained as that which the Lord himself produces. Thus, the deprivation of the receptive heart and the production of an obdurate heart can be thought of as one and the same process. In either way of expressing this concept, the Lord is regarded as the ultimate agent or cause, either of receptivity or obduracy.[180]

Restoration Texts
In the prophetic tradition, the hope is expressed that some day God will replace Israel's hard and disobedient heart with a heart of understanding and obedience. There are several texts that promise the restoration of spiritual sensitivity and discernment.

According to Jeremiah, all the people will have a heart to know God (24.7; 31.34; 32.38-40). In Jer. 31.33 a poignant expression of this sentiment is found:

> But this is the covenant which I will make with the house of Israel after those days, says the Lord: I will put my law within them, and I will write it upon their hearts; and I will be their God, and they shall be my people (RSV).

Similar pasages are found in Ezekiel, the prophet of the exile (RSV):

> And I will give them one [or 'a new'] heart, and put a new spirit within them; I will take the stony heart out of their flesh and give them a heart of flesh, that they may walk in my statutes and keep my ordinances and obey them; and they shall be my people, and I will be their God (11.19-20).

> A new heart I will give you, and a new spirit I will put within you; and I will take out of your flesh the heart of stone and give you a

heart of flesh. And I will put my spirit within you, and cause you to walk in my statutes and be careful to observe my ordinances (36.26-27).

What is common to all of these texts concerned with spiritual restoration is the idea that obduracy is a moral and spiritual condition from which recovery is possible only through God's intervention. Although these are positive texts, looking to an ideal age, they bear eloquent testimony to the problem of obduracy.

Summary

By way of summary, it is fair to say that whereas there are several texts similar to Isa. 6.9-10, none outside the book of Isaiah goes quite so far in expressing the idea that God on occasion will harden the hearts of his own people for purposes of judgment. Underlying this severe text is the conviction that God is sovereign and absolute, and is not bound to a particular people, but is Lord over all peoples. This means that God is free to harden Israelites, as well as Gentiles. (This does not mean that God is capricious; it means that because he is holy, God will not tolerate sin.) Other prophetic texts express the conviction that God's people are at times obdurate, or that God himself must give a heart of understanding to his people so that they can perceive, but only Isa. 6.9-10 explicitly states that God hardens his people in order to prevent repentance, and so render judgment certain. It is a text that represents a high point in the Old Testament's struggle to affirm God's sovereignty and a truly monotheistic faith. Finally, we have also found that in the book of Isaiah in particular, and the Old Testament in general, the idea of Israelite obduracy is tempered by the hope of an eventual softening, sometimes with respect to a remnant, that will lead to repentance, renewal, and restoration. In the chapters that follow the question of how this provocative text was understood by subsequent generations of believers will be explored.

Chapter 2

ISAIAH 6.9-10 IN QUMRAN[1]

Introduction

The Great Isaiah Scroll of Qumran is quite interesting. Not only does it provide us with a pre-Masoretic text, but it provides us with some exegetical insight into the methods of interpretation employed by the Qumran sectaries. Because of their apocalyptic–eschatological hermeneutic which led them to believe that everything prophetic in the scriptures spoke to and of them, the community of the last days, they interpreted the prophets (and many of the Psalms) according to their own experiences.[2] But, as will be seen below, the community had no room for prophetic self-criticism since, after all, they constituted the 'righteous remnant'.[3] In view of this orientation, we should not be surprised to find that the text of Isa. 6.9-10, as well as 6.13, has undergone some important modifications.

A. *Isa. 6.9-10 in 1QIsaiah*[a]

Because of the presence of several variants which have significant bearing on the translation of the passage, it is necessary to provide the Hebrew text. The text is as follows (col. 6, ll.2-5):

ויואמר לך ואמרתה לעם הזה
שמעו שמוע ועל תבינו
ראו ראו ועל תדעו
השם לב העם הזה
ואוזניו הכבד
ועיניו השע
פן יראה בעיניו
ובאוזניו ישמעו
בלבבו יבין
ושב ורפא לו

Before a translation and interpretation can be offered, several important variants must be taken into account. In v. 9 the Qumran text both times reads על instead of אל. In v. 10 the final ן of השמן has been omitted, and in the last line of this verse ולבבו became ולבבו by misplacing the copula. (This reading is also attested by 4QIsa[f].) In either location it would be pronounced ו. In the first and last examples, the variants may be explained as resulting from scribal confusion due to the similar sounds of the radicals in question. The other example could conceivably represent a scribal error in that the final ן was accidentally omitted, as may be suggested by the presence of the medial מ, rather than the final ם (השמ rather than השם). It is conceivable, then, that all of these textual variants[4] are scribal errors and thus the text was never intended to read any differently from what we have preserved in the MT. However, W.H. Brownlee has argued that the combination of these particular variants goes beyond mere coincidence, but points to a new understanding of the Isaianic text.[5] Whereas it is possible that the final ן of השמן has been omitted accidentally, which would explain why the scribe wrote מ when it should have been final, it might be argued that the scribal error lay not in omitting the final ן, but in inadvertently copying the medial מ, instead of writing final ם, since the medial was in all probability in the text before him. (Another possibility is that the final ן was apocopated, but that is unlikely and does not satisfactorily explain the presence of the medial מ.) In isolation it would be impossible to decide, but taken with the other variants of 1QIsaiah[a] and with other readings at Qumran, it does seem likely that השמ is a deliberate variant.

However, the problem arises as to how השמ should be pointed, if it is assumed to be the intended reading, e.g., is it הַשָּׂם (qal participle of שים, 'that which is set' or 'established') or הָשֵׁם (hiphil imperative of שמם, 'make appalled')?[6] F.J. Morrow favors the hiphil imperative pointing, since שמם so pointed in 1QH 7.2-3 makes the most contextual and grammatical sense.[7] As an example of the verb שמם appearing with לב ('heart'), he cites Ps. 143.4, ישתומם לבי ('my heart is appalled'). For similar reasons, and because of his understanding of the 1QIsaiah[a] passage as a whole, Brownlee also prefers the hiphil imperative pointing.[8] I am inclined to agree with Brownlee and Morrow. It would seem to be the most likely option to understand השמ in 1QIsa.[a] 6.4 (MT 6.10) as a hiphil imperative, and as a deliberate scribal alteration.[9] If so understood, the remainder of the variants then fall into place along the lines that Brownlee has suggested. At this point we shall examine Brownlee's interpretation and then bring in some other recent discussion on this text. He offers this translation:

9   [And he said. 'Go, and say to this people:]
        "Keep on listening, *because* you may understand;
        Keep on looking, *because* you may perceive!"
10   *Make* the heart of this people *appalled*:
        Stop its ears
        and turn away its eyes—
        lest it see with its eyes
        and hear with its ears.
        Let it understand in its heart
        and return and be healed.'[10]

According to Brownlee's interpretation, it would appear that these textual modifications have completely transformed the meaning of the Hebrew text. He has made the following observations in light of these noted variants:

(1) First of all, the negative particle אל of the MT has become the causal על (an abbreviation of על אשר) thus changing the meaning from 'not' to 'because'. Brownlee suspects that this variant, as well as the others, is intentional and is not the result of confusion on the part of the scribe between two words that sound alike.[11] Instead, the scribe has taken advantage of the fact that these words do have a similar sound, in order to facilitate and even justify the new reading. It would seem that the same thing can be said for all of the variants under consideration.

(2) By omitting the final ן from השמן ('make fat') the resultant variant is השם (the hiphil imperative of שמם meaning 'make appalled'; see Isa. 52.14),[12] a word which occurs frequently in the Prophets (see Jer. 2.12-13; 18.16; 19.8; 49.17; 50.13; Ezek. 26.16; 27.35; 28.19). What meaning this variant contributes will be discussed shortly.

(3) Finally, as noted by Brownlee, the ו is omitted (actually, it has been replaced with ב, another sound-alike) before the last line 'so that the force of the negative particle "lest" is broken, so that "*and (lest)* it understand" becomes "Let it understand"'.[13]

In support and clarification of his interpretation Brownlee cites

1QH 7.2-3 in which there are several related vocabulary items:

> Turn my eyes from seeing evil,
> my ears from hearing of murder.
> Make my heart appalled [השם] at evil thoughts.[14]

The occurrence of the words 'eyes', 'ears', 'heart', and especially השם, should be noted. Brownlee has pointed to another relevant text from Isaiah (33.15) where the righteous person is described as one

> who stops his ears from hearing of *murder*,
> and shuts his eyes from looking upon *evil*.[15]

Brownlee concludes that 'from this passage the words "evil" and "murder" were drawn by the hymn writer as the unexpressed (but understood) objects of the verbs in Isa. 6.10'.[16] Thus the text of 1QIsaiah[a] is to be read:

> Make the heart of his people appalled (at evil)
> > stop its ears
> > and turn away its eyes—
> lest it see (evil) with its eyes
> > and hear (of murder) with its ears.[17]

The effect of these variants is to redirect the entire thrust of the Isaianic passage. The passage no longer proclaims a word of judgment aimed at promoting and intensifying spiritual obduracy; rather, its purpose is to warn and aid the elect in protecting themselves from evil.[18]

B. *Isa. 6.13 in 1QIsaiah[a]*

Now that the altered thrust of vv. 9-10 has been observed and explained, what is to be made of vv. 11-13 that describe the destruction and desolation of the land? In v. 13 we encounter two more interesting variants in 1QIsaiah[a] that bear on this question. The text is as follows (column 6, ll. 8-10):

8 ועוד בה עשיריה ושבה והייתה

9 לבער כאלה וכאלון אשר משלכת מצבת   במה זרע הקודש

10 מצבתה

In all of the literature concerning this verse[19] not enough attention has been given to the wide space between מצבת and במה, according to

J. Sawyer.[20] He has argued that this gap is not accidental, but signifies a new thought beginning with the word במה.[21] He suggests that במה may be understood as the interrogative 'how?', and so the final clause of v. 13 should read: 'How can the holy seed be its stump?'[22] The second important variant is the addition of the definite article. 1QIsaiah[a] reads זרע הקודש instead of the indefinite זרע קדש of the MT. The insertion of the article ה has the effect of calling attention to the question of who is the 'holy seed', a question which was very important to the Qumran sectaries. These minor changes, according to Sawyer, have given Isa. 6.13 a new meaning, one that would have been quite acceptable in Qumran. Taking into account the larger context, the meaning is as follows: verses 9-10 make up an exhortation to 'this people' (i.e., the members of the Qumran community) to understand and to avoid impiety. Verses 11-13ab describe the terrible destruction for those who have not understood and obeyed (i.e., the religious establishment of Jerusalem). Verse 13c then concludes with the sarcastic question: 'How can the holy seed be *its* stump?' The 'holy seed' is Qumran and the 'stump' is the Jerusalem establishment. This interpretation becomes a reversal of the establishment's remnant theology. The rhetorical question, 'How can. . .?' is to be answered, 'It cannot be!'

Brownlee, however, has interpreted the significance of the space between מצבת and במה differently. Unlike Sawyer, he does not understand במה as an interrogative ('how?'), but as a longer spelling of the preposition and pronominal suffix בם ('in [or among] them').[23] He too understands the space as meant to introduce a new thought, but not as Sawyer concluded. The space is intended to call to the attention of the reader a new thought which he might otherwise miss in the Hebrew.[24] 1QIsaiah[a] should read:

> And though a tenth remain in it, it in turn shall be for burning like a terebinth and like an oak, when (their) stalk sheds (leaves)[25]—(so shall there be) among them the holy seed, its stalk.[26]

According to this translation, the Qumran sectaries probably are to understand themselves as 'the holy seed' that survives among the people of Israel.[27] Brownlee's translation is grammatically quite different, and it is not easy to decide which approach is best. But even if we cannot choose one over against the other, it is clear that the Qumran community identified itself as 'the holy seed' (as well as the 'stalk'), which will remain no matter how severely Israel is judged. The motivation for the alteration is two-fold. First, it offers an attack against the Jerusalem establishment. It will be destroyed, but the 'holy seed' (i.e., Qumran) will be spared. Secondly, the Qumran community had no place for prophetic criticism. Since, as their hermeneutical rule, prophetic texts applied to them and to their situation, especially such a significant one as Isaiah 6, it was unthinkable that Isaiah would be asked by the Lord to speak words that promoted obduracy among his people. So the wording was altered slightly, bringing in an understanding clarified further in other related texts. The result of this adjustment is that the message of condemnation has been transformed into an exhortation to righteousness. Such exegetical practice is due to an aversion to prophetic criticism on the part of the Qumran sectaries, for as yet no example of prophetic criticism understood as leveled against themselves has been found in the writings of Qumran.[28] Their hermeneutic simply did not allow for such self-criticism.

C. *The Obduracy Idea in Qumran*

Although Isa. 6.9-10 in 1QIsaiah[a] no longer has anything to do with obduracy, the idea is present elsewhere in the writings of Qumran, but never in reference to the eschatological community. Several references to being 'stubborn' are found, for example, in the *Manual of Discipline* (1QS) and the *Cairo–Damascus Document* (CD). In the latter document we are told that the angels fell 'because they walked in the stubbornness of their hearts' (CD[A] 2.17-18).[29] While in Egypt the Israelites 'walked in the stubbornness of their hearts' (CD[A] 3.5; cf. 3.11-12; 8.8). The document goes on to warn contemporary Israelites: 'The same applies again—in the future as it did in the past—to all who commit their hearts to idolatry and walk in the stubbornness of their hearts' (CD[B] 2.9-10). In the *Manual of Discipline* the person who would join the eschatological community must 'walk no more in the stubbornness of a guilty heart' (1.6; cf. 5.4-5). The one who persists in 'walking in the stubbornness of his heart' will be refused entry into the community (2.25-26). Obduracy derives from, or at least characterizes, a 'spirit of perversity': 'To the spirit of perversity belong... blindness of eyes, dullness of ears, stiffness of neck and hardness of heart' (4.11). Here most of the language of obduracy appears. Obduracy is also characteristic of the person who quits the community: 'If a man's spirit waver so far from the basis of the community that he betray the truth and walk in the stubborness of his own heart...' (7.18-19); and: 'If a man... quit the general body in order to walk in the stubbornness of his own heart, he is never to return to formal membership in the community' (7.22-24). In the *Thanksgiving Hymns* (1QH) it is said of the religious establishment: 'In the stubbornness of their hearts they wander astray and go seeking Thee through idols... Then with stammering tongue and with alien lips they speak unto Thy people, seeking guilefully to turn their deeds to delusion' (4.15-17). It is interesting to note that Isa. 28.11 has been alluded to, a passage also quite critical of the religious establishment: 'By men of strange lips and with an alien tongue the Lord will speak to this people'.

At Qumran there is the belief that the 'spirit of truth' enlightens one's heart and gives one a heart for God (cf. 1QS 4.2-3). Similarly, God himself must open the 'eyes' for one to understand his truth fully: '[Were it not for Thy grace,] I could not have seen this thing. [For how can] I look on [Thy glory] except Thou open mine eyes? How hear [the words of Thy truth] [except Thou unstop my ears?]. Behold, my heart was amazed that thus the word was revealed to one with ears unattuned, and that a [wayward] heart [was suffered to grasp these things]' (1QH 18.17-21; see also 11.25-29). In col. 2 of one of the fragmentary texts from cave four that Gaster has called, 'Prayer for Intercession',[30] we read: '[We beseech Thee, to tu]rn us again unto Thee with all our heart and soul, and so to plant Thy teaching in our hearts that we depart not from it to right or left, Thou having cured us of madness and blindness and bewilderment of heart'.[31] Here Deut. 28.28 has been alluded to, a text in which an Israel prone to wander is warned: 'The Lord will smite you with madness and blindness and confusion of mind'. The implication of these texts is that the eschatological community of Qumran has been delivered from these maladies. Their eyes and ears are open; their heart has been turned to God.

Summary

In the Hebrew tradition preserved in the MT, the prophet is commanded by the Lord to deliver a message whose intended effect is to render the people obdurate. The people are to be made insensitive to their spiritual bankruptcy and the disastrous consequences of it. In its historical context Isaiah's message is an example of 'prophetic critique' within the community. The Isaiah text of Qumran, however, provides a most remarkable effort at circumventing the original meaning. In a sense, the Qumran text also is a softening of the meaning of the Hebrew. But it is a complete transformation of the text, which now no longer has the prophet speaking an oracle in order to promote obduracy. Instead the prophet admonishes the righteous (the Qumran sectaries) to take heed during the troubled times that lie ahead. Those upon whom the disaster will come (the Jerusalem religious establishment) are in error if they suppose themselves to be the righteous remnant. Although the idea of prophetic self-criticism appears to be absent at Qumran, the obduracy idea is applied in various ways to non-members (and former members) of the sect.

Chapter 3

ISAIAH 6.9-10 IN THE SEPTUAGINT

Introduction

The oldest, and probably most important,[1] written translation of the Hebrew Bible is the Greek version called, due to the legendary tradition of its origin, the 'Septuagint' (LXX). Originally the name was applied to the Pentateuch only (c. third century BCE), but eventually was applied to the remainder of the canonical books (first century BCE) and the apocryphal books as well (first century CE). The Greek of the LXX is not pure koine, but a koine style abounding with Hebraisms. As a translation the Pentateuch is basically accurate and literal, though frequently it paraphrases anthropomorphisms which might be offensive to the more philosophically-minded Jews (particularly those of Alexandria).

Isaiah is written in good koine style, but as a translation it is paraphrastic, a fact which has been observed by I.L. Seeligmann.[2] Moreover, Seeligmann has demonstrated that the translator has certain pat translations for various Hebrew words, which he tended to use mechanically 'without any notice being taken either of the context in which it occurred, or of current Greek idiom'.[3]

A. *Isaiah 6.9-10 in the LXX*[4]

The LXX text of Isa. 6.9-10 reads as follows:

9 καὶ εἶπεν, Πορεύθητι καὶ εἰπὸν τῷ λαῷ τούτῳ,
Ἀκοῇ ἀκούσετε[5] καὶ οὐ μὴ συνῆτε καὶ βλέποντες βλέψετε καὶ οὐ μὴ ἴδητε.[6] 10 ἐπαχύνθη[7] γὰρ ἡ καρδία τοῦ λαοῦ τούτου,
καὶ τοῖς ὠσὶν αὐτῶν[8] βαρέως ἤκουσαν καὶ τοὺς ὀφθαλμοὺς αὐτῶν[8] ἐκκάμμυσαν,

To See and Not Perceive

μήποτε ἴδωσιν τοῖς ὀφθαλμοῖς καὶ τοῖς ὠσὶν ἀκούσωσιν καὶ τῇ
καρδίᾳ συνῶσιν καὶ ἐπιστρέψωσιν[9] καὶ ἰάσομαι[10]
αὐτούς.

The RSV (i.e., its translation of Mt. 13.14b-15, which is the
quotation of the LXX) translates as follows:

> 9 And he said, 'Go and say to this people:
>   "You shall indeed hear but never understand,
>   and you shall indeed see but never perceive".
> 10 For this people's heart has grown dull,
>   and their ears are heavy of hearing,
>   and their eyes they have closed,
> lest they should perceive with their eyes,
>   and hear with their ears,
> and understand with their heart
>   and turn for me to heal them'.

The LXX has significantly altered the complexion of the Hebrew
text. Several observations may be made:

(1) As in the Hebrew, the Greek verbs are reinforced by respective
cognates.[11] However, the LXX has made a very important change
when it uses the futures 'you will hear' and 'you will see' to translate
the Hebrew imperatives 'hear' and 'see' respectively.[12] The prophet
is no longer *enjoining* the people to become obdurate, but is
predicting that they will remain obdurate. This change removed
much of the sarcasm and judgmental tone. That this is the idea
behind the translation is confirmed, I believe, by changes that are to
be observed in v. 10.

(2) The passive 'has grown dull'[13] alters significantly the causative
meaning of the Hebrew 'make fat'. As it stands in the LXX, 'the heart
of this people' has become the subject rather than the object. With
respect to the presence of underlying hiphils, Seeligmann comments:
'In common with some of his colleagues, the translator has
consciously tried to give expression to the causative character of the
הפעיל forms. This is done in the purest manner when the infinitive of
the verb in question is made into the object of ποιεῖν'.[14] As examples
he cites Isa. 42.16 and 43.23. He also notes that 'frequently Greek
verbs expressing a causative notion are simply chosen' (e.g., 41.22,
εἰπεῖν; 43.9, ἀναγγέλειν).[15] However, there are times when the
translator does not wish to preserve the causative idea of the hiphil.

Instead, as has been pointed out by Seeligmann, he 'uses. . . passive forms of the verb, thereby completely altering the construction and even the meaning' of the text.[16] Unfortunately, Seeligmann does not discuss Isa. 6.10 in this connection, but it would seem that this text is a prime example of this tendency on the part of the translator. As the translator now has it, it is not the preaching of the prophet that causes the heart to be fat, but the prophet preaches *because* (γάρ) the heart is already fat.[17]

(3) The causal conjunctive γάρ is employed in order to underscore the change from active agency (as in the MT) to a passive condition. Therefore, the anticipatory message, 'You shall indeed hear but never understand', etc. is appropriate not because the Lord intends to harden the hearts of the people, but because the heart of the people has already become hardened.

(4) The verbs 'hear' and 'close' are probably gnomic, and may be translated in the present tense as the RSV has done. Again, as in the case of 'has grown dull', the subject, along with the responsibility, has been transferred from the prophet to the people.

(5) The context of 'lest' in the LXX is not the same as it is in the Hebrew, because the alterations already noted have changed the subject. In its Greek context 'lest' expresses the purpose of the people, not of the Lord speaking through his prophet. The people hear with difficulty and have shut their eyes *so that they* do not have to perceive with their eyes, hear with their ears, discern in their heart, and repent.

(6) As has already been mentioned, the LXX does not preserve an equivalent for the last clause of v. 13 in the MT ('a holy seed is its stump'). However, the reading, σπέρμα ἅγιον τὸ στήλωμα αὐτῆς, is provided by Aquila, Symmachus, Lucian, and *C*. Theodotion and Origen mark the clause with asterisks. Seeligmann thinks that the phrase may be authentic.[18] As has already been discussed above in Ch. 1, the omission of this clause in the LXX is probably accidental.[19]

It is clear from these observations that the LXX translator(s) of Isaiah wished to tone down the judgmental aspect of their Hebrew text. Indeed, such a command from the Lord would have been quite embarrassing. In the MT the prophet is commanded by the Lord to 'make the heart of this people fat', and so to prepare them for judgment. The opportunity for repentance is now past and so part of the judgment itself is to make the people all the more insensitive to the gravity of the situation and, consequently, to make them all the more culpable. However, in the LXX the prophet is to speak a message that *predicts* the people's insensitivity, not promotes it. It is because the people itself has hardened its heart and shut its eyes that the unfortunate result is blindness to its sin and coming judgment. Although the Lord would be willing, he is not able to heal the people, since it will not repent.

B. *Isaiah 6.9-10 in the Greek Recensions*

The LXX fell into disfavor among Jews primarily because of its use by Christians. The recension of Aquila (*c*. 130 CE) and the revision of Theodotion (*c*. 190 CE) were produced in order to make available to the Jewish community new Greek versions in which passages, particularly those well-suited to Christian exegesis, were modified (usually so as to be more literal). On the other hand, Symmachus (*c*. 170 CE), in all probability a Christian, had no such motivation. Unfortunately, all that remains of his recension are fragments from the *Hexapla*.

There is, however, evidence that would suggest the existence of at least one Jewish recension in the first century CE. In 1952 a Ta'amire bedouin found in a cave a Greek scroll of the Minor Prophets.[20] Subsequent excavators identified the cave as Nahal Hever, and found nine additional fragments of the scroll.[21] Shortly after the scroll's discovery D. Barthélemy published the fragments and suggested an early second-century CE date (i.e., during the bar-Kochbah revolt).[22] However, C.H. Roberts and P. Kahle have argued that the scroll should be dated between 50 BCE and 50 CE.[23] Barthélemy has concluded that the scroll is not an independent translation of the Hebrew, but is a recension of the LXX and, as such, represents a step toward the later recensions of Aquila, Symmachus, and Theodotion.[24] What is significant is that this scroll provides evidence 'not only that the Septuagint circulated in Palestine, but that it circulated in Palestine long enough and widely enough to undergo revision within Palestine'.[25]

Whereas the texts of Aquila and Theodotion are in agreement with LXX Isa. 6.9-10, Symmachus provides an interesting version of v. 10:[26]

ὁ λαὸς οὗτος τὰ ὦτα ἐβάρυνε,
καὶ τοὺς ὀφθαλμοὺς αὐτοῦ ἔμυσε,
μήπως ἴδῃ ἐν τοῖς ὀφθαλμοῖς αὐτοῦ,
καὶ ἐν τοῖς ὠσὶν ἀκούῃ,
καὶ ἡ καρδία αὐτοῦ συνῇ,
καὶ ἐπιστραφῇ, καὶ ἰαθῇ.

This people has closed its ears
> and shut its eyes,
lest it should see with its eyes,
> and hear with its ears,
> and its heart discern,
> and it turn and be healed.

A few observations may be made:

(1) The clause describing the heart apparently has been omitted, though this abbreviation may be due to Theodoret.

(2) 'Closed' (βαρύνειν) is the verbal cognate of the adverb βαρέως read by the LXX, and means literally 'to weigh down' or 'to depress'. ἐβάρυνε corresponds more closely to the MT's הכבד than does βαρέως ἤκουσαν of the LXX. (The verb occurs frequently, and appears to be synonymous with σκληρύνειν, cf. Exod. 7.14; 8.11 [8.15, RSV], 28 [32, RSV]; 9.34). However, as in the LXX, so also here the responsibility for the inability to hear rests squarely upon the people.

(3) Finally, Symmachus uses the passive 'be healed', which probably reflects the sense of the Hebrew more exactly than does the LXX.

Although the text of Symmachus is at variance with the LXX in a few places, the meaning is essentially the same. It is the people who have closed their eyes and ears. Thus, the Greek text traditions are in basic agreement with regard to the question of who is responsible for the obduracy of the people.

C. *Isaiah 6.9-10 and Related Old Testament Texts in the LXX*

The modifications of Isa. 6.9-10 in the LXX and the rescensions have been observed. It is the purpose here in this section to examine the other obduracy passages, some of which were discussed above in Chapter 1, in which significant differences from the Hebrew can be detected. Significant differences are detected in the following two texts.

Isa. 29.9-10. In the LXX v. 9 is abbreviated thus: 'Faint and be amazed, and have a hang-over, not from liquor, nor from wine'. In this abbreviated form not only has the Hebrew parallelism been lost, but the meaning, in that the references to blindness has been omitted, has been softened somewhat as well. In v. 10, however, there are significant alterations to be observed: 'for the Lord has poured out upon you a spirit of deep sleep, and will close their eyes and [the eyes] of their prophets and their rulers, they who see the secret things'. The second person of the Hebrew has given way in the LXX to the third person ('their') in the second part of the verse, and the Hebrew preterite ('and he closed') is rendered in the future ('and he will close'). It would appear that the Greek translator wished to avoid the obvious sense of the Hebrew text in which the Lord is depicted as the cause of blindness in his people. Instead, the Lord will close the eyes of others ('they'), presumably Israel's enemies, though it is possible that the reference is to Israel's wayward prophets. In any case, at the very least the use of the third person would suggest that the wicked represent a group other than the whole people.

Isa. 42.18-20. The LXX translates vv. 18 and 20 accurately enough, but there are a few modifications in v. 19: 'and who is blind except my servants, and deaf except those who rule them? Even the servants of God were blinded'. For some reason the Greek translator renders the singular עַבְדִּי as οἱ παῖδες μου. It is true that the translator may have felt that the word was to be read as plural (i.e., עֲבָדַי), but as a rule he has understood it as a singular (cf. 41.8; 42.1; 44.1, 2; 45.4; 49.6; 52.13).[27] Also, as a general rule the translator uses παῖς for עבד (two exceptions would be his use of δοῦλος in 49.3, 5). The translator may have altered the number from the singular to the plural *ad sensum* in order to identify the 'servant' more closely with the people of Israel, rather than with the Messiah.

2 Esdras 3.20-22. Although not discussed above in Chapter 1, the text of 2 Esdras 3.20-22 provides another example of the obduracy idea as it had come to be understood in the later tradition of the Greek Bible. The RSV translates:

Yet thou didst not take away from them their evil heart, so that thy
law might bring forth fruit in them. For the first Adam, burdened
with an evil heart, transgressed and was overcome, as were also all
who were descended from him. Thus the disease became permanent;
the law was in the people's heart along with the evil root, but what
was good departed, and the evil remained.

Reflected here is the belief, found in the prophetic tradition (see
Ezek. 11.19-20; 36.26-27), that a discerning heart must be provided
by God. In the context of 2 Esdras, this passage explains why Israel
was conquered by Babylon (see v. 27).

Wis. 4.14b-15. Also not discussed above in Chapter 1 is Wis. 4.14b-
15 (4.15, RSV), a text that bears some relation to the other Old
Testament obduracy texts. The RSV translates:

Yet the peoples saw and did not understand,
    nor take such a thing to heart,
that God's grace and mercy are with his elect,
    and he watches over his holy ones.

The text falls within a larger passage concerned with the death of the
righteous (4.7-5.23). In 4.10-15 Enoch is cited as a righteous man
who lived, comparatively speaking, only a 'short time' (4.13), having
been removed 'from the midst of wickedness' (v. 14). His early death
apparently was an act of mercy, intended to spare him from this
wickedness, 'yet the peoples saw and did not understand. . . ' That is,
the peoples failed to perceive that his early death in this case was a
reward for his righteousness, and not evidence that human morality
is of no consequence to God. The clauses, 'Yet the peoples saw and
did not understand, nor take such a thing to heart', bear some
affinities with the other obduracy texts, but they do not say that the
obdurate condition of the wicked was in any way brought on by
God.

Summary

It is apparent that the LXX translator of Isaiah wished to tone down
the harshness of the Hebrew text. Not only is this seen in Isa. 6.9-10,
but even in other obduracy texts as well. Thus, it would appear that
his rendering of 6.9-10 is not an isolated instance, but reflects an
overall tendency to soften the aspect of judgment against Israel.

It is to be observed that those texts in Isaiah which speak of the *Lord* hardening the heart of the people reveal the greatest amount of paraphrastic activity when compared to the other related obduracy texts. Whereas the LXX translators provide fairly literal translations of Isa. 43.8; 44.18; 63.17; Jer. 5.21-23; Ezek. 12.2; and Deut. 29.1-3, in two of the instances where God himself is viewed as actually producing obduracy, that is, Isa. 6.9-10 and 29.9-10, the Greek translator of Isaiah has modified the text. It is probable that our Isaiah translator found such theology objectionable, and so wished to mitigate the harshness of the Hebrew text. (Even in the case of 44.18, a passage addressed to the heathen idol makers, 'because' is used with the verb in the passive). Since most of the other related obduracy texts in the prophetic tradition described the people as obdurate of their own accord, there was more than enough precedent for such modification. Thus, the strongly expressed monotheism of Hebrew Isaiah is blunted. The assertion that obduracy and destruction are decreed by God reflects a more fully monotheistic understanding, but shifting these realities onto the shoulders of the people misses the whole point of the stress upon God's sovereignty. This is not to say that the Isaiah translator has retreated to some sort of polytheism; on the contrary, he was undoubtedly more careful to safeguard Yahweh's ontological unity than Isaiah himself. But the hermeneutics operating when Isaiah preached and wrote were not the hermeneutics of the time and place when our translator was at work. At issue was not the unity of God. At issue was the disturbing notion that the God who had given his people *torah* would ever intentionally harden his people. To this question the Greek translator gave a negative answer.

Chapter 4

ISAIAH 6.9-10 IN THE TARGUM

Introduction

The Hebrew word Targum means 'interpretation' or 'translation', used with respect to the Aramaic translation of the Hebrew Bible. Because of the importance of Torah and the conviction that it must be made meaningful to the average Jew, so that he could understand and obey it, the synagogue adopted the practice of reading the sacred text in Hebrew and then giving an Aramaic paraphrase that would be more intelligible to the laity. It is possible that the origin of this practice is in view in Nehemiah 8 where Ezra's scribes explained the meaning of the Hebrew text to an Aramaic-speaking Jewish people. These Targumim, then, were oral in their origin, but gradually assumed a fairly fixed form before being committed to writing sometime before the fifth century CE.[1]

The Targums vary in their adherence to the Hebrew. In its translation, Targum Onqelos is quite literal, Targum Jonathan is much more interpretive, and 'Pseudo-Jonathan' is replete with popular stories and legends. What these Targums have in common is the tendency to modernize archaic names, and to explain figurative/anthropomorphic language. But for the present purposes, the most significant tendency to observe is, as J.F. Stenning has noted, that frequently the condemnation of Israel offered by the prophets is transferred to the enemies of Israel.[2] A similar type of 'softening', as we shall see, has taken place in Targum Jonathan's version of Isa. 6.9-10 (and v. 13).

A. *Isaiah 6.9-10 in Targum Jonathan*[3]

The text of Isa. 6.9-10 in Targum Jonathan reads:[4]

ואמר איזיל ותימר לעמא הדין   9
דשמעין משמע ולא מסתכלין
וחזן⁶ מחזא⁵ ולא ידעין:
טפיש לביה דעמא הדין   10
ואודנוהי יקר
ועינוהי טמטים
דלמא יחזון בעיניהון⁷
ובאודנהון ישמעון
ובליבהון⁸ יסתכלון
ויתובון וישתביק להון:

9   And he said, 'Go, and speak to this people
    who hear indeed but do not comprehend,
    and see indeed but do not understand.

10 Make the heart of this people dull,
    and make their ears heavy,
    and shut their eyes;
    lest they see with their eyes,
    and hear with their ears,
    and understand with their heart,
    and turn again, and it be forgiven them'.

There are a few notable differences between the Targum and the MT:

(1) Verse 9 no longer contains a separate unit functioning as that which the prophet is to speak. Rather, in the Targum it has become a relative clause modifying עמא הדין ('this people'). This modification has been brought about by the insertion of the relative prefix ד. It is true that ד may introduce final clauses as well as relative clauses and so in effect approximates ὅτι or ἵνα ('that', or 'in order that'), but for a final meaning in this context we would expect imperfect verbs.[9] The alteration brought about by the insertion of ד has the effect of softening the aspect of divine agency in v. 10. The people are described as *already* obdurate. Thus, the assignment of the prophet is simply to increase their callousness. Also, it has the effect of isolating a particular sub-group. Those whom the prophet is to harden consist of those who are spiritually insensitive. It is not the *whole* people that is to be hardened, but only those 'who hear, but do not comprehend, and see, but do not understand'.[10] In contrast to this group stands the righteous remnant described in v. 13, a verse in

which much haggadic activity is to be observed (see comments below). Among this remnant probably are those 'that have not sinned', according to the targumist's addition in 10.21.

(2) There are two other significant changes in v. 9. The imperatives found in the MT disappear (they are replaced with participles and perfects), and the second person plurals are shifted to the third person plural. Both changes reflect, of course, the insertion of the relative ד.

(3) In v. 10 the verb שבק ('to forgive') replaces the Hebrew text's רפא ('to heal'). This reading occurs only in the Targum and in no other early text tradition (with the exception of Mk 4.12, in which the Greek equivalent ἀφεθῇ is found). It is possible that שבק was used because it conveys the more literal intention of the statement than the metaphorical רפא (see also *Tg.* Isa. 53.5).

(4) Similarly, the pa'el imperative טפיש ('to make dull' or 'obdurate') reflects a more literal understanding of the verse than the metaphorical השמן ('to make fat') of the MT.

(5) The telic use of דלמא would be equivalent to the use of פן in the Hebrew text. There is, however, the possibility that דלמא should be understood in a conditional sense. This conditional idea appears elsewhere in the Isaiah Targum, where there is no conditional idea present in the Hebrew: 'Behold. . . signs and portents *will be. . . upon* Israel,—*that if they see and repent, the decree which was decreed against them—that they go into exile so as not to appear before* the LORD of hosts. . . *—will be void*' (8.18); '*If the wicked repent, will they not be called* my servant, even *the sinners, against whom* I sent *my prophets? But the wicked are about to be repaid the retribution of their sins, except that if they repent they will be called* the servants of the LORD' (42.19).[11] The reference to seeing, repenting, and going into exile in 8.18 may very well be an allusion to Isa. 6.10-13; perhaps even an interpretation of it. If so, we should read 6.10 in light of 8.18, which would argue for understanding דלמא as conditional, instead of telic. In any case, it is evident that the rabbis understood this conjunction to mean 'unless' (or 'until').[12] If the targumist did in fact intend דלמא to be understood conditionally, the passage would read: 'Go, and speak to this people who hear but do not comprehend. . . Make the heart of this people dull . . . unless they see . . . and turn again, and it be forgiven them'. If this is what the targumist intended, then the severity of the passage has been mitigated significantly.

B. *Isa. 6.13 in the Targum*

In v. 13 the targumist has greatly elaborated on the 'holy seed':

> 'And a tenth shall be left in it, and they shall again be for
>   burning;
>   like the terebinth and like the oak,
>   which appear to be dried up when their leaves fall,
>   though they are still moist enough to preserve a seed from
>   them.
> So the exiles of Israel shall be gathered together,
>   and they shall return to their land;
>   for the holy seed is their plant.'

Whereas the first half of the verse is translated literally, in the second half there is some noteworthy paraphrase that calls for comment:

(1) The MT's 'stump [of the terebinth or oak] that remains standing' is replaced by the clause, 'which appear to be dried up when their leaves fall'. This clause may have something to do with the reading of the Vulgate (*quae expandit ramos suos*) or that of 1QIsaiah[a] ('when the stalk sheds [leaves]'), but whence its origin is not easily determined.

(2) More significantly, the clause, 'though they are still moist enough to preserve a seed from them', mitigates the severity of the picture of judgment, and anticipates the reference to the 'holy seed'. In 1.4 the targumist refers to the Judahites as a 'holy people' and a 'beloved seed'.

(3) Inspired by the imagery of the Hebrew text, the targumist believes that the passage has something to do with the promise to gather the exiles. This passage is one of several passages in the Isaiah Targum that is concerned with the theme of exile and return. A few examples may be cited:[13] In MT 42.7 the Lord promises to 'bring out the prisoners from the dungeon', while in the Targum he will 'bring forth the exiles from among the Gentiles, where they are like prisoners'. In MT 46.11, in reference to God's plans for Cyrus, the Lord will call 'a bird of prey from the east, the man of my counsel from a far country'. But the Targum transforms the passage to read: '(I am he) that says to gather exiles from the east, to bring openly as a swift bird from a far land the sons of Abraham my chosen'. Finally, in MT 66.9 the Lord asks: 'Shall I, who cause to bring forth, shut the

womb?' But in the Targum we find this interpretive paraphrase: 'I, God, created the world from the beginning, says the Lord, I created all men; I scattered them among the nations. I am also about to gather your exiles...' (see also 51.11; 53.8; 54.7).

The targumist apparently understands the exiles in contrast to the group that hears and see, but does not understand. This does not mean that they are without a measure of spiritual blindness or guilt. It means only that they make up the righteous remnant that will return from the exile and, once again, be fruitful in the land of Israel. Indeed, the targumist describes the remnant, for the most part, as 'disobedient and rebellious' (1.6), in need of repentance and of being refined, cleansed, and purified from their sins (8.18; 10.21-22; 53.10). They will be a people who, when God comes to save them, will finally see the law and heed the words of the prophets (35.4-5).

C. *Isaiah 6.9-10 and Related Old Testament Texts in the Targum*

It would be useful to survey briefly the other obduracy texts in the Isaiah Targum for purposes of comparison. We are interested to see if what was observed in Isa. 6.9-13 is in line with the Targum's theology elsewhere.

Isa. 29.9-10. At least one significant difference from the Hebrew is to be noted in the Targum's rendering of the passage. B.D. Chilton's translation of the text reads as follows (with targumic variations italicized):

> 9 Delay, be astounded, *be confused* and *appalled*! They are drunk, but not with wine; they stagger, but not with *old wine*.
> 10 For the LORD *cast among* you a spirit of *deception*, and has *hidden himself from* you, the prophets, *the scribes and the teachers who were teaching* you *the teaching of the law* he has *hidden*.[14]

According to the targumist the Lord has not blinded the prophets and the seers. He has only removed them from the people, and has thus deprived the people of their instruction in Torah.[15] To underscore the aspect of instruction, 'seers' is replaced by 'scribes' and 'teachers' (which, of course, are rabbinic terms). Obviously, an element of judgment still remains, but it lacks the severity of that found in the Hebrew.

Isa. 42.18-20. In this passage several significant variations are also to be found. Chilton has translated the text as follows:

> 18 *You wicked who are as* deaf, *have you no ears? Hear!* And *you sinners who are as* blind, *have you no eyes? Consider and* see! 19 *If the wicked repent, will they not be called* my servant, even *the sinners, against whom* I sent *my prophets? But the wicked are about to be repaid the retribution of their sins, except that if they repent they will be called* the servants of the Lord. 20 You see many things, but do not observe them; *your* eyes are open, but *you do* not *listen to teaching.*[16]

The deaf and blind of v. 18 are qualified as the 'wicked' and as 'sinners'. There is no such qualification in the Hebrew. The reading, 'consider and see', instead of 'look and see', as in the Hebrew, probably has arisen from the importation of אסתכלו from the related text of Isa. 6.9-10. Verse 19 displays the greatest difference from the MT. Rather than being a reference to Israel collectively as the Lord's servant, the Targumic reading refers only to those Israelites who are 'servants' because of their repentance, an idea not even hinted at in the Hebrew (see also the Targum at 29.10).[17] This tendency to avoid collective condemnation was seen with reference to Isa. 6.9-13 where the prophet was commanded to harden those *who* will neither hear nor perceive.

Although it is not part of the text under consideration, it is interesting to note the self-serving modification found in the following verse (i.e., v. 21). The MT reads: 'The Lord was pleased, for his righteousness' sake, to magnify his law and make it glorious'. However, the Targum reads: 'The Lord is pleased to justify Israel; he will magnify those who observe his law, and will strengthen them'.

Isa. 43.8. In this passage we find some noteworthy modifications. Chilton translates:

> He brought *the* people *from* Egypt, who are *as* the blind, yet have eyes, who are *as* deaf, yet have ears![18]

The element of obduracy remains, but the passage has been historicized. God does not call for the people to be brought forth (as in the Hebrew), but reminds his people that he is the one who had brought them forth from Egypt. Chilton notes that the targumist has alluded to the great exodus event in order 'to express his certainty that God would act' (see also 51.9).[19] The targumist also qualifies the description of obduracy by saying that the people were '*as* the blind' and '*as* the deaf'. (The Hebrew reads: 'the people who are blind. . . who are deaf').

Isa. 44.18. The Targum of Isa. 44.18 presents a few variants of interest. Chilton translates:

> They know not, neither do they discern; for their eyes *are* shut so that they cannot see, so that they cannot understand *with* their heart.[20]

In the Hebrew the sense is active ('for he [God] has smeared over [טח] their eyes'), while here in the Targum the sense is passive (מטמטמן, the same word used in 6.10). This may be no more than the divine passive, in which case the meaning would be no different from that of the Hebrew, but it could point to another instance in which the obduracy idea in the Isaiah Targum is blunted.

Isa. 63.17. In this passage also the Targum has made a few noteworthy alterations. Chilton translates:

> O LORD, why *will* you *despise* us, *to* err from ways *which are correct before you as the gentiles who have no portion in the teaching of your law? Let not* our heart *be turned* from your fear; return *your shekhinah to your people* for the sake of your servants, *the righteous, to whom you swore by your Memra to make among them* the tribes of your heritage.[21]

Here we again encounter the targumist's interest in the law and the shekinah. For our purposes, however, the interesting modification is the Targum's 'Let not our heart be turned from your fear', which in the Hebrew reads: '[Why] do you harden our heart, so that we do not fear you?' Whereas the Hebrew clearly implies that God has hardened the heart of his people, the Targum transforms the question 'why' into a petition that says nothing about hardening. Although the sense of the Hebrew is not completely lost, it is clear that the obduracy idea has been mitigated.

Summary

The Targum has mitigated the harshness of the Hebrew text in two ways, possibly three. First, the relative ד is inserted and the imperatives become indicatives, thus transforming something that the prophet was to bring about into a description of the hardened condition of the people. In all probability the targumist has in view a limited group, a group that is obdurate. In this light it is more understandable that the prophet is commanded (v. 10) to make 'this' people obdurate, for it is the judgment they deserve. Secondly, the idea of the 'holy seed' has been greatly expanded in typical haggadic style, with the effect of reinforcing the idea of remnant and consolation in the text. Thirdly, if דלמא is to be understood conditionally, then the prophet is only to harden the hearts of the people if they do not repent.

The Targum in various ways has also blunted the obduracy hermeneutic of Hebrew Isaiah in the other passages (29.9-10; 42.18-20; 43.8; 63.17). It would appear that the targumist is reluctant to have a blanket condemnation levelled against all of Israel, her prophets included.[22] There is a tendency to make a distinction between those who were faithless and wicked and those who were faithful and righteous. It is primarily the wicked who are hardened and called deaf and blind.[23] But the targumist is not being entirely unfaithful to the theology of the Book of Isaiah. After all, Isaiah itself proclaims a righteous remnant (cf. 4.2-4). The targumist is, of course, interpreting Isaiah, but the point is that apparently the targumist did not appreciate the severity of Isaiah's prophet critique. Because of his absolute sovereignty, God was able and fully entitled to pour out a spirit of stupor upon his prophets, to harden the hearts of his people as a whole, and to call his servant Israel 'blind'. The targumist does not accept this idea without careful qualification.

But this is not to say that the targumist's updating is completely wrong-headed or without value.[24] Since there really is no longer a nation of Israel (as he writes), but a Jewish people scattered throughout the world, the way of forgiveness and righteousness is always open for those who 'return'. Since Israel does not exist as a nation, it is scarcely possible to judge her as a whole. Thus, the emphasis has shifted from the collective idea to the individualistic idea. In this respect the theology of the targumist is something like the theology of the New Testament.

Chapter 5

ISAIAH 6.9-10 IN THE PESHITTA

Introduction

The Syriac (or Peshitta, which is Syriac for 'simple'), though of uncertain date, is an important translation of the Hebrew Bible. The origin of the Peshitta is also uncertain, but it has been suggested that the Syriac Pentateuch has certain linguistic affinities with the Palestinian Targum, which could in turn suggest dependence of the former upon the latter.[1] Other scholars have noted that certain passages of the Peshitta may even antedate the Targum.[2] So far as its relationship to the LXX and its recensions is concerned, the Greek versions seem to have influenced the Peshitta in a sporadic fashion only. The Syriac version seems to be more closely tied to the Hebrew than is the LXX in many instances. Nevertheless, as in the case of the LXX, the translation of the Peshitta varies from quite literal to rather free paraphrase. Most paraphrastic of all is the rendering of Chronicles, which contains midrashic elements, and which is in some ways similar to the Targums.

A. *Isaiah 6.9-10 in the Syriac*

The Syriac text of Isa. 6.9-10 reveals the influence of the Aramaic and the LXX:[3]

9	*w'mr ly zl 'mr l'm' hn'*
	šm'w mšm' wl' tstklw
	whzw mhz' wl' td'wn.
10	*'t'by lh gyr lbh d'm' hn'*
	w'dnwhy 'wwr w'ynwhy š'
	dl' nhz' b'ynwhy wnšm' b'dnwhy wnstkl blbh
	wntwb wnštbw lh.

9	And he said to me, 'Go—say to this people:
	"Hear indeed, but do not comprehend,

see indeed, but do not understand".

10   For the heart of this people has become dull,[4]
         and their ears are heavy,
         and their eyes are closed;
         lest they see with their eyes,[5]
         and hear with their ears,
         and understand with their heart,
         and turn again and it be forgiven them'.

The following observations may be made:

(1)   The use of the nominal *mšm'* (lit. 'a hearing'), which is
       analogous to ἀκοῇ of the LXX, equals the Targum's משמע,
       which is used because Aramaic and Syriac do not use the
       infinitive absolute form. The same is true of *mḥz'* ('a
       sight').

(2)   The verbs *tstklw* ('comprehend') and *td'wn* ('understand')
       are pe'al imperatives. Thus, at this point, the Syriac text is
       in essential agreement with the MT.

(3)   The syntax of v. 9bc is like that of the MT and the LXX in
       that these lines make up what the prophet is to speak. The
       Targum, which introduces these clauses with the relative ד,
       is not followed.

(4)   In v. 10 there are two more factors that suggest a relationship
       with the LXX. First, the ethpa'al *'t'by* ('has become dull') is
       the equivalent of the LXX's ἐπαχύνθη.[6] Secondly, the
       conjunction *gyr* unquestionably reveals direct dependence
       upon the LXX's γάρ. The sense of the Peshitta is virtually
       identical to that of the LXX.

(5)   However, *wnštbw* ('and it be forgiven') likely follows the
       Targum's וישתביק.[7]

It would appear that both Targumic and Septuagintal elements are
represented in the Peshitta. Because of its similar reading in v. 10,
the Peshitta yields about the same sense as the LXX: the prophet is to
speak the word of obduracy, because the heart of the people is
already insensitive.

B. *Isaiah 6.9-10 and Related Texts in the Syriac*

Most of the relevant Old Testament obduracy texts in the Syriac
follow the Hebrew fairly closely (Deut. 29.3; Isa. 43.8; Jer. 5.21, 23;

Ezek. 12.2; Zech. 7.11-12). However, a few noteworthy variations appear in some of the Isaianic passages.

Isa. 29.9-10. Whereas imperatives are employed in v. 9 in the Hebrew, the Syriac has indicatives ('. . . they are drunken. . . they stagger. . . '). Also, both verses in the Syriac are in the third person (v. 10: 'For the Lord has poured out upon them. . . '), rather than in the second person as in the Hebrew. Finally, whereas the Hebrew states that it is the Lord who shut the eyes, the Syriac states that it was the deep sleep that shut the eyes. The meaning, however, is essentially the same.

Isa. 42.18-20. In v. 18 in the Hebrew, the blind man is enjoined to look and see, but in the Syriac he is to understand and see. It is probable that this reading is derived from the Targum, which also reads, 'understand and see'. It is possible that 'understand' (אסתכלו originally) found its way into this passage because of its affinities with Isa. 6.9, where both words also occur. In v. 19b the Syriac reads, 'the ruler', instead of 'my dedicated one' as in the Hebrew. This variant reading likely derives from the LXX's reference to 'those who rule' (οἱ κυριεύοντες). Finally, in v. 20a in the Syriac the Lord tells his servant, 'I gave you counsel'. But the Hebrew reads: 'You see many things'. This variation again reflects the LXX, which uses βούλομαι. Despite the variations, the Syriac has essentially the same meaning as the Hebrew.

Isa. 44.18. In the Hebrew the heathen cannot see or discern because God (the implied subject) has smeared (טוח) over their eyes. But the idea is passive in the Syriac, 'their eyes are shut'. The passive probably derives from the LXX (ἀπημαυρώθησαν), or perhaps from the Targum (מטמטמון, the same word used in 6.10). The difference may not be significant, especially if no more than the divine passive is intended. However, it is possible that what we have here is another instance in which the obduracy idea is blunted somewhat.

Summary

Because this chapter is the last one that examines an ancient version of Isa. 6.9-10, it will be useful briefly to summarize all of the versions that have been considered. In the MT the Lord commissions his prophet Isaiah to proclaim a message calculated to produce and promote obduracy for purposes of judgment. The Greek versions, however, shift this responsibility from the Lord and his prophet to the people itself. It is in this sense that the thrust of the MT has been softened. This is even the case in the recension of Aquila, which normally follows the Hebrew more closely than does the LXX. The Targum preserves the imperatives of v. 10, but re-defines the 'people' as those 'who' hear and see, but do not understand. This group stands in contrast to the group that is described as the 'holy seed'. The Peshitta has basically the same thrust as the LXX. The prophet is to speak his paradoxical message to the people because their heart has become obdurate. Thus, the Peshitta also has preserved a softened version of the Hebrew Text. In the case of the Qumran version the text has been re-directed altogether, in that the pious are admonished to avoid sin so as not to be included among those who face the terrible destruction that is described in vv. 11-13, and who falsely regard themselves as the holy seed.

It would appear that the versions do not transmit the idea, as it is found in the MT, that the Lord has commissioned his prophet Isaiah to proclaim a message calculated to produce and promote obduracy. In a broad sense, then, there exists unanimity among these versions in that obduracy is viewed as the responsibility of the people, and can never be thought of as God's intention with respect to his own people.

Chapter 6

ISAIAH 6.9-10 IN PAUL

Introduction

Strictly speaking, the text of Isa. 6.9-10 does not appear in the writings of Paul. However, it is quite possible that the references to the hardening of Israel in Rom. 11.7 and 2 Cor. 3.14 are in fact allusions to the text (ἐπωρώθη[σαν]). This possibility is strongest in the case of Romans, and is supported by the observation that in the very next verse (i.e., 11.8) Paul provides a conflated quotation of the related obduracy texts, Deut. 29.4 and Isa. 29.10. Furthermore, the verb πωροῦν (as opposed to παχύνεσθαι) appears in the fourth evangelist's paraphrase of Isa. 6.10 (cf. Jn 12.40), and is the word used by Mark in language recalling the logion in 4.11-12, which contains the paraphrase of Isa. 6.9-10 (see 3.5; 6.52; 8.17-18). Moreover, Paul's citation of Isa. 53.1, in the context where he discusses Israel's 'hardening' (10.16), may reflect a Christian tradition that involves Isa. 6.9-10, for it is possible that a version of this tradition appears in Jn 12.38-40 where Isa. 53.1 and 6.10 are cited together to explain Jewish unbelief. Lastly, it should be noted that in the tradition of Acts, Paul quotes Isa. 6.9-10 (see Acts 28.25-27), which could point to a tradition where it was remembered that the apostle had used the text to explain Jewish unbelief. In any case, Paul's use of the similar texts, Deut. 29.4 and Isa. 29.10, and his explanation of Jewish unbelief as due to a condition of spiritual blindness call for examination of these passages in this chapter.

A. *The Obduracy Theme in 1 and 2 Corinthians*

In the Corinthian correspondence, the Old Testament obduracy theme finds expression in the ideas of lack of wisdom (1 Cor. 2.6-16) and hardened minds (2 Cor. 3.14-16). The first passage, although perhaps not an obduracy passage strictly speaking, does bear some relation to the idea, and so warrants discussion.

1 Cor. 2.6-16. As to the problems at Corinth to which the apostle addresses himself, it will have to suffice here to note only that Paul apparently wishes to impress upon his readers the fact that inherent to his supposedly simple gospel (as apparently his detractors would regard it) is God's profoundest wisdom (1.18–2.5), a wisdom which only the spiritually mature can understand (2.6-3.1, 18-20). It is a wisdom, Paul teaches his Corinthian converts, that 'none of the rulers of this age understood. . . for if they had, they would not have crucified the Lord of glory' (2.8). Paul goes on to argue that this wisdom is only to be had from God who imparts it through his Spirit (2.10-13). This wisdom, Paul argues, cannot be obtained through the normal channels of human observation and reasoning, 'as it is written':

> What no eye has seen,
>   nor ear heard,
>   nor the heart of man conceived,
> what God has prepared for those who love him (2.9).

The quotation appears to be a conflation of various parts of Isa. 64.4; 52.15; 65.17; and Sir. 1.10.[1] The first part of the quotation ('What. . . heard') is clearly derived from Isa. 64.4, but from the Hebrew (64.3: '. . . the ears heard not, the eye did not see a god besides you. . . '), and not from the LXX (64.3: '. . . we did not hear nor did our eyes see a god except you. . . ').[2] The similar passage, Isa. 52.15, if alluded to at all, perhaps accounts for the presence of the relative pronouns. The middle portion of the quotation ('nor. . . conceived') may possibly derive from Isa. 64.17b, though whether from the LXX (65.16b) or the Hebrew is scarcely evident.[3] The last clause likely derives from Sir. 1.10b: '. . . he [God] supplied her [wisdom] to those who love him'. The fact that the last part agrees with Paul's quotation exactly (τοῖς ἀγαπῶσιν αὐτόν), and that Sirach, as Paul, also refers to wisdom, would increase the probability that this passage is indeed in view. We should not assume, however, that Paul is the originator of this curious conflation of materials. Scholars have pointed to numerous close parallels in various apocalytic and pseudepigraphal writings, though most post-date Paul's letter.[4] The appearance of a close parallel in Pseudo-Philo's *Biblical Antiquities*

(26.13b) provides first-century evidence of the existence of this tradition, a tradition with which the apostle was apparently familiar.[5] But this is not to say that Paul is dependent on Pseudo-Philo (or vice versa). In all likelihood, both of these first-century writers were drawing upon a fairly well known apocalyptic wisdom tradition.[6]

The point that the apostle is trying to make comes out clearly in the subsequent verses. Only the spiritually mature person can fathom God's wisdom (2.15), whereas for the 'natural man', on the contrary, spiritual things are foolish (2.14). It is interesting that Paul states that the natural man 'is not able to understand' (οὐ δύναται γνῶναι), an idea possibly related to the fourth evangelist's interpretation of Isa. 53.1 and 6.10 (John 12.39: οὐκ ἠδύναντο πιστεύειν).[7] In any case, the obduracy theme appears to underlie Paul's thinking in this passage.

2 Cor. 3.14-16. The obduracy idea is expressed more forcefully in 2 Cor. 3.14-16. Paul only touches on it briefly, and then only as a digression from his main thought concerning the ministry of the new covenant (see 3.7-4.6), but what he does say is of significance.

> But their minds were hardened; for to this day, when they read the old covenant, that same veil remains unlifted, because only through Christ is it taken away. Yes, to this day whenever Moses is read a veil lies over their minds; but when a man turns to the Lord the veil is removed (RSV).

C.K. Barrett thinks that the first clause, ἀλλὰ ἐπωρώθη τὰ νοήματα αὐτῶν, alludes to Isa. 6.9-10.[8] That may be, but the expression, 'to this day', also likely alludes to the similar phrase in Deut. 29.4 (Deut. 29.3 in Heb. and LXX), although again it appears that the LXX itself may not be the specific source.[9] V.P. Furnish has noted that Paul uses the verb πωροῦν only here and in Rom. 11.7, where a conflation of Deut. 29.3[4] and Isa. 29.10 is quoted (see further comments below).[10] He argues that since this verb is used in the Johannine citation of Isa. 6.10 (John 12.40) an Old Testament passage that has influenced the other two texts, it appears 'that Paul is dependent here (and in Rom. 11) on some familiar, Christian apologetic formulation'.[11] I am inclined to agree. In 4.3-4 Paul resumes the veil theme and states: 'the god of this world has blinded [τυφλοῦν] the minds of the unbelievers, to keep them from seeing the light of the gospel' (v. 4). Thus, we have here in 3.14 and 4.4 the two verbs (τυφλοῦν/πωροῦν) found in John 12.40. (There is a difference, of course, in that in John it is God who has blinded his people, whereas here in Paul it is the 'god of this world').

The point that apparently Paul is attempting to articulate is that Israel's hardened condition has prevented her from recognizing the marvelous work that God has done before them in Christ. If Paul does indeed intend to allude to Deut. 29.1-3, then he may mean that contemporary Israel, like ancient Israel, has an inherent inability to discern God's redemptive activity. This inability is to be explained and described in terms of the 'hardened heart'. The references to the 'veil' (vv. 13, 14, 15, 16) contribute further to the idea of obduracy in implying blindness. (By it Paul also suggests that the old covenant has been superseded by the new one in Christ).[12] The only cure for the problem is repentance, a 'turning to the Lord', at which time the veil is removed.[13]

B. *The Obduracy Theme in Romans 9–11*

Romans 9–11 constitutes a major section in what many consider Paul's most significant writing. In this section Paul attempts to clarify the relationship of Jews and Gentiles within the context of the history of salvation. The one unmistakable theme running throughout the section is the theme of God's sovereignty. Following E. Käsemann, we may divide the section as follows: introduction (9.1-5); the validity and provisional goal of divine election (9.6-29); Israel's guilt and fall (9.30-10.21); and the mystery of salvation history (11.1-36).[14] The three major divisions reflect the past, present, and future, i.e., Israel's past election, present unbelief, and future restoration. It is interesting to observe that the obduracy idea runs throughout these chapters of Romans.[15]

Just as the prophets of the Old Testament cited sacred tradition in order to understand the present situation, so Paul cites Israel's sacred tradition[16] in order to find meaning in his own perplexing situation. In 9.6-13 Paul argues that election is God's sovereign right, and illustrates this point by noting that before their birth Jacob the younger was chosen over Esau the older (vv. 11-13; cf. Mal. 1.2-3). God does this, Paul reasons, because as Creator he may have mercy upon whom he wishes to have mercy (vv. 14-16; cf. Exod. 33.19). Paul then cites the example of Pharaoh, whom God raised up in order to demonstrate his power (v. 17; cf. Exod. 9.16).[17] Paul concludes: 'So then he has mercy upon whomever he wills, and he hardens [σκληρύνειν] the heart of whomever he wills' (v. 18).[18] In v. 19 Paul gives expression to the objections he feels most people would have with such an argument, and so appeals to God's right as Creator. In language recalling Isa. 29.16 (cf. also Isa. 45.9), Paul argues that the pot does not have the right to answer back to the potter (vv. 20-21). God has the absolute right to make vessels either for mercy or for destruction (v. 22). This last statement, beginning with the protasis, 'What if God. . . has endured. . . the vessels of wrath', has no concluding apodosis. However, it is not difficult to imagine what it must be: 'It is God's right'.[19]

What is important in Paul's argument is the tangent in which he introduces the idea of the inclusion of the Gentiles into God's plan (9.23-24). Paul builds his case for the inclusion of the Gentiles by appealing to two texts from the Old Testament (v. 25, cf. Hos. 2.23; v. 26, cf. Hos. 2.1 (LXX 1.10]). Now Gentiles may be included in the membership of the children of God, but at the same time only a remnant of Israel 'will be saved' (v. 27, cf. Isa. 10.22-23). Because of Israel's unbelief, God has judged his people, sparing but a remnant (vv. 28-29, cf. Isa. 1.9).[20] Because of his absolute sovereignty, God may choose whom he wills and he may harden whom he wills. As we shall see in the subsequent argument, Paul believes that through faith the Gentiles may enter the company of the elect, while because of their unbelief and hardened hearts, Jews have left this company.

In the second division (i.e. 9.30–10.21), Paul probes the problem of present Jewish unbelief. He reasons this way: on the one hand, Gentiles who historically have not pursued righteousness obtained righteousness through faith, but Israel, on the other hand, who historically has pursued a righteousness based upon the works of the law did not obtain righteousness (vv. 30-31). They did not pursue righteousness through faith, but rather stumbled over a stumbling stone (i.e., the need for faith apart from works, v. 32). It is significant that the verses Paul cites in order to clarify and support his assertion are Isa. 8.14 and 28.16.[21] Paul's quotation is a conflation of these texts and is similiar to that in 1 Pet. 2.6-8.[22] His quotation is closer to the Hebrew than it is to the modified version found in the LXX:[23]

> Behold, I am laying in Zion a stone that will make men stumble,
>   a rock that will make them fall;
> and he who believes in him [*or* it] will not be put to shame (RSV).

It is apparent that Paul has interpreted the first part of Isa. 28.16 in light of Isa. 8.14. The foundation stone of the first passage becomes a stumbling stone when understood in terms of the second passage.[24] Paul's interpretation may be related to the eschatological–messianic interpretation of Isa. 28.16 at Qumran.[25] The quotation itself consists of the opening line of Isa. 28.16, a fragment of Isa. 8.14, and the last line of 28.16. The appearance of καταισχύνειν is the only evidence of contact with the LXX, otherwise the quotation is closer to the Hebrew. In its translation of Isa. 8.14, the LXX appears to be underscoring the possibility of averting judgment: 'If you have confidence in him he shall be to you a sanctuary, and not as a stone for stumbling. . .'[26] Nevertheless, in light of 28.16b ('He who believes will not be in haste [*or* ashamed]') the interpretation really does not miss the mark. What Paul assumes is that the stone (אבן) of both passages refers to the same thing. In view of Jewish unbelief, Paul concludes that the costly foundation stone is the same stone which causes men to stumble and to be offended. According to Paul's argument, it is the concept that righteousness may be obtained through faith, as opposed to works that has caused his fellow Jews to stumble (vv. 30-32).[27]

The remainder of the section (10.1-21) attempts to explain this faith and how it comes about. Whereas righteousness based upon the law requires strict observance of the law, to which Paul's fellow Jews adhere zealously, but ignorantly,[28] righteousness based upon faith is realized in the reception of the gospel (vv. 5-9).[29] Any man, without racial distinction, may call upon the Lord and be saved (vv. 10-13), for faith will not give cause for disappointment (v. 11, cf. Isa. 28.16b). In the next few verses Paul explains the necessity of the missionary enterprise as follows: if people are to have faith, they must hear the gospel; if they are to hear, there must be a preacher; and if there is to be a preacher, one must be sent (vv. 14-15). At this point Paul returns to the problem of Jewish unbelief ('but they have not all heeded the gospel'), a problem which is anticipated by scripture: 'Lord, who has believed our report?' (v. 16, cf. Isa. 53.1). Paul has made a smooth transition from v. 15 to v. 16 by quoting the two passages from Isaiah (i.e., 52.7, 'how beautiful are the feet of those who preach good tidings'; and 53.1). It is likely that Paul believed that the two passages were closely linked (ἀκοή is used in both, probably representing an example of exegesis based upon *gezera šawa*): the apostle who brings good tidings will, nevertheless, encounter unbelief. Thus, Paul finds his own missionary experience clarified by these Isaianic texts.[30] The section concludes with a series of quotations illustrating Israel's obstinacy toward God (v. 21), and her jealousy when God reveals himself to others (vv. 18-20).

In the third section (11.1-36) Paul returns to the question of what will happen to Israel in view of her present obdurate condition. In vv. 1-2a Paul reaffirms Israel's election (cf. v. 29; 9.4-5). Once again Paul finds in scripture an explanation for his experience. Just as in the days of Elijah the prophet, when all but a few had turned to Baal, so now all but a few have rejected the Gospel (vv. 2b-4, cf. 1 Kgs 19.10, 18). What is left is a remnant, chosen by God's grace, which for Paul is yet more evidence that salvation is not of works (vv. 5-6, cf. 2 Kgs 19.4 where King Hezekiah requests that the prophet Isaiah pray for 'the remnant that is left').[31] Whereas the elect 'obtained it' (ἡ δὲ ἐπέτυχεν), the 'rest were hardened' (οἱ δὲ λοιποὶ ἐπωρώθησαν; v. 7, cf. v. 25).[32] What Paul means by this last phrase, which recalls σκληρύνειν of 9.18 and which may be an allusion to Isa. 6.9-10,[33] is made clear by his conflated citation of LXX Deut. 29.3 and Isa. 29.10 in v. 8:

> God gave them a spirit of stupor, eyes that should not see and ears
> that should not hear, down to this very day (RSV).

Most of the quotation comes from Deut. 29.3, with the phrase, πνεῦμα κατανύξεως, taken from Isa. 29.10. Paul understands the present lack of belief by the Jews as not only a fulfillment of these texts, but as a condition brought on by God himself. In this respect, Paul's understanding of these texts accords well with their original sense, especially in the case of Isa. 29.10. By citing Deut. 29.3 in which Moses reminds the people of Israel of all that God did to Pharaoh and warns them that they too lack discernment, the plight of unbelieving Israel becomes in some ways analogous to that of Pharaoh, who earlier had been described as hardened (9.18). Both Pharaoh and Israel have remained obdurate in the face of God's redemptive acts. Both Pharaoh and Israel are 'hardened'.[34]

To add further scriptural support to his bold assertion that most of Israel has been hardened, Paul quotes from an imprecatory Psalm (68.22-23 [Heb. 69.22-23]) in vv. 9-10, a text which also refers to unseeing eyes:

> Let their feast become a snare and a trap,
>   a pitfall and a retribution for them;
> let their eyes be darkened so that they cannot see,
>   and bend their backs for ever (RSV).

Paul follows the LXX fairly closely, but there are a few alterations worth mentioning. In the first line ἐνώπιον is omitted, and the phrase, καὶ εἰς θήραν, is inserted. In the second line Paul has reversed the prepositional phrases and has added the pronoun αὐτοῖς. The last two lines are quoted verbatim. The significant variant is the addition of καὶ εἰς θήραν. It is probable that θήρα ['trap'] comes from LXX Ps. 34.8 (Heb. 35.8), another imprecatory Psalm.[35] These verses from the two imprecatory Psalms are quite similar. The insertion of θήρα has enriched the quotation from LXX 68.23-24. The clause, 'let their eyes be darkened so that they cannot see', recalls the similar metaphorical language of the other obduracy texts (Isa. 6.9-10; 29.9-10; 42.18, 20; 43.8; 44.18; Jer. 5.21; Ezek. 12.2; Deut. 29.3). It is indeed significant that Paul has employed the imprecation on enemies. These verses only serve to bolster the hardening idea of the preceding Old Testament quotation. Not only does Paul believe that God has hardened his own people, as he has Israel's enemies of the past, but he has used language that has set them over against God as his enemy.[36] Indeed, the apostle later actually calls his fellow Jews 'enemies' (v. 28).

Whether or not Paul in v. 7 has in mind Isa. 6.10 is uncertain. But in view of his general argument in these three chapters, and especially in view of the quotations of Deut. 29.3/Isa. 29.10 and Pss. 68.23-24/34.8, the question is not overly important. What is important is that Paul has discovered in these texts evidence for viewing Israel's unbelief as ordained by God,[37] a view that is congruent with Isaiah's original preaching.[38]

In the remainder of the chapter Paul tries to explain why such a hardening should have taken place. The answer to this question is found in its result. Because of Jewish obduracy, the gospel has gone out to the Gentiles. The Jews have become enemies of God for the sake of the Gentiles (cf. v. 28). During this time of obduracy, described as a 'partial hardening', God's grace will continue to be extended to them 'until the full number of Gentiles has come in' (v. 25). When this time finally arrives, God will establish his covenant with the Jews and remove their sins (vv. 26b-27, cf. Isa.

59.20-21; Jer. 31.33). Thus, 'all Israel will be saved' (v. 26a). For Paul, the divine plan is evidence of God's mercy for all (vv. 31-32), for Jews and Gentiles alike (cf. 3.29-30).[39] Having reached the end of his line of reasoning Paul concludes with a eulogy of praise for God's wisdom and knowledge (vv. 33-36; compare 1 Cor. 2).

Summary

For Paul, as seen in 2 Cor. 3.14-16 and Rom. 9-11, the only explanation for Jewish rejection of the Christian gospel lay in the idea of the hardened heart as found in various Old Testament passages. Because Israel's heart is hardened, the eschaton is delayed, giving opportunity for the good news to go out to the Gentiles. The hardened heart, therefore, far from indicating failure, reveals God's wisdom in bringing about a universal salvation. The obduracy idea, as seen in 1 Cor. 2.6-16, appears to provide a broader explanation for general rejection of, or inability to, comprehend the Christian message.

Chapter 7

ISAIAH 6.9-10 IN MARK

Introduction

The logion in Mark that contains the paraphrase of Isa. 6.9-10 (Mark 4.11-12) has produced more discussion and disagreement than just about any other passage in the gospels. We are faced with a variety of questions: (1) What Old Testament version underlies the Marcan paraphrase? (2) How is it to be translated? (3) What does it mean in the context of the logion? (4) Was it originally a part of the larger context of Mark 4? (5) How has the evangelist Mark understood it, and how does it fit into his gospel? (6) Did Jesus utter this logion, and, if he did, (7) what did he mean by it? Other questions could be asked, but these, I believe, should be sufficient for our purposes. The first three questions are addressed in section A; questions four and five in section B; and six and seven in section C.

A. *The text of Isaiah 6.9-10 in Mark*

Isa. 6.9-10 is found paraphrased in Mk 4.12, and is the Old Testament text's earliest appearance in the New Testament. It reads:

ἵνα βλέποντες βλέπωσιν καὶ μὴ ἴδωσιν,
    καὶ ἀκούοντες ἀκούωσιν καὶ μὴ συνιῶσιν,
μήποτε ἐπιστρέψωσιν καὶ ἀφεθῇ αὐτοῖς.

'So that they may indeed see but not perceive,
    and may indeed hear but not understand;
lest they should turn again, and be forgiven' (RSV).

Mark's paraphrase is an abbreviation of the Isaianic text.[1] Corresponding parts of the LXX read as follows: 'You will indeed hear

and not understand, and you will indeed see and not perceive...
lest... they should turn and I heal them'. Although most of his
vocabulary is found in the LXX, Mark's paraphrase differs from the
LXX in four major ways. (1) Mark has placed the part that derives
from Isa. 6.9bc in the third person, while the LXX follows the second
person (but not the imperative) of the Hebrew. (2) The clauses of Isa.
6.9bc are reversed in Mark's quotation, with the 'seeing' clause
occurring first and the 'hearing' clause second. (3) Mark truncates
the Isaianic text by leaving out the portions describing the blindness
of the eyes, the deafness of the ears, and the undiscernment of the
heart. It is probable that this abbreviation has been made out of
grammatical concerns. The purpose for such abridgment, M. Black
argues, and I think correctly, was 'to complete the main thought of
the ἵνα clause' which introduced the quotation.[2] The quotation, as it
now stands, consists of coordinated ἵνα/μήποτε clauses. (4) As his
last clause in the quotation (i.e. Isa. 6.10), Mark has καὶ ἀφεθῇ
αὐτοῖς rather than the LXX's καὶ ἰάσομαι αὐτούς.

When we compare Mark's quotation with the text of the Targum,
we observe three important similarities. (1) The Targum also has
shifted v. 9 into the third person in order to accomodate the
syntactical alteration from direct speech to a relative clause. (2) Like
the Targum's rendering of v. 9, Mark's verbs are indicative, not
imperative. (3) The Targum has the equivalent of Mark's phrase, καὶ
ἀφεθῇ αὐτοῖς: להון ושתביק.[3] In view of these similarities most scholars
have concluded that Mark is here thinking of neither the LXX nor the
Hebrew, but of the Targum.[4]

Probably the most hotly debated question of exegesis in Mk 4.10-
12 has to do with the translation of the two conjunctives, ἵνα and
μήποτε. There is debate because these conjunctives usually express
the idea of purpose, an idea that many interpreters have over the
years found inappropriate to the context. The debate is important,
for how these two conjunctives are understood is crucial to the
meaning of the paraphrase. There are at least six suggestions that
have been made: (1) T.W. Manson believes that Mark's ἵνα is the
result of the evangelist's misunderstanding of the relative particle ד.[5]
He finds it inconceivable that Jesus would intentionally veil his
message with riddles, so Mark's logion must surely misrepresent the
original expression of Jesus. He states: 'As the text stands it can only
mean that the object, or at any rate the result, of parabolic teaching is

to prevent insight, understanding, repentance, and forgiveness. On any interpretation of parable this is simply absurd'.[6] Moreover, he believes that the logion contradicts the parable, in that it is not the efficacy of the sown word that is in question, but the response of those who receive it: 'In other words the efficacy of parables depends, not on the parables, but on the character of the hearers'.[7] Had Mark understood the particle ד properly, he would have written: 'But to those who are outside all things are in parables, who see but do not perceive', etc.[8] Manson then offers two possible interpretations of what μήποτε was likely supposed to have meant.[9] The first possible meaning would be that the final line of the logion read: 'For if they did [i.e., if they understood], they would repent and receive forgiveness'. The second alternative would be to take the Aramaic דלמא (which underlies μήποτε) in the sense of 'perhaps'. Thus, we read the text: 'Perhaps they may yet repent'. Manson concludes: 'The quotation from Isaiah is not introduced by Jesus to explain the purpose of teaching in parables, but to illustrate what is meant by οἱ ἔξω. . . the sort of character which prevents a man from becoming one of those to whom the secret of the kingdom is given'.[10] We can agree with Manson (and others) that the paraphrase of Isa. 6.9-10 in Mk 4.12 probably originated from the Aramaic version, but I see little validity in understanding Mark's ἵνα as his failure to translate properly the relative ד of the Aramaic text.[11] In any case, Mark's understanding of the logion is left unexplained.

(2) A half century ago M.-J. Lagrange took a different approach by suggesting that Mark's ἵνα 'est donc presque équivalent de ἵνα πληρωθῇ'.[12] However, he bases his conclusion on the prior assumption that Mark's version is but an abbreviated form of Matthew's text.[13] Jeremias also suggests that Mark's ἵνα 'almost amounts to an abbreviation of ἵνα πληρωθῇ',[14] and that it was not *Jesus'* purpose to be enigmatic, but that it was *God's* purpose, as revealed in the scriptures, to conceal the truth by means of the parables.[15] However, in a note he concedes that Manson's suggestion that ἵνα be understood as a relative pronoun is not only possible, but that the 'meaning is the same'.[16] With respect to μήποτε, Jeremias cites Rabbinic evidence where Isa. 6.9-10 is understood not as a threat of final hardening, but as a promise of forgiveness[17] (an understanding which is based upon the translation of דלמא/פן as 'unless').[18] Therefore, μήποτε in Mk 4.12 should be so understood.

This suggestion is plausible, but I wonder if in the Semitic mind there would be significant difference between ἵνα and πληρωθῇ, for both have telic meaning. What real difference in meaning is there between doing something in order to bring about an effect or doing something in order to fulfil a text that describes the same effect? In a study on quotation formulas, B. Metzger has noted that even when ἵνα is used with verbs of fulfilment, such as πληροῦν, ἀναπληροῦν, and τελειοῦν, the grammatical sense 'is probably telic'.[19] The notion of scriptural fulfilment does not obviate the telic meaning of ἵνα. Metzger has observed that 'the occurrence of certain events was held to be involved in the predetermined plan of God revealed in the Scriptures'.[20] The basic problem, however, that attends the view that ἵνα is an abbreviation of ἵνα πληρωθῇ is that the syntax of the ἵνα/ μήποτε construction is broken. Another solution should be sought.

(3) Another view that is often advanced understands ἵνα in the causal sense. T.A. Burkill has concluded that ἵνα should be understood as 'because' and μήποτε as 'perhaps'.[21] Similarly, C.F.D. Moule suggests that Mark is trying to say that Jesus' hearers prefer mysteries because they wish to remain ignorant.[22]

(4) Another alternative is to view Mark's ἵνα as having a consecutive function. C.H. Peisker has suggested that ἵνα may reflect the Hebrew consecutive למען ('that' or 'so that').[23] Therefore, with respect to the logion's context in the parable chapter, Peisker concludes that 'das Nicht-Verstehen ist also nicht in den Gleichnissen final intendiert, es ist. . . Resultat der Gleichnisreden Jesu'.[24] Similarly H. Anderson understands ἵνα as meaning 'with the result', and he also takes the μήποτε to mean 'unless'.[25] Recently B.D. Chilton has understood Mark's ἵνα in the sense of result.[26] Again, this solution is possible, but it really does not answer the problem of v. 11 ('but for those outside everything is in parables'), for this part of the logion also seems to imply purpose.

(5) It has also been proposed that Mark's ἵνα should be understood imperatively, in the sense of 'let them see. . .'[27] However, this meaning does not fit the syntax of the Marcan context well.

The problem that is basic to all of these attempts to interpret ἵνα and μήποτε in senses other than final is the observation that both Matthew and Luke omit the μήποτε clause, while the former replaces ἵνα with ὅτι. Had Mark's μήποτε meant 'unless', thus reflecting a common Rabbinic understanding of Isa. 6.10 (assuming that this understanding was as early as the first century CE), then why would Matthew and Luke omit the clause?[28] If μήποτε had such a meaning we would have expected the later evangelists to have retained it. To answer this objection by saying that μήποτε was ambiguous, in that it could mean either 'lest' or 'unless', and therefore the evangelists Matthew and Luke would have omitted it, concedes the point. After all, had the later evangelists been aware of the meaning 'unless', why could they not have replaced it with a term that unambiguously meant 'unless'? Such terms as ἐκτὸς εἰ μή, παρεκτός, or πλὴν ὅτι give plain expression to the idea of 'unless'. But apparently Matthew and Luke were not aware of any such meaning in Mark, and so found the clause, if not unacceptable, at least undesirable, and so omitted it. Much is the same in the case of Mark's use of ἵνα. Matthew and Luke were apparently unaware that the ἵνα may very well be a mistranslation of the Targum's relative ד, since neither corrects Mark by replacing it with οἱ. Nor was it obvious to Matthew and Luke that Mark's ἵνα was an abbreviation of ἵνα πληρωθῇ since neither takes that option (though Matthew later uses a similar formula in introducing his formal quotation of the LXX version of Isa. 6.9-10 in 13.14-15, a formula which is, however, quite common in Matthew, and likely not suggested to him by the presence of Mark's ἵνα). It is pointed out by some scholars that Matthew does in fact replace Mark's ἵνα with ὅτι; therefore Mark's ἵνα may be understood as causal and not final. But is this an instance where Matthew has merely clarified Mark's obscure causal meaning, or has the later evangelist attempted to redirect the Marcan thrust? (See the discussion of Matthean redaction in ch. 8 below.)

(6) The last alternative is to understand Mark's ἵνα and μήποτε clauses as final, or telic, in meaning. Several commentators have concluded that Mark's ἵνα (as well as μήποτε) must be understood as telic. E. Schweizer and W. Grundmann have translated ἵνα as 'in order that' and μήποτε as 'lest'.[29] After his discussion of the alternatives, V. Taylor concludes: 'Mark's meaning must be that for those who are not disciples the purpose of the parables is to conceal the truth and to prevent repentance and forgiveness'.[30] A.M. Ambrozic and E. Stauffer think that ἵνα and μήποτε are telic,[31] while W. Manson is willing only to admit that the former is telic while the latter means something like 'just in case',[32] which presumably has about the same meaning as 'lest'.

M. Black also understands Mark's ἵνα and μήποτε clauses as telic.
His succinct conclusion is worth quoting:

> Nothing is more certain than that Mark wrote and intended
> ἵνα. . . μήποτε: his original purpose is clear from the ἵνα clause; it
> is continued and reinforced by the μήποτε clause, which has been
> selected and adapted from the Old Testament quotation in order to
> be subordinated to the ἵνα clause. We are dealing not with direct
> quotation or misunderstanding of a quotation, but with intentional
> adaptation and interpretation of a quotation. Dr. Manson is
> probably right in suggesting that the words in the Old Testament
> passage on which the μήποτε clause there depends, 'Make the heart
> of this people fat. . . ', have been deliberately omitted by Mark, but
> not for the reason he gives (to avoid the implication that parable
> was intended to prevent forgiveness), but to enable the writer, by
> his adapted μήποτε clause, to complete the main thought of the ἵνα
> clause, that the purpose of parabolic teaching was to prevent
> repentance.[33]

In another relevant study, D. Daube has seconded the judgment of
Black. He concludes that Mark's logion only intensifies the division
between the enlightened elect and the outsiders who are 'destined to
grope in the dark'. He states:

> Actually, he [Mark] makes Jesus dwell on this division in the
> harshest terms: the outside world, Jesus says, is spoken to in riddles
> 'in order that they may see and not perceive, and hear and not
> understand'. There is no justification for mitigating this statement
> by declaring ἵνα due to a mistranslation from the Aramaic. . . .
> From the beginning, the form in question is anything but
> universalistic.[34]

Recent studies are tending to confirm the judgment of these
scholars. In his study of the Marcan community H.C. Kee has
concluded that the logion is to be rightly interpreted as telic in
meaning,[35] while G.R. Beasley-Murray has concluded that 'Mark
would not have hesitated to interpret the *hina* and the *mepote* as
expressive of purpose'.[36] Finally, J. Marcus has shown that the telic
idea of ἵνα fits meaningfully in the context of Mark 4 and of Mark's
gospel in general.[37] This will be discussed at greater length in the
section that follows.

Linguistic considerations aside, there are also five other reasons
why a final interpretation (which inevitably leads to the hardening,

or obduracy, theory of parables) for these clauses makes the best sense. (1) The obduracy idea in the Old Testament establishes more than enough precedent for such an idea. The Jewish people were reminded at every Passover observance of the drama of God hardening the heart of Pharaoh (Exod. 4-14). But the obduracy idea entails more than the exodus tradition. As seen already in Ch. 1, God confounds human wisdom (2 Sam. 17.4; 1 Kgs 12.15) and even, on occasion, deceives (1 Kgs 22.13-23). God is the source of knowledge or lack of it. Moses is told: 'Who has made man's mouth? Who makes him dumb, or deaf, or seeing, or blind? Is it not I, the Lord?' (Exod. 4.11). Those whom he deceives and hardens are not only the enemies of Israel, such as Pharaoh and King Sihon (Deut. 2.30), or Israel's foolish leaders, but even Israel herself (Isa. 6.9-10; 29.9-10; 63.17). In view of this tradition, a tradition that is a fundamental part of Israel's religious heritage, no objection against the final interpretation can be raised on the grounds that such an idea is foreign either to Jesus, or to Mark, or to the tradition that lies between them.

(2) The saying in Mk 4.24-25 comports well with a final interpretation of vv. 11-12. The warning in v. 24a implies danger, such as the threat of obduracy would warrant, while the principles of vv. 24b-25 ('more will be given' and 'what he has will be taken away') imply that it is God who gives and takes away divine insight. (The passive verbs are surely instances of the 'divine passive'). Furthermore, the floating saying, 'If any man has ears to hear, let him hear' (Mk 4.9, 23), connotes the same idea. It is God who gives 'ears to hear'. Those who do not 'hear', do not because God has not given them 'ears'.

(3) There are sayings in Q which reflect this same idea of God's sovereignty in the matter of revealing or withholding spiritual insight. This is evident in Lk. 10.21-22 where Jesus says: 'I thank thee, Father, Lord of heaven and earth, that thou has hidden these things from the wise and understanding and revealed them to babes; yea, Father, for such was thy gracious will. All things have been delivered to me by my Father; and no one knows who the Son is except the Son and any one to whom the Son chooses to reveal him' (cf. Mt. 11.25-27). Clearly this saying is rooted in the belief that the revelation of divine truth is at divine discretion. Moreover, in the beatitude that follows, one is left with the impression that the moral character of a person does not always determine whether or not one

is given divine revelation: 'Blessed are the eyes which see what you see! For I tell you that many prophets and kings desired to see what you see, and did not see, and to hear what you hear, and did not hear it' (Lk. 10.23-24). If divine insight was contingent upon human character, then the 'many prophets', who surely were as entitled as the disciples, would have seen and heard. Interestingly enough, Matthew senses the relevance of this saying for the question of why some do not understand Jesus' parables, and so places it in ch. 13 (vv. 16-17), his counterpart to Mark 4, right after his quotation of Isa. 6.9-10![38]

(4) The final interpretation applied by the fourth evangelist to Isa. 6.9-10 attests this understanding of Isaiah and the obduracy idea in non-Synoptic circles (John 12.38-40). (See discussion in Chapter 10 below.) Although quite possibly reflecting a later stage in theological development,[39] its presence suggests that the idea that the hearts of people were hardened by Jesus' ministry is not a Marcan aberration. (If John derived the idea from Mark, then there would be evidence that at least one early interpreter of Mark understood the ἵνα/μήποτε clauses as final.)

(5) Although Isa. 6.9-10 is not quoted in Paul, texts like it are (i.e., Isa. 29.10 and Deut. 29.3[4]), indicating, as can clearly be seen from the arguments of Rom. 9.6-29 and 11.1-10, that Paul also shared the view that God hardened the heart of his people to the Christian gospel. To be sure, Paul does not refer to Jesus' teaching (in parables or otherwise), but his theology at the very least indicates that at an early stage Christian thinking could entertain the sort of interpretation that we have suggested for the logion in Mk 4.11-12. One would think that in light of the general Jewish rejection of Jesus and the Christian gospel, a fact that surely vexed early Christian theologians (if not Jesus himself), the Old Testament obduracy motif, in its harshest form, would have suggested itself.[40] This, I believe, is what ultimately is responsible for the Marcan text in question.

If, then, the coordinated ἵνα/μήποτε clauses are final, and no compelling reason has been found to understand them otherwise, then the logion seems to be saying that the purpose for giving 'outsiders' all things 'in parables' is to prevent them from understanding, repentance, and forgiveness.[41] As Jeremias and others have pointed out, in such a context 'parables' must be understood as 'riddles', since the word apparently stands in contrast to the unfolding of a 'secret' (μυστήριον).[42] The disciples, the 'insiders', are given the secret of the kingdom of God, that is, the key to divine truth (to further truth according to vv. 24-25), but the outsiders are prevented from obtaining this knowledge. What such a logion means in its present Marcan context is the concern of the next section.

B. *The Context of Isaiah 6.9-10 in Mark*

Immediate Context
The problem begins with the observation that Mk 4.1-34 appears not to be a well-integrated unity. The composite nature of Mark 4 is readily apparent, and may be outlined as follows: (1) narrative introduction (vv. 1-2), (2) Parable of the Sower (vv. 3-8), (3) floating saying, 'He who has ears. . . ' (v. 9), (4) editorial introduction to logion (v. 10), (5) logion (vv. 11-12), (6) editorial introduction to explanation of parable (v. 13), (7) explanation of the Parable of the Sower (vv. 14-20), (8) other kingdom parables (vv. 21-32), and (9) parabolic description of Jesus' mode of teaching (vv. 33-34).

The first issue that confronts us has to do with the literary context of this logion. Is it part of the Sower Parable, or is it an independent piece of pre-Marcan tradition? Many scholars doubt that this logion originally had anything to do with its present context. W. Marxsen agrees with Jeremias that the logion is pre-Marcan[43] and has been inserted into its present context, but not erroneously as Jeremias contended.[44] Marxsen believes that the evangelist knowingly updated his text, in keeping with his broader theological interests.[45] The text does seem to support this view, for v. 10 leads into v. 13 quite naturally: '[They] asked him concerning the parables[46]. . . And he said to them, 'Do you not understand this parable? How then will you understand all the parables?' This rebuke of the disciples' ignorance occurs again in Mk 7.17-18: '. . . his disciples asked him about the parable. And he said to them, "Then are you without understanding?"' One suspects that in the original tradition, the request for an explanation immediately received a rebuke, followed by the explanation. This pattern is found undisturbed in 7.17-18. Thus, on form-critical grounds alone one suspects that the logion has later been placed into its present context. Furthermore, the logion does not provide a smooth logical link between the Parable of the Sower and its interpretation in vv. 14-20. If the question of the disciples is meant to ask why Jesus spoke in parables (as Matthew so interprets), a question which the logion appears to be answering, the parable's interpretation is unsolicited. If, however, the disciples are asking what the Parable of the Sower meant (as Luke so interprets), the logion itself is unsolicited. For linguistic reasons also some scholars suspect that the logion is foreign to its present context.[47] Therefore, on form-critical, contextual, and possibly linguistic grounds it seems that the logion is an intrusion. Moreover, there are historical considerations that also support this conclusion; but we shall return to them later.

If the logion is indeed an intrusion into its present literary context, then who put it there, the evangelist Mark or some tradent before him? Because the language of obduracy occurs elsewhere in Mark (3.5; 6.51; esp. 8.17-18), probably recalling the logion under consideration, and because of Mark's curious and unique understanding of Jesus' parables (4.33-34), which is likely a part of his larger secrecy scheme,[48] it is quite likely that the evangelist Mark is responsible for the present location and function of the logion.

But what contribution does the logion make to its narrower context in 4.1-34, and to its larger Marcan context? Let us turn first to the narrower context. Several reasons may be offered as to why the evangelist would have placed the logion into its present context. (1) Because Mark views the parables as not easily understood (4.33), but requiring private explanation (4.10, 34; cf. 7.17; 9.28; 13.3), and because the logion uses the word 'parables' (παραβολαί), making it relevant on linguistic grounds also, the placement of the logion between a question of the disciples and a rebuke of Jesus would serve the evangelist's interests. (2) Because Mk 4.1-34 constitutes the gospel's largest collection of parables, the insertion here of a logion that the evangelist regarded as having relevance for Jesus' parables in general would only seem natural. (3) Mark may also have sensed the relevance of the logion's emphasis on distinguishing two classes of people (i.e., insiders and outsiders)[49] for the parable's different types of soils. That is, both the logion and the parable describe those who receive the 'secret'[50] (or word) and those who do not.[51] (4) In view of prominence of the word 'seed' in the parable, as well as its identification as 'the word' (ὁ λόγος) in the parable's interpretation, and the presence of Isaiah 6 in the logion, it is possible that the evangelist may have in mind the 'seed' of Isa. 6.13. Just as the seed of

Isaiah 6 would emerge as a remnant from out of the obdurate masses, so the 'seed' of Jesus' preaching would produce obduracy in the masses, but guarantee the emergence of a remnant which responds in faith.[52]

It would appear then that the insertion of the logion into its present context serves the purpose of clarifying the nature of Jesus' parables (4.13; and teaching in general, according to 4.33-34). The evangelist wishes to show that at the heart of Jesus' parables is the 'word' (4.14, 15, 16, 17, 18, 19, 20), that is, the Christian proclamation which some embrace and others reject. Those who reject the Christian proclamation, according to Mark's presentation, do so because they are obdurate to its divine truth (4.11-12). Thus, in all likelihood Mark is attempting to apply Jesus' parables to his *Sitz im Leben*, a *Sitz* that probably involves rejection and intense persecution (4.17, and as seen especially in the passion predictions and in ch. 13). In a recent and compelling study, Marcus has argued that the logion in 4.11-12 must be understood against the sayings in vv. 21-22: '... nothing is hidden except [in order] that it should be revealed', etc.[53] For at least two reasons the texts (4.11-12; 4.21-22) should be viewed as related: (1) The similar usage of ἵνα in both contexts and (2) the injunction to hear immediately preceding vv. 10-13 (v. 9) and following vv. 21-22 (v. 23) are strong indications that the passages are mutually illuminating. Seen in this light, the point of vv. 11-12 seems to be that what is (now) hidden will eventually come to light. What exactly is to come to light will be considered in the next section.

General Context
We now turn to the question of the logion's context in the larger Marcan context. It was mentioned above that Mark apparently views the parables as not easily understood. On more than one occasion Jesus rebukes his disciples for their inability to understand them (4.13; 7.18). On other occasions, however, Jesus rebukes his disciples for failing to grasp some lesson arising out of Jesus' ministry in general. Two noteworthy episodes that relate to this theme come shortly after the feeding miracles. After walking on the water, the disciples were utterly astounded, 'for they did not understand about the loaves, but their hearts were hardened' (6.51b-52). The word for 'hardened' (πωροῦν), is that used to describe the hostile and unbelieving

response of the Pharisees earlier in 3.1-6 (πώρωσις in v. 5). Although 6.51-52 may not recall 4.11-12 (the themes are similar, but the vocabulary is different), it is likely that the similar incident following the second feeding miracle does. Again, confusion on the part of the disciples arises with regard to the significance of bread (8.14-16). Jesus rebukes them as follows (vv. 17b-18a):

> Τί διαλογίζεσθαι ὅτι ἄρτους οὐκ ἔχετε; οὔπω νοεῖτε οὐδὲ συνίετε; πεπωρωμένην ἔχετε τὴν καρδίαν ὑμῶν; ὀφθαλμοὺς ἔχοντες οὐ βλέπετε καὶ ὦτα ἔχοντες οὐκ ἀκούετε;
>
> Why do you discuss the fact that you have no bread? Do you not yet perceive or understand? Are your hearts hardened? Having eyes do you not see, and having ears do you not hear? And do you not remember? (RSV)

The references to the hardened heart, unseeing eyes, and unhearing ears recall many of the obduracy passages (Isa. 6.9-10; Jer. 5.21, 23; Deut. 29.3; Ezek. 12.2), with perhaps Isa. 6.9-10 and Jer. 5.21, 23 closest. Mark's reader cannot help but see a connection between 4.12 and this passage (i.e. 8.17-18), for there is key language common to both (βλέπειν, ἀκούειν, συνίημι). It would seem that not only are the 'outsiders' obdurate, but the disciples themselves suffer from the same affliction. There is a difference, of course, in that whereas the Pharisees openly oppose Jesus (as in 3.1-6 and elsewhere), the disciples do not, at least not intentionally (see 8.31-33). Interpreters have wrestled with this aspect of the Marcan secrecy idea. T.J. Weeden argued some years ago that because of a distorted view of Christian faith, in which some viewed themselves as the heirs of apostolic, miraculous power, the evangelist Mark attempted to discredit the apostles, especially Peter.[54] This he has done, explains Weeden, by showing how the disciples are obdurate to the true nature of Jesus' messiahship and of Christian discipleship, in that both involve suffering, even death. Without accepting every aspect of Weeden's thesis, it is evident that the evangelist has applied the obduracy idea to the disciples. It would appear that he has done this in order to show that prior to Easter all, Jesus' friends and enemies alike, suffered from the wrong concept of messiahship. The explanation for this consistent misconception, Mark tells us, is due to the biblical problem of the hardened heart.[55]

But the hardened heart is not without its redeeming features, for it significantly advances Marcan christology. Without the hardened heart, Jesus would not have been rejected and put to death; and had he not been put to death, there could have been no resurrection and no Christian gospel. The logion in 4.11-12 must be seen in this light. Marcus has concluded:

> God intends the outsiders to be blinded by Jesus' parables and his parabolic actions (4.11-12), so that they oppose him and eventually bring about his death; in his death, however, the new age of revelation will dawn. Thus the hiddenness of Jesus' identity (cf. the *hina* clause in 4.12) leads to his death, which in turn results in the open manifestation of his identity (cf. the *hina* clause in 4.22). The *hina* clauses in vv. 21-22, like the one in 4.12, refer to God's intention, and all of these *hina* clauses intersect at the cross.[56]

If the people have 'eyes' to see and 'ears' to hear, then they can recognize that in rejection and death, God's purposes are being accomplished; but even if they do not recognize the divine plan at work (as the disciples in Mark apparently do not), the light will dawn suddenly and dramatically at Easter.[57] Then God's purpose in promoting obduracy will become apparent. Then the disciples, who had misunderstood, resisted, forsaken, and denied Jesus, will once again 'see' Jesus, as the young man promises the frightened women at the empty tomb (16.5-8).

C. *The Context of Isa. 6.9-10 in Jesus*

Did Jesus actually utter the logion contained in Mk 4.11-12, and if he did was it spoken in reference to the parables? To these two related questions we now turn.

Because of its strangeness and relationship to the secrecy idea, there are several scholars who view this logion as inauthentic. C.H. Dodd found the logion (and the parable's explanation) not only out of place, but inauthentic after an analysis of its vocabulary. He observed that there are

> seven words which are not proper to the rest of the Synoptic record. All seven are characteristic of the vocabulary of Paul, and most of them occur also in other apostolic writers. These facts create at once a presumption that we have here not a part of the primitive tradition of words of Jesus, but a piece of apostolic teaching.[58]

R. Bultmann originally had seen the logion as no more than an editorial bridge linking the parable with its interpretation.[59] F.C. Grant believes that this logion represents Mark's theology in which it is understood that Jesus wished to withhold the truth from the unworthy, a view which, he notes, is common enough in the first-century Greco-Roman world.[60] Finally, F. Hauck and G. Haufe have also concluded that the logion is inauthentic, for it simply does not properly define the function of the parable.[61]

Other scholars, however, believe that the logion reflects an authentic word of Jesus. Manson believes that the logion, when corrected, is authentic.[62] Jeremias also believes that vv. 11-12 are authentic, and are thus pre-Marcan, but that originally they had a wider application than that of the parables.[63] The fact that the 'seeing' clause of Isa. 6.9 comes first (instead of the 'hearing' clause, as it is in Isaiah) suggests that what was originally in view was not the hearing of parables, but the observation of public ministry. Had the saying originally been concerned with parables, we should expect to find the traditional order of the clauses retained. Mark, Jeremias believes, inserted the logion into the present context because he had been misled by the catchword παραβολή, which in the logion itself means 'riddle' or 'enigma' but in the context of the parables means no more than a sermon illustration.[64] J. Gnilka has also concluded that the logion is authentic, but originally had nothing to do with the idea that the parables hardened the hearts of the hearers.[65] J.R. Kirkland agrees with Jeremias that the logion is very likely authentic,[66] but thinks that it reflects Jesus' genuine self-understanding that his teachings were 'sacred' and 'special', and so were to be dispensed in some mysterious manner.[67] In view of its puzzling qualities V. Taylor believes, like Jeremias, that the logion's best explanation is that it represents something that Jesus said, but is now out of place.[68] E.F. Siegman agrees that there is a ring of authenticity, but its location in Mark is problematic.[69] Others who have concluded that this logion reflects an authentic word of Jesus would include E.P. Gould, T.W. Manson, N. Perrin, W.L. Lane, B.D. Chilton, G.R. Beasley-Murray and J.A. Fitzmyer.[70]

In my estimation the logion does indeed derive from Jesus. Jeremias is probably correct that in its original context, 'in parables' meant 'in riddles'. The logion likely represents a saying in which Jesus summarized the net effect of his total ministry[71] in terms of the response of two groups of people: his disciples to whom the secret of the kingdom has been revealed (through Jesus' teaching and ministry), and 'outsiders' to whom Jesus' ministry and teaching remain obscure and unintelligible. J.W. Bowker in a recent study has argued that Mark's depiction of Jesus teaching crowds publicly, and his disciples privately, reflects common rabbinic practice of time.[72] Moreover, it is probable that Jesus viewed his ministry as one that would separate the 'wheat from the chaff', as the Baptist's depiction in Luke would indicate (3.16-17).[73] Recall also the Q saying in Mt. 10.34-36: 'Do not think that I have come to bring peace on earth; I have not come to bring peace, but a sword. For I have come to set a man against his father, and a daughter against his mother. . . ' (cf. Lk. 12.51-53).[74] This saying alludes to Mic. 7.6, which in rabbinic tradition was associated with the distress that would attend the advent of Messiah (cf. *m. Sot.* 9.15). It is likely that the understanding of Micah found in Q and in Mishna derives from a common exegetical tradition (since it is not too likely that Mishna in this instance has been influenced by Christian exegesis), with which Jesus would have been familiar, and in terms of which he may have understood his mission. In any case, it is quite likely that one certain historical aspect of Jesus' ministry is that of the fiery prophet and reformer. Such a logion as Mk 4.11-12 would fit very naturally in this context.[75]

F. Eakin has suggested that the logion possibly reflects Jesus' self-understanding because of the parallel experiences of the latter and of the Old Testament prophet, both of whose messages fell on deaf ears.[76] There is another aspect of the logion's affinities with the Targum that may. be relevant to this suggestion. Not only is there dictional coherence with the Aramaic tradition (i.e., 'forgiven' instead of 'heal'), but there is important thematic coherence as well.[77] This coherence is seen in Jesus' application of Isa. 6.9-10 to only a part of Israel, for the disciples are not among those who fall under the judgment of the Isaianic text. This idea seems to underlie the Targum (as argued above in Ch. 4). In the Targum, the prophet was to make obdurate those who do not hear or see. Similarly, Jesus' ministry makes obdurate those who are outside his circle of followers. Thus, to whatever extent that Jesus' identified with the message and experience of Isaiah, the words of Isaiah seem to have been appropriated from the Aramaic tradition. It also should be noted in passing that there is some evidence of tradition associating Isaiah with parables, which apparently is in reference to his vision described in Isaiah 6: 'And the rest of the vision of the Lord, behold, it is recorded in parables in my words which are written in the book which I openly proclaimed' (*Ascen.* [*Mart.*] *Isa.* 4.20).

Finally, one might inquire as to whether or not Jesus intended the saying to be understood literally. Whereas it is quite possible that Mark understood it in a literal sense, the observation of Jesus' frequent use of hyperbole could suggest that his saying is meant only to be rhetorical, perhaps with a sense of irony.[78] Nevertheless, rhetorical or not, an element of judgment was likely intended.

Summary

Isa. 6.9-10 has made a significant contribution to Mark's theology. This Old Testament text, couched in the 4.11-12 logion, contributes to Mark's secrecy theme, a theme that seems to revolve around the obduracy idea. With it the evangelist shows how Jesus' understanding of messiahship and discipleship was misunderstood by friend and foe alike. However one understands Marcan christology,[79] and I have no intention of probing this question further than what has been touched on in this chapter, it seems clear that Isa. 6.9-10, paraphrased in 4.12 and 8.18, and perhaps alluded to in 3.5 and 6.52, functions as a vital factor.

Although we are on less certain footing with regard to Jesus' use of Isa. 6.9-10, in my view it seems permissible to suggest that Jesus may have cited this Old Testament text as a way of summarizing and explaining the negative response of many of his contemporaries toward his ministry. If so, then his usage likely led to the early Church's usage of this specific text, and to the development of what might be called a 'theology of obduracy' (such as we find in Romans 9-11, Acts and John).

Chapter 8

ISAIAH 6.9-10 IN MATTHEW

Introduction

Isa. 6.9-10 is quoted twice in Matthew. The first quotation (cf. 13.13b) is a paraphrase based upon Mk 4.12. The second quotation (cf. 13.14b-15) is taken from the LXX verbatim. In section A we shall examine the first quotation as it is presented in Matthew. Our concern here is chiefly textual and grammatical. We shall not examine Matthew's quotation of the LXX, since that has already been done in Chapter 3 above. We shall, of course, take it into consideration as we study Matthew. In section B we shall examine the theological context of Isa. 6.9-10 in Matthew.

A. *The Text of Isa. 6.9-10 in Matthew*

Matt. 13.13b reads as follows:

> ὅτι βλέποντες οὐ βλέπουσιν καὶ ἀκούοντες οὐκ ἀκούουσιν οὐδὲ συνίουσιν.

> Because seeing they do not see, and hearing they do not hear, nor do they understand (RSV).[1]

A few observations are in order: (1) The first difference in comparison with Mark's paraphrase is the substitution of 'because' (ὅτι) for 'in order that' (ἵνα). Jesus does not speak parables *in order that* his hearers may not understand, but *because* they do not understand.

(2) Matthew follows Mark in that the 'seeing' clause comes first, but he has abbreviated both clauses by reducing them to simple clauses, i.e. the καὶ μή clauses are omitted, and the subjunctives (βλέπωσιν/ἀκούωσιν) become negated indicatives (οὐ βλέπουσιν/οὐ ἀκούουσιν). The effect is a more streamlined rendering.

(3) Matthew has omitted Mark's μήποτε clause. This modification is particularly significant as we shall see below. For Matthew, the abbreviated paraphrase serves as an introduction to a formal quotation of the Isaianic text, which follows א verbatim.[2] That the evangelist has added a formal quotation of LXX Isa. 6.9-10 is significant to our understanding of his adaptation of the Marcan paraphrase.

The differences in Matthew are not unimportant, but amount to a thorough reworking of the Marcan text. What is to be made of these differences?

B. *The Context of Isa. 6.9-10 in Matthew*

Immediate Context

Comparison of the Marcan and Matthean contexts reveals several noteworthy differences. I shall attend only to those that are most likely to bear some relationship to the evangelist's reworking of the logion containing the paraphrase of Isa. 6.9-10. Ten points of interest will now be considered.

(1) In Matthew the question posed by the disciples is different. The disciples ask not 'concerning the parables', but *why* Jesus teaches in parables (13.10), which is Matthew's attempt to move more smoothly into the saying about parables (13.11). It is possible that Matthew has understood Mark's plural use of 'parables' (in 4.10, 11) in the sense of mode or manner of teaching. He may also have sensed that a reference to parables was uncalled for, since Jesus had told but one parable. Moreover, by having Jesus ask *why*, Matthew will be able more easily to introduce into the logion the sense of cause. In any case, Matthew sensed the awkwardness of Mark's text, and has attempted to smooth it out. Even so, the train of thought remains somewhat obscure. The way Mt. 13.11 reads, Jesus does not answer the question. Moreover, the insertion of the gain or loss saying at this point (Mt. 13.12=Mk 4.25) only postpones Jesus' answer. In Mt. 13.13, however, Jesus finally does answer the question: 'This is why I speak to them in parables, because. . .'[3] Furthermore, in modifying Mark this way, C.E. Carlston notes that he 'has removed the motivation for the explanation of the Sower'.[4] According to Matthew's version, the disciples do not ask about what the parable means, though Jesus tells them anyway; they only wanted to know why he taught the way he did.

(2) The Matthean Jesus also gives a different answer. In Mark we are told: 'To you has been given the secret of the kingdom of God, but for those outside everything is in parables' (4.11). But in Matthew Jesus says: 'To you it has been given to know the secrets of the kingdom of heaven, but to them it has not been given'. There are several differences that ought to be commented upon. First, Matthew states that the disciples (i.e., 'you') have been given to *know* the secrets of the kingdom. The insertion of γνῶναι, a favorite word in Matthew (compare Mt. 10.26 with Mk 4.22; 12.7 with Mk 2.23-28; 16.3 with Mk 8.11-12), suggests that knowledge is a key element in discipleship, which is one of Matthew's themes (also note 13.51-52).[5] Secondly, Matthew states that the disciples have been given to know the *secrets* rather than the singular 'secret' of his Marcan source. Carlston suggests that the plural implies that the disciples understand Jesus' teaching as a whole.[6] This could be, for it is in keeping with Matthew's generally more positive view of the disciples, both here (as seen in the omission of Mk 4.13 and the inclusion of the beatitude in 13.16-17), and throughout his gospel (see 16.16-19). At the very least, the plural number would point to the variety of lessons to be learned from the seven kingdom parables found in Matthew 13.[7] Thirdly, Matthew replaces 'those outside' with 'them'. The effect of this substitution is to narrow the gap between believers and unbelievers. Unlike Mark, who is probably less optimistic about his church's external relations, Matthew (who, it should be remembered, emphasizes the missionary enterprise) wishes to tone down the distinction.[8] This is not a matter of compromise, but a matter of diplomacy. Fourthly, Matthew says that 'it has not been given', rather than 'everything is in parables'. Here Matthew wishes to avoid Mark's peculiar view of Jesus' parables. They may be profound, and perhaps less clear than non-parabolic teaching, but they are not riddles; nor are they intended to obfuscate Jesus' teachings (see Mt. 13.34-35).

(3) Matthew inserts Mark's saying on gaining or losing (4.25) between the two verses of the logion (i.e., Mt. 13.11=Mk 4.11; Mt. 13.12=Mk 4.25; Mt. 13.13=Mk 4.12). This alteration is deliberate and has affected the meaning of the logion taken over from Mark. By bringing this saying forward, Matthew has given the disciples added incentive to pay close attention to his teaching, for in so doing their knowledge will be multiplied. The threat of losing what one has, however, anticipates Matthew's paraphrase of Isa. 6.9-10 in the next

verse. Those who are not Jesus' disciples, because of their spiritual insensitivity, are only bewildered further by Jesus' parables, and so lapse deeper into ignorance.[9]

(4) Mt. 13.13 explicitly states the reason why Jesus speaks in parables ('This is why [διὰ τοῦτο] I speak to them in parables'). Not only does this statement make it clear that what follows is Jesus' answer to the original question, but it serves as an editorial seam, enabling Matthew to resume his Marcan source.

(5) Matthew replaces Mark's ἵνα with ὅτι, thus changing the sense from purpose to cause. It is possible that Matthew's ὅτι is recitative, in which case Jesus says, 'This is why I speak to them in parables: "Seeing they do not see... nor do they understand"'. In either way, however, the meaning is essentially the same. In Matthew's version, obduracy logically precedes the prophetic word. As it now stands, the prophetic word only describes an existing condition, it does not bring it about, or even advance it.[10] Nevertheless, in view of v. 12, Matthew may understand Jesus to be saying something to the effect: 'I speak parables to them, instead of plain teaching, because they are obdurate', as if to say that obdurate people deserve only parabolic teaching.[11] The parables do not promote obduracy, they only make it easier to remain obdurate, and so to 'lose what one already has'. If this interpretation is correct, then in light of the warning in v. 12, there remains a certain sense of judgment.

(6) Matthew formally introduces and quotes LXX Isa. 6.9-10. The fulfilment formula, one which the evangelist uses frequently, also adds to the sense that the people's obduracy is an existing condition, as if the Matthean Jesus says: 'They are an obdurate people, therefore in their case, Isa. 6.9-10 has been fulfilled'. This is the only example where a Matthean fulfilment quotation is uttered by Jesus himself.

(7) The verbatim quotation of the LXX, which of course Mark lacks (but see Acts 28.26-27), only confirms the Matthean sense that obduracy is a prior condition, and not one brought on by the prophet or, in the gospel context, by Jesus. (LXX: 'For the heart of this people has become fat', instead of as it is in the Hebrew: 'Make the heart of this people fat'; see discussion of the meaning of LXX Isa. 6.9-10 in Chapter 3 above). Although God, through the message of Jesus, no longer directly brings about the condition of obduracy, its condition, nevertheless fulfills God's purposes.[12]

(8) Matthew appends a composite beatitude (vv. 16-17), likely drawn from Q (see Lk. 10.23-24 and Mt. 11.25-27; cf. John 8.56; Heb. 11.13; 1 Pet. 1.10-12). The presence of this beatitude underscores the disciples' status as recipients of the 'secrets of the kingdom'. *Their*[13] eyes and ears, in contradistinction to the blind eyes and the deaf ears of the quotation, 'are blessed because they do see. . . and hear'. It is interesting to note that the order of the seeing/hearing clauses is the same as their order in the logion (v. 13), rather than in the order of hearing/seeing, as found in the Old Testament. It may be that this beatitude, like the logion itself, derives from an authentic saying of Jesus that had to do more with his (observable) ministry in general than with his parables in particular.[14]

(9) The status of the disciples is greatly enhanced, not only by virtue of the beatitude itself, but also by virtue of the omission of Mk 4.13: 'Do you not understand this parable? How then will you understand all the parables?' Matthew probably feared that these questions in effect placed the disciples too close to the company of those who are obdurate, and so elected to omit them altogether. This concern is in keeping with his overall attempt to portray the disciples in a more positive light.[15] (See further discussion below.)

(10) Mt. 13.34 is a redaction of Mk 4.33-34. To it is appended another 'fulfilment' quotation. Whereas in Mark's version there remains the sense that the parables are hard to understand ('. . . as they were able to hear it'), in Matthew this idea has vanished. Moreover, Matthew says nothing at this point about Jesus giving private explanations to the disciples. (In Matthew, private instruction is less frequent). This omission is probably due to the evangelist's wish to avoid the implication that the disciples, like the crowds, were unable to understand the parables. In v. 35 Matthew adds a quotation from Ps. 78[77].2 that shows that Jesus' habit of teaching 'in parables' fulfilled 'what was spoken by the prophet'. Although his quotation exhibits a mixture of traits from the LXX and the Hebrew, the plural 'in parables', derived from the LXX, renders the text particularly suitable for the Matthean context.[16] Moreover, the appearance of 'hidden' anticipates the Parable of the Hidden Treasure in v. 44. The sense seems to be that Jesus speaks parables, and in so doing reveals truths about things, such as the kingdom of God, that have heretofore remained hidden.

General Context

We now turn to the question of how the obduracy idea functions elsewhere in Matthew's gospel. Three passages of interest shall be considered.

(1) In the healing of the man with the withered hand (Mk 3.1-6; Mt. 12.9-14), Matthew omits Mark's 'and he looked around at them with anger, grieved at their hardness of heart' (3.5). It is likely that Matthew has omitted this detail, not because he wished to be more conciliatory toward the Pharisees, but because he was hesitant to describe Jesus as angry, a disposition that the evangelist may have deemed inappropriate for his Lord.[17] Moreover, in light of the quotation of Isa. 42.1-4 in vv. 18-21, in which the chosen servant is described as quiet and gentle, such anger would have seemed out of place. That the 'scribes and Pharisees' are considered obdurate elsewhere in Matthew is plainly evident by their castigation as 'blind guides of the blind' (see 15.14; 23.16, 17, 19, 24, 26).

(2) When Jesus walks on water in Mk 6.48-51, the disciples respond in fear (v. 49) and amazement (v. 51), 'for... their hearts were hardened' (v. 52). However, in Matthew's version of this episode (14.25-33), the picture is changed dramatically. The evangelist admits that the disciples were initially terrified (v. 26), but when Jesus 'immediately' speaks, reassurance returns (v. 27). This assurance is seen in Peter's bold offer to join his Lord out on the water (vv. 28-29), an experiment that results in a lesson on faith (vv. 30-31).[18] The Matthean episode concludes with the disciples worshipping Jesus, and confessing him to be God's Son (v. 33). Nothing could stand in sharper contrast to the picture that we have in Mark where the terrified disciples learn nothing about faith and make no such confession. There they are portrayed instead as ignorant and obdurate.

(3) Finally, in his account of Jesus's rebuke of the disciples for failing to understand the meaning of the 'bread' (16.5-12), Matthew makes two major changes. First, he says only that Jesus asked: 'Do you not yet perceive?' This rebuke is considerably more mild than what we find in Mark: 'Do you not yet perceive or understand? Are your hearts hardened? Having eyes do you not see, and having ears do you not hear?' (8.17b-18a).[19] Secondly, he explains what it was that the disciples had not learned about the 'bread', namely, that his reference to yeast in v. 6 was only figurative. The disciples are

rebuked for misunderstanding his warning—thinking that he referred to literal bread—and for failing to realize that the fact that they had forgotten to take bread (v. 5) would surely present no problem for one like Jesus who had miraculously multiplied loaves and fish on two previous occasions. Their lapse was due to 'little faith', not to 'hardened hearts'. In sharp contrast to Mark's version, in which the disciples are once again left in an obdurate condition, Matthew says of the disciples in v. 12: 'Then they understood. . . '[20]

Summary

Although the obduracy idea in Matthew is understood differently from the way it is in Mark, it nevertheless plays an important part, for it also explains why some people are unable to recognize the purposes of God. In his presentation of the idea, Matthew is careful (1) to avoid any implication that the disciples are obdurate, or (2) that Jesus' word produces obduracy. The evangelist does, however, view Jesus' enemies as obdurate, especially the Pharisees (and so deserving of parabolic teaching only), but the responsibility of this obduracy lies wholly with them.

Chapter 9

ISAIAH 6.9-10 IN LUKE–ACTS

Introduction

Isa. 6.9-10 is quoted twice in Luke–Acts. The paraphrase found in Lk. 8.10b is based upon Mk 4.12. The formal quotation found in Acts 28.26-27 is based upon the LXX.

A. *Isa. 6.9-10 in Luke*

The Text of Isa. 6.9-10

Luke's version of the paraphrase of Isa. 6.9-10 is found in the parables context. The text reads:

ἵνα βλέποντες μὴ βλέπωσιν[1] καὶ ἀκούοντες μὴ συνιῶιν,

'So that seeing they may not see, and hearing they may not understand' (RSV)

The following grammatical observations may be made: (1) Unlike Matthew, Luke retains Mark's ἵνα, and so, in all probability, retains the telic sense (more on this below). (2) Like Matthew, he has omitted the μήποτε clause, but, unlike Matthew, he has not appended a formal quotation of the Isaianic text. Thus, Luke's paraphrase is briefest of all. (3) Luke has abbreviated his Marcan source somewhat differently from the way that Matthew did. Like Matthew, he has reduced the 'seeing'/'hearing' clauses to simple clauses rather than compound clauses. But the evangelist has left the verbs in the subjunctive mood. (4) There is virtually no evidence, as is argued by D. Wenham, for seeing the shorter versions of Matthew and Luke as witnesses to a non-Marcan source (with Mark's paraphrase but an expansion of the Matthean version).[2] Both of the secondary evangelists have taken up and omitted different parts of Mark's paraphrase in an effort to streamline it and, what is more significant, to alter its meaning, as further analysis of the Lucan redaction will demonstrate.

Luke's redaction of the Marcan logion is not nearly as involved as it is in Matthew. It consists primarily of abbreviation and stylistic revision.[3] However, seen against the Lucan context in which other changes have taken place, some significant differences in emphasis will be observed. We turn now to a consideration of the context of Isa. 6.9-10 in Luke.

Immediate Context of Isa. 6.9-10 in Luke
Not every difference or peculiarity in the Lucan version will be taken into account. What is of interest are those differences (or similarities) that point to Luke's understanding of Isa. 6.9-10 and the Old Testament obduracy idea. The following observations may be made:

(1) In contrast to Mark (and Matthew) the question of the disciples pertains directly to the Parable of the Sower (8.5-8) that Jesus has just uttered: 'His disciples asked him what this parable meant' (8.9). Luke's revision is only natural, since Jesus will shortly provide an interpretation of the parable. Since Luke has taken this option, he abbreviates the logion, concentrating, instead, on its interpretation. (This contrasts with Matthew, who attempted to answer the question why Jesus spoke in parables. Therefore, Matthew greatly expanded the Marcan logion.) Even so, the logion fits the context so awkwardly that one wonders why the evangelist did not elect simply to omit it altogether. However, Luke may have retained it since the obduracy idea, as we shall see, plays a significant role in his theology.

(2) Like Matthew, Luke refers to *knowing* the plural *secrets* of the kingdom of God. As in the case of Matthew, 'to know' puts emphasis on learning, while 'secrets' probably entail the various details of Jesus' teaching, and not simply, as in Mark, the single idea that the kingdom is present in Jesus.[4]

(3) Also like Matthew, Luke has omitted the offensive reference to 'those outside', preferring the innocuous 'the rest'. It is likely that the evangelist wishes to reduce the gulf between the disciples and the crowds.[5] This is in keeping with Luke's emphasis that the 'word of God' (8.11) is for all.[6]

(4) Luke retains Mark's in parables, 'but there is no evidence that for him it meant anything other than the ordinary parables spoken

by Jesus'.[7] But in what sense is 'in parables' antithetical to being given the knowledge of the 'secrets'? The saying demands some kind of contrast. Therefore, it seems likely that although Luke does not view them as incomprehensible, or at least nearly so (which apparently Mark does), he probably does understand them as requiring careful thought.[8]

(5) Because he has retained Mark's ἵνα, the logion still seems to mean that the reason that Jesus speaks in parables is to render his hearers obdurate. Although the consecutive sense, denoting result rather than purpose, is grammatically possible, I suspect that it is final here in Luke for many of the reasons cited above in the discussion of ἵνα in Mark.[9] This is likely also because of Luke's use of the infinitive γνῶναι, which in the Lucan context (but not in the Matthean) is probably an instance of the infinitive of purpose. As such, it stands roughly parallel to the ἵνα. In other words, the Lucan Jesus is saying: 'To you it has been given (in order that you may) know. . ., but to the rest (it has been given) in parables, in order that seeing they should not see. . . ' Being given information about the kingdom 'in parables' is not 'to know'.

(7) Luke omits Mark's μήποτε clause. The omission of this clause makes it clear that Luke does not share the view that Jesus' parables are designed to prevent repentance and forgiveness.[10] Jesus' use of parables may be designed to prevent the 'rest' from knowing the secrets of the kingdom (a knowledge reserved for disciples), but it is not designed to prevent repentance and forgiveness. More on the significance of this omission will be seen in the next point.

(8) One item in Luke's version of the parable's interpretation calls for comment. With regard to the first group of people who hear the word, but do not respond fruitfully, Mark says only: 'When they hear, Satan immediately comes and takes away the word which is sown in them' (4.15). But Luke puts it: 'The ones along the path are those who have heard; then the devil comes and takes away the word from their hearts, that they may not believe and be saved' (8.12).[11] The last clause, 'that [ἵνα] they may not believe and be saved', is a Lucan addition that could represent the evangelist's substitution for Mark's μήποτε clause ('lest they should turn again, and be forgiven'), which he had omitted earlier.[12] In other words, Luke is saying that whereas *Jesus* does not prevent forgiveness and salvation, the *devil* does.

(9) It is possible that Luke has placed the material about those who are his 'true mother and brothers' here in vv. 19-21 as a substitution for Mark's enigmatic sayings in 4.33-34. Rather than emphasizing the difficulty of Jesus' parables, and the need for his disciples to receive private explanation, Luke offers this material, which he has taken from Mk 3.31-35, in order to emphasize his theme concerned with obeying the 'word of God'. The saying of v. 21 also implies that the word can be heard and understood.[13] There is nothing strange or inexplicable about it.[14]

These observations lead to the conclusion that Luke does not share Mark's view that the purpose of Jesus' parables is to prevent repentance and forgiveness. What Luke seems to be saying instead is that whereas the disciples of Jesus receive full disclosure of the details pertaining to the kingdom of God, those who have not chosen to follow Jesus receive no more than parables. The implication is that not until one becomes a disciple of Jesus will one receive all the truth. Furthermore, the reason that some people fail to heed Jesus' word and to follow him is because the devil snatches away the message. This the devil does, so that they will not believe and be saved.

General Context of Isa. 6.9-10 in Luke
We now turn to the question of how the obduracy idea functions elsewhere in Luke's gospel. Several passages shall be considered.

(1) The account of the man with the withered hand (Mk 3.1-6) occurs in Lk 6.6-11. Luke omits Mark's 'with anger, grieved at their hardness of heart' (Mk 3.5), and simply says: 'And he looked around on them all, and said to him. . . ' (Lk. 6.10).[15] The omission of Jesus' anger is in keeping with the evangelist's portrait of Jesus.[16] Because of this omission, retention of the reference to the Pharisees' hardened hearts at this point would have been awkward. However, the thought is not entirely absent in the Lucan version. In 6.11, a verse which Luke has completely rewritten, Jesus' enemies are described as 'filled with fury'. Luke uses the word ἄνοια, which literally means 'mindless rage'. What the evangelist has done is to reserve his description of the scribes and Pharisees until the miraculous cure has taken place. As the story now reads, they not only oppose Jesus when confounded by superior logic (v. 9), but they oppose him even after a dramatic example of miraculous power (v. 10). Furthermore, since this episode is likely to be taken with the one that precedes it (both

are concerned with what is lawful on the Sabbath),[17] the Lucan description is probably placed at the end of the section as a general summary of the Pharisaic response to Jesus. Although Luke does not say that the scribes and Pharisees have 'hardened hearts', his reference to them as possessed with 'mindless rage' is scarcely less descriptive of obduracy.

(2) The accounts of the disciples' fear and lack of understanding following the feeding miracles (Mk 6.49-52; 8.16-21) are both omitted in Luke. Whereas the omission of the second episode is due to the fact that this portion of Mark is part of the larger section that Luke omits (Mk 6.45-8.26, sometimes called 'Luke's Big Omission'), it is likely that he has omitted the first episode, although providing an account of the feeding miracle itself (9.10-17), because of its negative portrayal of the disciples.

(3) Elsewhere in Luke, however, the disciples are chastened for their lack of understanding, but it is never viewed as a debilitating or permanent condition. In 9.54 the disciples, alluding to Elijah (2 Kgs 1.9-16), ask Jesus if they should call fire down from heaven as judgment upon the unresponsive Samaritan village. Jesus, however, rebukes them (v. 55). This dramatic incident likely is intended to call the reader's attention to the theme of God's mercy, a theme that runs throughout Luke's central section that this pericope inaugurates. In 24.11 the disciples do not believe the report of the woman who had just returned from the empty tomb, a theme that is no doubt traditional (cf. Mt. 28.17). That this condition of post-Easter unbelief is only temporary, however, Luke makes quite clear in the rest of ch. 24. The two on the road to Emmaus do not recognize the risen Jesus initially because 'their eyes were kept from recognizing him' (v. 16). After breaking bread, Jesus calls them 'foolish men, and slow of heart to believe all that the prophets have spoken!' (v. 25). Jesus then explains to them the scriptures (vv. 26-27). When Jesus appears a second time he asks his disciples, 'Why are you troubled, and why do questionings arise in your hearts?' (v. 38). Jesus then 'opened their minds to understand the scriptures' (vv. 45-47). In these examples it is clear that Luke views the disciples' spiritual imperceptivity as only temporary and primarily due to their discouragement and bewilderment following Jesus' death (see vv. 19-24). This interpretation is confirmed when we examine Luke's versions of the passion predictions. After one of the predictions, Mark tells us that the disciples

'did not understand the saying, and they were afraid to ask him' (9.32). But Luke puts it this way, 'But they did not understand this saying, and it was concealed from them, that they should not perceive it; and they were afraid to ask him about this saying' (9.45). In Mk 10.32 the disciples are 'amazed' and 'afraid' with regard to Jesus' passion prediction. In Lk. 18.34, however, we are told that 'they understood none of these things; this saying was hid from them, and they did not grasp what was said'. Both passives, 'it was concealed' and 'it was hid', are probably divine passives. That is, God withheld from the disciples the full implications of Jesus' passion predictions. In putting the disciples' response to the predictions this way, Luke prepares the reader for the disciples' failure to respond quickly in faith and understanding to the Easter announcement. On the whole, Luke's portrait of the disciples is consistently more positive than that found in Mark.[18]

By way of summary, it can be said that in Luke the obduracy idea is present, but it is not presented in quite the same manner as in Mark. It seems to apply to the various characters of the Lucan account as follows: (1) The enemies of Jesus, such as the scribes and Pharisees who plot his destruction, are controlled by senseless hatred. Their murderous actions, as we learn in Acts 2.23, are part of God's 'definite plan'. They represent the opposite of what Luke regards as the 'noble minded' (see Acts 17.11). Although the distinctive vocabulary of obduracy is not used, the Lucan depiction seems to presuppose the general idea. (2) The 'rest', that is, those who are not Jesus' disciples (which would include enemies and 'impressed unbelievers'), are not privileged to full disclosure of kingdom truths. (3) Unlike Mark, in Luke only a softened version of the obduracy idea is applied to the disciples. They are unable to understand fully because it was God's will that they not know more fully until the risen Christ should explain the scriptures to them. At no time do they oppose Jesus, and at no time does Jesus regard them as having 'hardened hearts', 'blind eyes', or 'deaf ears'. It is likely that Luke regards all of the various types of response to Jesus as part of God's ordained plan.

B. *Isa. 6.9-10 in Acts*

The Text of Isa. 6.9-10

Like Matthew, the quotation of Isa. 6.9-10 in Acts 28.26-27 follows the LXX ℵ verbatim. The quotation in Acts, however, contains the first part of Isa. 6.9: 'Go to this people, and say'. The inclusion of this part of Isaiah is particularly appropriate in light of the missionary thrust of Acts. The LXX rendering, as discussed above in Ch. 3, suggests that the hardening process is due to the people, and not to God or to the prophet through whom God speaks. Whether the LXX version in this instance represents precisely what Luke wishes to say is a moot point, since the LXX is the only version of the Old Testament that the evangelist ever quotes.

Immediate Context of Isa. 6.9-10 in Acts
The immediate context of the formal quotation in Acts 28 is significant. The following observations may be made. (1) The setting involves Paul's attempt to persuade fellow Jews of the truth of the Christian proclamation. All day long Paul tries 'to convince them about Jesus both from the law of Moses and from the prophets' (v. 23). This idea of a comprehensive witness from the scriptures was seen in the last chapter of Luke's gospel (24.27, 44-45). (2) According to the evangelist, what prompted Paul's recitation of this Old Testament text was the response of unbelief: 'Some were convinced by what he said, while others disbelieved' (v. 24). To these unbelievers Paul declares: 'The Holy Spirit was right in saying to your fathers through Isaiah the prophet. . . ' (v. 25). (3) After the quotation, Paul admonishes his fellow unbelieving Jews: 'Let it be known to you then that this salvation of God has been sent to the Gentiles, they will listen' (v. 28). This concluding remark only epitomizes what had been characteristic of the church's experience in general, and of the Pauline mission in particular. This theme will be traced in the next section.

General Context of Isa. 6.9-10 in Acts
The obduracy idea in Acts appears to be part of the author's larger understanding of the sovereignty of God. That is, the stubbornness that led to Jesus' crucifixion was part of God's plan. The development of this understanding may be sketched by touching on the following passages: (1) In reference to Judas Iscariot's betrayal of Jesus, Peter tells the assembled disciples, 'the scripture had to be fulfilled' (1.16). The use of ἔδει πληρωθῆναι makes it clear that the evangelist understood Judas' act as in some sense foreordained.

(2) As has already been mentioned, in his Pentecost sermon Peter tells his audience that their act of crucifying Jesus was 'according to the definite plan and foreknowledge of God' (2.23). Peter reiterates a similar idea in his sermon from Solomon's portico, when he says: 'I know that you acted in ignorance, as did also your rulers. But what God foretold by the mouth of all the prophets, that his Christ should suffer, he thus fulfilled' (3.17-18; cf. v. 21).

(3) After being warned by the High Priest and other religious authorities not to preach Jesus any longer, Peter and his Christian friends sing in praise to God, citing Ps. 2.1-2 which describes the futility of foreign kings and peoples who oppose God and his Messiah (4.25-26). The Christians go on to recount how the rulers, both Jewish and Gentile, had 'gathered against' Jesus 'to do whatever [God's] hand and [God's] plan had predestined to take place' (vv. 27-28).

(4) In Stephen's speech the theme of obduracy appears. In 7.25 we are told that the Hebrews 'did not understand' that Moses was to be their deliverer (see also v. 35). During the wilderness wanderings the people 'refused to obey him' (v. 39), instead wishing to offer sacrifices to idols (vv. 40-41). Stephen's speech concludes with this scathing criticism:

> 'You stiff-necked people, uncircumcised in heart and ears, you always resist the Holy Spirit. As your fathers did, so do you. Which of the prophets did not your fathers persecute? And they killed those who announced beforehand the coming of the Righteous One, whom you have now betrayed and murdered, you who have received the law as delivered by angels and did not keep it' (vv. 51-53).

Here we find many of the elements that concern us. The Jewish forefathers are called 'stiff-necked, uncircumcised in heart and ears'. These are all obduracy terms. Of special significance is to observe that Stephen links the tradition of persecuting the prophets to the experience of Jesus, something that Jesus himself had done in Luke's gospel (see 13.31-35). Moreover, there is reference to the 'law' that is not kept. In the Lucan context it is possible that this is to be understood as failure to believe in Jesus, of whom the law and the prophets spoke (see Lk. 24.27, 44-46; Acts 28.23).

(5) A major turning point takes place in Acts 13. In this chapter Paul replaces Peter as the central character. But of greater significance

is the shift from the Jewish mission to the Gentile mission. On his first missionary journey, Paul preaches a sermon at the synagogue of Antioch of Pisidia (vv. 16-41). In his sermon, the apostle briefly recounts Jewish history and the events surrounding Jesus. After announcing that Jesus has been raised up, and that in him there is forgiveness of sins, Paul concludes his sermon with a warning: 'Beware, therefore, lest there come upon you what is said in the prophets: "Behold, you scoffers, and wonder, and perish; for I do a deed in your days, a deed you will never believe, if one declares it to you"' (vv. 40-41). Paul's foreboding citation of Hab. 1.5 anticipates the Jewish unbelief described in vv. 44-45. Because of this unbelief Paul declares: 'It was necessary that the word of God should be spoken first to you. Since you thrust it from you, and judge yourselves unworthy of eternal life, behold, we turn to the Gentiles' (v. 45; see also 18.6). True to Paul's word, and to Isa. 49.6 which he quotes in v. 47, the Gentiles rejoiced and 'glorified the word of God; and as many as were ordained to eternal life believed' (v. 48). What we have here is something that approximates the opposite of ordained obduracy. Not only are acts of obduracy, such as executing God's Anointed, part of God's will, but so is faith.

(6) Finally, in 19.9 some of the members of the synagogue at Ephesus are described as those who 'were stubborn [σκληρύνειν] and disbelieved, speaking evil of the Way'. Therefore, Paul withdraws from the synagogue, conducting his ministry, instead, from the school of Tyrannus.

C. *Is Luke's Use of Isa. 6.9-10 Anti-Semitic?*

From time to time scholars have suggested that to one degree or another the Lucan writings are anti-Semitic. However, nothing close to a scholarly consensus has emerged, viz., either that Luke is anti-Semitic or that he is not.[19] In a series of recent studies J.T. Sanders hopes to demonstrate once and for all that Luke–Acts is indeed anti-Semitic.[20] He contends that Luke is not merely anti-Judaic (that is, opposed to the Jewish religion), but that he actually hates the Jewish people, and so is anti-Semitic in the fullest sense.[21] In my judgment, not only is his exegesis of many of the relevant passages questionable, his entire approach is flawed by a failure to assess comparatively intra-Jewish polemic and sectarian controversy. Sanders does not fail to assess the relevant items adequately; he does not assess them at all. Supposed evidence of Luke's hatred of the Jews pales in comparison to the real thing. For example, Pharisees believed that the Sadducees were unclean (*m. Nid.* 4.2) and destined for hell (*1 Enoch* 38.5; 95.3; *m. Sanh.* 10.1; *b. Ber.* 58a; *Roš. Haš.* 17a). The rabbis hated the uneducated Jews, or *'am ha-areṣ* (Jn 7.47-49; *m. Dem.* 2.2, 3; *b. Pesah.* 49b), while the latter hated the former in return (*b. Pesah.* 49b). Of course, the covenanters of Qumran hated all Jews who were not members of their community (1QS 1.9-10), prayed that apostates never be forgiven (1QS 2.4-9), and eagerly anticipated the future judgment of the wicked of Israel (1QH 4.18-20). Indeed, the members of Qumran believed that they would take part in punishing those outside their community (1QpHab 5.3-5). John the Baptist called his fellow Jews a 'brood of vipers' in grave danger of judgment (Mt. 3.7b-10; Lk 3.7b-9). Paul, the Christian Jew, regarded his fellow non-Christian Jews as hardened (Rom. 11.7; 2 Cor. 3.12-4.6) and as God's 'enemies' (Rom. 11.28), who oppose and displease God (1 Thess. 2.14-16). This type of polemic, however, reflects intra-Jewish debate, that is, who is right and who is wrong and what are the consequences. This polemic has nothing to do with racism, anti-Semitic or otherwise.

Obviously Luke believes that apart from faith in Christ, the Jews are lost (Acts 2.38; 3.17-26; 4.8-12), but this does not mean that he hates the Jewish people and wishes for their destruction,[22] any more than it does in Paul. There is simply too much material in Luke–Acts that runs counter to such a conclusion. One thinks of the canticles of the birth narrative, which are filled with pro-Jewish sentiments (Lk. 1.33, 54-55, 68-79; 2.25, 30-31). Even at the crucifixion, the dying Jesus says, 'Father, forgive them; for they know not what they do' (23.34).[23] Elsewhere Jesus' execution is partially excused on the grounds of ignorance (Acts 3.17; 13.27; 17.30). The martyred Stephen also forgives his executioners (Acts 7.60). These utterances stand in sharp contrast to the dying words of condemnation uttered by the seven sons in 2 Macc. 7 (esp. vv. 14, 17, 19). Moreover, Luke's references to non-Christian Jews as 'brethren' simply make no sense, if the evangelist were anti-Semitic (Acts 2.29; 3.17; 7.2; 13.26, 38; 22.1, 5; 23.1, 5, 6; 28.17, 21).[24] Luke's usage of the word 'brethren' in addressing non-Christian Jews is very much in keeping with its usage in Jewish sources, where on occasion a rabbi cries out, 'Hear me, O brethren of the house of Israel' (*t. Yoma* 1.12), and then exhorts his brethren to do or not to do such and such a thing (see also *t. Šeb.* 8.2; *Sipre Num.* § 161 [on 35.34]; *b. Ketub.* 28b; Rom 9.3). Furthermore, Luke's reference to Pharisees (Acts 15.5; 26.5), Sadducees (Acts 5.17), and Christians (Acts 24.5, 14; 28.22) as 'sects' (αἵρεσις) is only additional evidence that this evangelist viewed himself as a participant in intra-Jewish debate, if not in some sense a part of Israel.

The present task, however, is not to review at length the thesis of Professor Sanders, which has been done elsewhere,[25] but to examine the function of Isa. 6.9-10 in Luke-Acts, a function which Sanders has found to contribute significantly to Lucan anti-Semitism. With this issue in mind, let us reconsider the two contexts in which this prophetic text is cited.

It has already been observed that Luke abbreviates the Marcan paraphrase of Isa. 6.9-10. By retaining Mark's ἵνα, the Lucan evangelist has retained the telic idea, but his omission of 'outsiders' and the μήποτε clause significantly mitigates the severity of the Marcan version. Why Luke would make these changes if he were anti-Semitic is not easy to understand. In any case, Sanders does not comment on this passage, which is probably an indication that he himself does not view the function of this passage as anti-Semitic in this context.

It is the function of the formal quotation of Isa. 6.9-10 in Acts 28.26-27, however, that has occasioned most of the attention. For his concluding episode, the Lucan evangelist has Paul meet with 'the local leaders of the Jews' one last time. Paul explains to them why he is in custody (vv. 17-20). The Jewish leaders report that they have heard nothing official from Jerusalem, although they are aware that Christianity is widely spoken against, and that they desire to hear more (vv. 21-22). On the appointed day, Paul testifies concerning Jesus and the kingdom of God, arguing from the law of Moses and the prophets (v. 23). Some are convinced, while others do not believe (v. 24). In view of the lack of a believing consensus, Paul quotes Isa. 6.9-10 (vv. 25-27). Paul then adds this commentary. 'Let it be known to you then that this salvation has been sent to the Gentiles; they will listen' (v. 28). Sanders believes that because the 'some' of v. 24 are only 'persuaded' and not actually converted, and because Paul quotes Isa. 6.9-10, Luke views all Jews as obdurate, rejected of God, and without hope.[26] There are problems, however, with both of these conclusions. First, there is no good reason not to understand those who were persuaded [πείθειν] as actual believing Christians. The same word is used in Acts 17.4: 'And some of them were persuaded [πείθειν], and joined Paul and Silas. . .' That these persuaded ones are regarded by Luke as Christians is seen in 17.10, where they are called 'brethren', a word that Luke uses regularly in reference to Christians.[27] The positive response of some Jews in Acts 28.24 therefore suggests that the evangelist has not closed the door on all Jews.[28] After other declarations to turn to the Gentiles, Paul continued to go to Jews (13.46-14.1; 18.6-19). Indeed, 28.30 explicitly says that Paul 'welcomed all who came to him'. In view of Paul's previous declarations and subsequent continued evangelism of Jews, we should assume that the 'all' of v. 30 includes Jews, as well as Gentiles. Secondly, Isa. 6.9-10 is not quoted to show that God has rejected Israel. The passage simply does not say this. Rather, this prophetic text explains why the nation of Israel as a whole ('this people') has not believed the Christian message.[29] According to Luke, Jewish unbelief does not mean that Christianity is wrong. Jewish unbelief, on the one hand, fulfils scripture (thus fending off the charge that Christian claims are false)[30] and, on the other, justifies the Gentile mission (which is the Lucan Paul's main point in v. 28).[31]

The function of Isa. 6.9-10 in Luke–Acts is not anti-Semitic, but it *is* anti-Judaic. Luke believes that apart from faith in the risen Christ, Judaism is incomplete and inadequate. His non-ecumenical fundamentalism may be offensive to modern people of faith, but the charge of anti-Semitism is unwarranted.

Summary

The obduracy idea, that is, blindness to divine truth, seems to play a major role in Lucan salvation history. This is seen in the crucifixion of Jesus, which makes forgiveness of sins possible, and in the persecution of the church, which causes her to spread to the Gentiles. The obduracy idea, in various nuances, is employed to interpret various features of the Christian experience. It is applied to particular individuals and classes of individuals. The Pharisees and various religious leaders are called 'mindless', 'stubborn', or 'stiff-necked' toward Jesus or the apostolic proclamation. For their part, the disciples are slow to understand, in need of having the scriptures opened to them. As for Isa. 6.9-10 in particular, it seems to be the text that explains not Jesus' use of parables, but why the Jews rejected the Christian proclamation. As it stands in Acts 28, the chapter that concludes Luke's two-volume narrative, Isa. 6.9-10 appears to be the single most important biblical witness to the early Church's experience of Jewish rejection and unbelief.

Chapter 10

ISAIAH 6.9-10 IN JOHN

Introduction

Isa. 6.10 is paraphrased in John 12.40. It will be argued that John 9.39b represents an allusion to Isa. 6.9 (as well as other similar Old Testament texts), and so it will be cited along with John 12.40.

A. *The Text of Isa. 6.9-10 in John*

The text reads:

9.39 ἵνα οἱ μὴ βλέποντες βλέπωσιν
καὶ οἱ βλέποντες τυφλοὶ γένωνται.

12.40 τετύφλωκεν αὐτῶν τοὺς ὀφθαλμοὺς
καὶ ἐπώρωσεν αὐτῶν τὴν καρδίαν,
ἵνα μὴ ἴδωσιν τοῖς ὀφθαλμοῖς
καὶ νοήσωσιν τῇ καρδίᾳ
καὶ στραφῶσιν, καὶ ἰάσομαι[1] αὐτούς.

9.39 that those who do not see may see,
and that those who see may become blind (RSV).

12.40 He[2] has blinded their eyes
and hardened[3] their heart,
lest they should see with their eyes
and perceive with their heart
and turn for me to heal them (RSV).

The following grammatical and textual comments are in order: (1) Although John 9.39 lacks the 'hearing' clause, it is probable that Isa. 6.9 is in view. This is likely for several reasons. (1) Throughout the fourth gospel emphasis is placed on seeing rather than hearing, especially in the immediate context in which Jesus has healed a blind man. Also, the element of hearing is likewise omitted from the paraphrase of Isa. 6.10 in John 12.40. (Although the quotation of Isa. 53.1 in John 12.38 involves the idea of 'hearing'). (2) τυφλός of 9.39 links the quotation to τυφλοῦν of 12.40. (3) There are several thematic parallels between chs. 9 and 12, which would suggest a relationship between the quotations, e.g., rejection of signs (cf. 9.16; 12.37) and threats of excommunication (cf. 9.22; 12.42; more on this below). However, this is not to deny the possibility of influence of other related passages, for it will be shown that John's paraphrase of Isa. 6.10 in all probability has been influenced by a variety of related texts. In the case of John 9.39, the language of Isa. 29.18 is recalled where the prophet proclaims that 'the deaf will hear' and 'the eyes of the blind will see [οἱ. . . ὀφθαλμοὶ τυφλῶν βλέψονται]' (cf. Isa. 29.10).

(2) In John's quotation of Isa. 6.10, the imperative of the original Hebrew has been realized: God *has* blinded their eyes and has hardened their heart. The telic force of this quotation is unmistakable, especially when viewed in its context.

(3) In addition to the novel presence of τυφλοῦν, the evangelist uses πωροῦν rather than the expected παχύνεσθαι. Both verbs are similar in meaning, the former being derived from ὁ πῶρος, a word used in connection with ancient medical reference to the callousing of the bone after an injury (Latin: *callus*). Thus, both convey the idea of thickening. The appearance of πωροῦν may be due to its wider circulation in early Christian circles (e.g., Mk 3.5; 6.52; 8.17; Rom. 11.7).

(4) In a study published in 1947, C.K. Barrett concluded that this quotation of Isa. 6.10 is probably best understood as having been derived from an acquaintance with the Targum.[4] But in his later commentary he instead opted for the Hebrew text, which he thinks the evangelist was loosely quoting from memory.[5] C. Goodwin noted that the last three words (καὶ ἰάσομαι αὐτούς) exactly agree with the LXX, and that the arrangement of the clauses 'looks like the effect of quoting from memory'.[6] In view of these two observations he concludes that 'we have no reason to doubt that the LXX was the source he knew, and we need not consider seriously the possibility of his using some freak version that rendered the Hebrew in this way'.[7] Likewise, E.C. Hoskyns judged that the last three words were proof enough that John's citation was based upon the LXX.[8] C.C. Torrey also believed that the LXX lay behind the quotation.[9] However, C.F.

Burney thought that John's quotation may in fact be dependent upon an unpointed Hebrew text, which could explain the presence of John's past tenses rather than the expected imperatives.[10] This view that John may in fact have had the Hebrew either before him, or at least in mind, has received some recent support. E.D. Freed has basically agreed with the view of Burney that the quotation was based upon the Hebrew text, although he does suggest that the last part was influenced by the LXX.[11] R. Schnackenburg also follows Burney, but, like Freed, sees ἰάσομαι as a deviation.[12] J. O'Rourke has suggested that John's quotation may very well have been dependent upon the Hebrew, with the variations to be explained in terms of his deliberate pesher exegesis.[13] Whether John had the Hebrew before him or the LXX or the Targum,[14] it should not be assumed that the fourth evangelist had no other text in mind than Isa. 6.10. It could very well be that the evangelist had in mind other related texts as well. Compare, for example, the following texts from the LXX:

> Behold, all are blind
> they do not know how to think (Isa. 56.10)

> Hear, you deaf,
> and look, you blind, that you may see (Isa. 42.18)

> The servants of God became blind (Isa. 42.19)

> The Lord has given you to drink a spirit of stupor
> and he will close their eyes (Isa. 29.10)

ἐκτυφλοῦν and τυφλοῦν are present in Isa. 56.10 and 42.19, respectively, which could account for the appearance of τετύφλωκεν in John's citation. Whereas these occurrences are in the passive voice, the verbs of 29.10 are active (note the perfect πεπότικεν). In LXX Isa. 29.14 even stronger language is used in depicting the Lord as the author of spiritual blindness: 'I shall destroy the wisdom of the wise and the discernment of the discerning shall I hide'.[15] Although the verb πωροῦν and its cognate πώρωσις occur a few times with καρδία in the New Testament (cf. Mk 3.5; 6.52; 8.17; Eph. 4.18), and twice in *Hermas* (cf. *Man.* 4.2.1; 12.4.4), never once does this combination occur in the LXX. The presence of πωροῦν with καρδία here in John's citation of Isa. 6.10 and similar usage elsewhere in the New Testament may suggest an early Church formulation or *testimonium*, as some scholars have argued.[16]

I conclude that the fourth evangelist freely composed the quotation from Isa. 6.10 and certain other related Isaianic passages (possibly reflecting an early Christian *testimonium*) to suit his own theological purposes. One important purpose was to show that it was God (and not the people) who caused the obduracy, and so brought on Jewish unbelief. In this respect John's version is closer in spirit to the MT than it is either to the Targum or to the LXX.

B. *The Context of Isa. 6.9-10 in John*

Immediate Context

The immediate context of the allusion of Isa. 6.9 in John 9.39 is the healing of the man born blind (vv. 1-7), and the ensuing controversy with the Pharisees (vv. 13-34). The allusion appears to mean that Jesus will give the truth ('sight') to the innocent ('the blind'), but will withhold it ('become blind') from the guilty ('those who see'). This is seen by the introduction to the allusion: 'For judgment I came into this world, that [ἵνα]. . . ' (v. 39a). It seems that this statement indicates that this effect is Jesus' *purpose* and not simply a *result* of his ministry. In this episode, it is the man born blind who gains true (in)sight, while the Pharisees who have eyesight, but lack insight, are those who are truly blind. The contrast between the blind man and the Pharisees is dramatic. 'Three times the former blind man, who is truly gaining knowledge, humbly confesses his ignorance (12, 25, 36). Three times the Pharisees, who are really plunging deeper into abysmal ignorance of Jesus, make confident statements about what they know of him (16, 24, 29)'.[17]

The immediate context of the quotation of Isa. 6.10 in John 12.40 is the summary unit consisting of 12.37-43. In this unit the evangelist explains why Jesus' ministry, despite the confirming signs that have attended it, has been rejected. It has been met with unbelief, he says, 'in order that [ἵνα] the word of the prophet Isaiah might be fulfilled' (v. 38a). The evangelist then cites LXX Isa. 53.1 verbatim implying that Jewish unbelief was predicted in the scriptures. However, according to vv. 39-40 this unbelief is not only predicted, but is actually produced by God: 'For this reason they were unable to believe [οὐκ ἠδύναντο πιστεύειν], because again Isaiah has said, "He [God] has blinded their eyes. . . "' The telic force of the Isa. 6.10 quotation is plainly evident.

It is interesting to observe further what the evangelist appears to have done with his two quotations from Isaiah. The linkage of the two passages is probably an example of *gezera šawa* in which passages with similar vocabulary are expounded together.[18] In this case, both quotations are bound closely together with πάλιν. Furthermore, when the evangelist says, 'Isaiah said these things because[19] he saw his glory[20] and spoke of him' (v. 41), he probably refers to both passages, and not only to 6.10. It is also probable that the evangelist was aware of the vocabulary common to both Isaianic passages (i.e., 6.1-13 and 52.13–53.12).[21] This is likely because the two key words, ὑψοῦν and δοξάζειν, are found at the beginning of the LXX version of the Suffering Servant Hymn, and are found together in John 12 (vv. 23, 28, 32, 34). Whereas in 6.1 it is the Lord who is high and lifted up, in 52.13 it is the Servant who is high and lifted up. Furthermore, in both Isaianic passages an element of obduracy is present. In Isa. 6 the prophet is commanded to preach a message of obduracy, while in Isa. 53 the prophet wonders who has believed. Since it is likely that the fourth evangelist viewed Jesus as the incarnation of God's shekinah (see 1.14),[22] it is probable that here he is saying that Isaiah saw Jesus,[23] God's glory and God's Servant, high and lifted up (or, in the language of the LXX, which in this case the evangelist appears to be following, 'lifted up' and 'glorified'),[24] and prophesied a message of obduracy. This prophecy of obduracy is fulfilled in the ministry of Jesus.

General Context
The following points should serve to clarify what function Isa. 6.9-10 and the obduracy idea have had in the fourth gospel: (1) There is present in John a pervasive theme of mystery and misunderstanding,[25] a theme that is facilitated by the obduracy idea. A few examples may be cited. In 1.10-11 the world and his own people fail to recognize and accept the Word.[26] In 2.19-21 the 'Jews' misunderstand Jesus' statement about raising up his 'temple' in three days. In 3.1-15 the ignorance of Nicodemus, a 'teacher of Israel' is exposed. In 6.60-66 some of Jesus' disciples find his teaching 'hard' (σκληρός), and cease following him. In 8.27 Jesus' opponents do not understand him. Many other examples could be cited. When one comes to 12.37-43 where the obduracy idea finds clear expression, one can hardly be surprised that despite all of Jesus' signs, few of the religious

authorities believed. Thus, it would appear that the obduracy idea is but a part of the larger Johannine scheme of misunderstanding.

(2) The allusion to Isa. 6.9 in John 9.39 makes an important contribution to the 'signs' theme in the fourth gospel. The allusion to this text establishes the moral that Jesus' enemies are blind to the display of God's power in Jesus. The blindness of the Pharisees to the significance of Jesus in this episode anticipates the summary in 12.37-43. Moreover, there are a few noteworthy parallels between these chapters. Not only is the sign of John 9 recalled by the comment in 12.37 that the signs of Jesus were met with general unbelief, but the fear of being cast out of the synagogue is emphasized in both chapters. In 9.22 the healed man's parents are afraid of the 'Jews' because of the decision to excommunicate anyone who confesses Jesus as the Christ. Similarly, in 12.42 the evangelist claims that many of the rulers believed in Jesus, but on account of the Pharisees would not confess it, lest they, too, be cast out of the synagogue.[27] Thus, the explanation of obduracy in ch. 12 has been illustrated by at least one of the specific 'signs'.

(3) The Isaianic quotations in 12.37-41, an important transitional unit in John,[28] suggest that the obduracy motif plays a major literary and theological role in the gospel of John. Its literary function is seen in that it is the unit that summarizes Jesus' ministry of signs (chs. 2-11), and prepares the reader for the passion account that follows (chs. 13-20). Theologically, this unit shows that Jesus' ministry of signs has been unsuccessful in persuading the Pharisees (sometimes dubbed 'the Jews') that Jesus is truly the Christ of God. By quoting Isa. 53.1 the evangelist[29] shows that this response of unbelief was predicted in scripture. By quoting Isa. 6.10, especially in the way he does, the evangelist attempts to show that this obdurate response was God's intention.[30] Seen in the light of Johannine christology, it would appear that the rejection of Jesus was God's plan so that his Son could be lifted up and, in being lifted up, return to the Father.[31] It is likely that D.M. Smith's suggestion is correct that this theme should be understood as an apologetic aimed to answer Jewish criticism.[32]

(4) Recent scholarship has suggested that Jesus is presented as the prophet like Moses.[33] This is likely so, for there are numerous verbal and thematic parallels with portions of the Pentateuch. In view of this typology it is quite probable that the evangelist would see Jewish

hard-heartedness toward Jesus' ministry of signs in terms of Israelite obduracy toward Moses and the signs produced through him. One is reminded of Deut. 29.2-4 where Moses tells the people of Israel: 'You have seen all that the Lord did before your eyes in the land of Egypt, to Pharaoh and to all his servants and to all his land, the great trials which your eyes saw, the signs [LXX σημεῖα], and those great wonders; but to this day the Lord has not given you a mind to understand, or eyes to see, or ears to hear'.

Summary

It would appear that Isa. 6.9-10 and the obduracy idea have played a major role in the theology of the fourth gospel. Unlike Mark, in which the parables of Jesus are uttered to produce obduracy, in John it is Jesus' ministry of signs that bring this about. However, John does not say that Jesus' signs actually cause obduracy. He only states that Jesus' signs result in obduracy because that is what the scriptures predict and what God makes happen.

Chapter 11

ISAIAH 6.9-10 IN THE RABBIS[1]

Introduction

In the preceding chapters a formal analysis of the various Jewish and Christian text traditions of Isa. 6.9-10 was undertaken. Whereas the interpretation of this text, as reflected in the text traditions themselves, was for the most part implicit, we now turn to an examination of the explicit interpretation of the Isaianic text in what may be termed the 'post-canonical' period. In this chapter we shall examine the interpretation of Isa. 6.9-10 in Rabbinic writings. In the next chapter we shall examine its interpretation in the writings of the Church fathers. Such literature, although admittedly post-biblical, may preserve interpretations and traditions derived from the first century CE, or even earlier, and so could help clarify the direction that some of the text traditions and exegeses eventually took.

As a case in point, one might cite G. Vermes who has provided useful examples of the fruitful insights into biblical interpretation to be gained by studying admittedly late and chronologically uncertain Rabbinic sources.[2] Through a careful analysis of the midrashic process of 'rewriting' the Bible, the modern exegete can often be successful in uncovering early interpretations, some of which are lurking within the canonical scriptures themselves. What may be very subtle in the biblical text, and consequently easily overlooked, may be called to our attention when it is discovered in greater detail in later Rabbinic sources.[3] In the present study, however, the emphasis falls chiefly on comparative analysis. In what way is rabbinic interpretation like or unlike the interpretations that have been observed in the Old Testament text traditions and in the New Testament writers? This question addresses our major concern.

To See and Not Perceive

A. *The Idea of Obduracy in Early Jewish Writers*

At the outset of this section it is interesting to note that this particular text in Isaiah occurs very rarely in Rabbinic literature. In fact, among other early Jewish authors, e.g. Josephus and Philo, it is not to be found at all. In Philo the verb παχύνειν occurs twice, both times in citations of Deut. 32.15.[4] The adjectival synonym σκληρός occurs twice in somewhat relevant discussions. In *De Fuga et Inventione* (42) Philo believes that ignorance is the cause of hardness, while in *De Specialibus Legibus* (1.304-307) he provides a brief discussion of the supposition that 'some are uncircumcised in heart' and consequently are admonished by the law (νόμος) to 'circumcise the hardness' of their hearts. This hardness of heart, Philo tells us, is nothing other than allowing one's mind (νοῦς) to be 'unbending and exceedingly unruly'. This definition is completely in keeping with the biblical data. In an extended commentary on Gen. 2.25 and 3.1 (*Legum Allegoria* 2.53-70), Philo metaphorically refers to the inability to see or hear (2.69):

> Do you not observe that the mind which thinks that it exercises itself is often found to be without mental power, in scenes of gluttony, drunkenness, folly? Where does the exercise of mind show itself then? And is not perceptive sense often robbed of the power of perceiving? There are times when seeing we see not and hearing [we] hear not [ὁρῶντες ἔστιν ὅτε οὐχ ὁρῶμεν καὶ ἀκούοντες οὐκ ἀκούομεν], whenever the mind, breaking off its attention for a moment, is brought to bear on some other mental object.[5]

What Philo appears to be describing here (and in the larger context) is in a certain sense a sort of moral obduracy that is brought on by moments of profligacy and foolishness. Although it is possible that here he intends to echo the language of some of the Old Testament obduracy passages (such as Isa. 6.9-10; Jer. 5.21; or Ezek. 12.2), he apparently does not have the biblical idea of obduracy in mind, for his discussion evidences little affinity with the theological import of the obduracy passages.[6]

B. *Isaiah 6.9-10 in the Rabbis*

The earliest appearance of Isa. 6.9-10 in the rabbinic literature is in *Mekilta de-Rabbi Ishmael*.[7] In order to understand the point of its usage of Isaiah, it will be necessary to trace the midrash from the beginning. The point of departure is Exod. 19.2a: 'And when they set out from Rephidim and came into the wilderness of Sinai...' According to one interpretation, Israel's sin, repentance, and forgiveness are hinted at in these geographical references, that is, Israel sinned and was forgiven in Rephidim and later would sin and be forgiven in Sinai.[8] Citing Ps. 81.7 ('I tested you at the waters of Meribah', alluding to Exod. 32.1-14), it is deduced that God knew all along that Israel would be obstinate. When he 'saw the children of Israel' (Exod. 2.25a), God knew that they would provoke him in the future. When he 'knew their condition' (Exod. 2.25b), God realized that in the future his people would blaspheme. Yet God, knowing that his people would deal with him falsely (despite what is said in Isa. 63.8a), remained Israel's Savior (as is said in Isa. 63.8b). Though Israel lies to God and has a faithless heart (Ps. 78.36-37), God is still willing to forgive (Ps. 78.38). Isa. 6.10 is then cited as another example of this principle: 'Make the heart of this people fat... and turning'—repentance achieving its task—'be healed'. The absence of the conjunction ('lest'), which is probably deliberate[9] (as the rabbinic exegesis yet to be examined will confirm), obliterates the idea of purpose. In this form the quotation parallels Ps. 78.36-38 more closely. That is, Israel's heart on occasion may become fat, but when she turns (or repents), she will be healed (or forgiven, as it is in the Isaiah Targum; see also *b. Meg.* 17b). In the context of *Mekilta* Isa. 6.10 is yet one more example of the Israelite cycle of obduracy followed by forgiveness.

Isa. 6.9 is not quoted in the Babylonian Talmud, while 6.10 is cited but three times. Of these citations only two bear any significance for our concerns. In *Roš. Haš.* 17b, Isa. 6.10 is cited in the context of a discussion of the 'power of repentance that... rescinds a man's final sentence' of judgment.[10] Rabbi Johanan's understanding of this text is quite interesting in that he believes that the announcement of the judgment (i.e. 'Make fat...') implies the offer to the people for them to repent. If one repents in the interval, that is, after announcement but before the judgment, one is forgiven. This interpretation is possible because the conjunction פן is apparently understood as 'unless' (perhaps following דלמא in the Targum and μήποτε in the LXX, both of which may have the conditional meaning). Therefore, Isa. 6.10 means that the prophet is to make the people's heart fat unless (or until) they repent and are healed (i.e., forgiven). There is no hint in Johanan's use of this text, that hardening is for the purpose of preventing repentance.[11]

In *b. Meg.* 17b, Isa. 6.10b ('lest they . . . be healed') is cited twice. The first citation is intended to explain, even justify, the sequence of benedictions in the *Amidah*. The fourth benediction begins, 'Thou grantest to man understanding', while the fifth begins, 'Bring us back, O Father'. The talmud asks: 'What reason had they for mentioning repentance after understanding? Because it is written, "Lest they, understanding with their heart, return and be healed"'.[12] (A similar exegesis appears in *y. Ber.* 2.3). The second citation of Isaiah, however, is more relevant for our concerns. Ps. 103.3-4a is cited in order to demonstrate that healing and redemption come after forgiveness. Isa. 6.10 is then cited, and we are told that healing 'refers not to the healing of sickness but to the healing [power] of forgiveness'.[13] Here the Targum is presupposed. This exegesis, like that in *Roš Haššana* considered above, does not understand מן in the sense of 'lest', but probably in the sense of 'unless' or 'until'.

The interpretation of Isa. 6.9-10 in *Seder Elijah Rabbah* (or *Tanna Debe Eliyyahu*) 16 (82-83) flatly contradicts the interpretation that it was God's desire to render the people obdurate. The words of the prophet Isaiah are not to be taken literally, for he spoke sarcastically. The teacher explains:

> If the idea should enter your mind that the Holy One in having Isaiah say this did not, God forbid, desire the repentance of Israel, consider the parable of a mortal king who had an only son dwelling in a principality, to whom he sent an emissary with instructions to say to the prince: 'Why not slaughter many bullocks, many kids of the flock, eat their flesh and drink much wine?' The apparent purpose of the instructions was to encourage the prince to drowse and be slothful in working his fields or irrigating the fields that needed water. Of course, the real purpose of the instructions was to make the prince repent of his slothful life, and with the emissary go forth to work in the field, so that the father would then come and take satisfaction in his son.[14]

The Midrash goes on to say that Isaiah knew full well what was meant, for he was aware of the prophecies of Jerusalem's bliss (Zech. 2.8-9 and 8.4 are cited). 'Therefore, knowing that God wished him to be sarcastic as a means of making Israel aware of the extent of its folly, Isaiah kept silent and said no more than, "Lord, how long?"' (Isa. 6.11).[15]

In what may be an allusion to Isa. 6.9, a midrash in *Gen. Rab.* 91.6 (on 42.1) says that after the loss of Joseph, Jacob lost his prophetic gift. The result of this loss was that Jacob 'saw yet did not see, heard yet did not hear'. The idea here, however, has nothing to do with obduracy.

It seems that the original idea of the Hebrew text is completely lost, or at least unacceptable, in the rabbinic literature. Isa. 6.9-10 is no longer a threat of judgment, but has become, as J. Jeremias has remarked, 'a promise' of forgiveness.[16]

The Medieval Jewish commentators generally agree with the earlier rabbinic interpretation. In his tenth-century Arabic translation, Saadia Gaon (882-942)[17] significantly alters the meaning of v. 9: 'Listen to what you will not understand. Watch for what you will not know'.[18] This rendering approximates that of the LXX. Saadia does, however, retain the imperatives of v. 10 ('make heavy', 'close', 'shut up', respectively). The idea now is that the people are urged to pay attention to that which they have not heeded. Failure to do so, it is implied, will result in the stern consequences of v. 10.

Rabbi Solomon ben Isaac (1040-1102, known by the acronym 'Rashi')[19] gave the following interpretation to v. 10: 'Their heart is becoming increasingly hard. . . in order that they should not understand'. That is, the people harden their hearts so that they will not have to understand. This view is taken up in greater detail by Rabbi David Kimhi (1160?-1235?, known by the acronym 'Radak'). He explained the text in 'two ways'. The first way was the apparent way in which the verbs are understood as imperatives. The passage would then mean: 'When the sinner wants to sin, God keeps him from the paths of salvation until the sinner receives his punishment'. Kimhi cites the examples of Pharaoh and King Sihon, of whom it is said that 'God hardened [their] spirit and made [their] heart arrogant'. The second way was to view the imperatives of v. 9 as futures (as did Saadia and the LXX) and to follow the lead of the targumic reading, 'and do not perceive. . . and do not understand', as implying that the individual *can* perceive and understand, if he is only willing. The verbs of v. 10 are treated as indicatives so that the text may now be understood: 'You hear the words of the prophets, but do not understand; you see the miracles, but do not comprehend. You are hardening your heart and plastering over your eyes. . . *because* [כי] you do not want to repent and be forgiven'. Kimhi favors the second way of interpreting the text. In fact, A. Cohen notes this argument of Kimhi's in arguing his own case that the 'verbs' in question were really meant to be adjectives, and thus only served the function of describing the sick condition of the people.[20]

C. *Related Passages in the Rabbis*

A few of the related obduracy passages, surveyed above in Chapter 1, also occur in the rabbinic writings. The following may be considered.

Deut. 29.3[4]. In *b. Abod. Zar.* 5a the rabbis discuss the ingratitude of their ancestors at the time of the exodus and wilderness wanderings. Commenting on the words of Moses in Deut. 29.3-4[4-5] ('I have led you forty years in the wilderness. . . but to this day the Lord has not given you a mind to understand, or eyes to see, or ears to hear'),[21] Raba said: 'From this you can learn that it may take one forty years to know the mind of one's master'.[22] This, of course, is not the meaning of the text, or context, at all. The point of Deuteronomy is that even after forty years of seeing God's mighty works (as described in 29.1-2[2-3]), the people remain obdurate.

Another interpretation suggests that Israel does not have a mind to understand because they kept silent when God exclaimed: 'Who will grant that they had such a heart' (Deut. 5.26[29]).[23] Because Israel did not answer, 'You Master, grant it', they did not receive a heart prone to obedience.[24] Similarly, R. Johanan laments that Israel did not at that moment at Sinai ask that the inclination to evil be forever rooted out.[25] Because they did not, the words of Deut. 29.3[4] describe how the matter now stands.[26] R. Meir, however, thinks that Deut. 5.26[29] implied only that God wished that Israel's earlier expression of fidelity (Deut. 5.24[27]) were truly meant.[27]

Pseudo-Jonathan's interpretive paraphrase of Deut. 29.3[4] is noteworthy: 'And the Word of the Lord has given you a heart not to forget, but to understand; eyes, not to blink, but to see; ears, not to be stopped, but to listen with. Yet you have forgotten the law with your heart, and have blinked with your eyes, and have stopped your ears, to this day'. The sense of the passage has been dramatically altered. The point that is being made, as is seen in the second half of the verse, is that Israel's obduracy is her own doing, not God's. Although God has provided his people with an understanding heart, seeing eyes, and hearing eyes, they do not utilize them. This change is reminiscent of the LXX's rendering of Isa. 6.10: 'For the heart of this people has become fat. . . they have closed their eyes. . . ' Israel may still be obdurate, but it is so, not because God has withheld an understanding heart, etc.

Isa. 1.3. The rabbis believe that the great sin of making the golden calf was done by proselytes, and not by Israelites, since Exod. 32.8 reads, 'This is your God, O Israel' (implying that non-Israelites are speaking), instead of, 'This is our God' (implying that Israelites are speaking). Israel, however, was not without sin, for the people allowed the proselytes to commit the evil. Israel was ignorant (Isa. 1.3 is cited) and foolish (Jer. 4.22 is cited), but should have known better.[28] The Isaianic text appears in another exegesis of the golden calf. Aaron cast a gold plate, upon which was inscribed the holy name, into the fire, and out came the golden calf. 'The calf came out lowing, and the Israelites saw it, and they went astray after it. Rabbi Jehuda said: Sammael [or Satan, cf. *Tg. Ps.-J.* Exod. 32.24] entered into it, and he was lowing to mislead Israel, as it is said, "The ox knoweth his owner"' (Isa. 1.3).[29]

Isa. 29.9-10. Commenting on Adam's sleep, the rabbis find four kinds of sleep, or 'torpor'. The fourth kind, which is relevant for the present discussion, is the 'torpor of folly'. Isa. 29.9-10 describes this torpor: 'Stupefy yourselves, and be stupid!' etc.[30] Elsewhere Isa. 29.10 is cited along with several other obduracy texts. The following midrash follows a pattern of sin, punishment, restoration. Because Israel sinned with the eye (Isa. 3.16 is cited, 'The daughters of Zion. . . walk. . . with wanton eyes'), she is smitten in the eyes (Isa. 29.10 is cited, 'The Lord. . . has closed your eyes'); yet she will be comforted by the eye (Isa. 52.8 is cited, 'They shall see, eye to eye, the Lord returning to Zion'). Because she sinned with the ear (Zech. 7.11 is cited, 'They stopped their ears'), she will be smitten in the ear (Isa. 42.18 is cited, 'Hear you deaf'), yet she will be comforted by the ear (Isa. 49.20 is cited, 'The children of your bereavement shall yet say in your ears').[31] Another interesting exegesis of Isa. 29.10 finds a promise of freedom hinted at in this otherwise judgmental passage.

The exegesis begins with Exod. 21.26: 'When a man strikes the eye of his slave. . . and destroys it, he shall let the slave go free for the eye's sake'. Since freedom is the result of striking an eye, it therefore follows that freedom will result from the judgment described in Isa. 29.10: 'For the Lord. . . has closed your eyes'.[32]

Isa. 63.17. In an interesting midrash, Isa. 63.17 ('O Lord, why dost thou make us err from thy ways and harden our heart?') is cited to explain why the sons of Jacob treated their young brother Joseph so poorly. When the Midianites (מִדְיָנִים) passed by (Gen. 37.28), the evil strife (מְדָנִים) of the brothers passed, and so they spared Joseph's life. In reflecting on this sad episode in Israel's early history, R. Judah ben R. Simon recites Isa. 63.17 and then confesses: 'When Thou desiredst, Thou didst inspire them with love; and when Thou desiredst, Thou didst inspire them with hate'.[33]

Jer. 5.23. Commenting on Eccl. 1.16 ('Spoke with my own heart'), the rabbis list several ways in which the heart can act or be. The heart can see, hear, speak, walk, etc. The heart can also become proud (Deut. 8.14 is cited); it rebels (Jer. 5.23 is cited); it can be stubborn (Deut. 29.18 is cited); and it can become hard (Prov. 28.14 is cited).[34]

Zech. 7.11-12. It was noted above how Zech. 7.11 ('They stopped their ears', etc.) was employed. The second verse in this obduracy passage occurs elsewhere: Israel sinned with her heart (Zech. 7.12 is cited, 'They made their hearts like adamant'), was punished with her heart (Isa. 1.5 is cited, 'and the whole heart faint'), and is comforted with her heart (Isa. 40.2 is cited, 'Bid Jerusalem take heart').[35]

It is apparent that in various ways the severity of these texts is mitigated. In Deut. 29.3[4] the people did not receive an understanding heart because *they* did not ask for one. (or, they did receive one, but did not use it to advantage). In Isa. 29.9-10 a promise of deliverance is found because God's judgment is directed against the 'eyes'. Because Israel sinned with her ears (Zech. 7.11) and with her heart (Zech. 7.12), restoration and comfort will come to her through her ears and heart. Although in the case of Isa. 63.17 it is admitted that God himself on occasion will inspire hatred, it is not admitted that he causes his people to be obdurate toward himself.

Summary

It has been observed above (Chs. 1-5) that there has been a variety of modifications introduced into the various Jewish versions of Isaiah. The common ingredient in all of these efforts is the attempt to mitigate the severity of the text. When the text is found in Rabbinic literature (and its appearance is rare) it is understood as having to do with a promise of forgiveness and not a threat of final hardening. Within the Jewish history of interpretation of Isa. 6.9-10, then, a complete transformation has taken place. The prophetic criticism of the eighth-century prophet Isaiah, which announced final judgment, has been transformed into a promise of forgiveness. Rabbinic interpretation of the related obduracy passages generally conforms to this tendency.

There are two possible explanations for the infrequency of Isa. 6.9-10 in Rabbinic literature, and for its distinctive interpretation when it does appear. First it might have been because of its exploitation by early Christian interpreters.[36] The Rabbis wished not to call attention to the text at all, or at least to explain it in terms other than obduracy. Secondly, it may have been the harshness of the text itself that was found to be offensive and contrary to Jewish hermeneutic and theology. For whichever reason, and it may have been both, the Rabbis interpreted Isa. 6.9-10 contrary to its original sense. Such moralizing has already been observed in 1QIsaiah[a], in the LXX, and in the Targum. In any case, it is not insignificant that such a poignant text as Isa. 6.9-10 occurs but rarely in Rabbinic literature and not once conveying its original sense.

Chapter 12

ISAIAH 6.9-10 IN THE FATHERS[1]

Introduction

Much of what was said in the Introduction to the preceding chapter applies here. Study of patristic usage of Isa. 6.9-10 is undertaken in order to help clarify emerging trends in early Christian theology and to determine in what ways patristic usage continues, intensifies, or modifies New Testament usage of this text.

A. *The Text of Isaiah 6.9-10 in the Fathers*

Before examining the fathers' explicit interpretation of Isa. 6.9-10, it would be worthwhile to survey the texts and versions that they used. The Greek fathers usually attest, as would be expected, the LXX, though not always without some variation, while the Latin fathers attest the 'Old Latin'. Jerome's version, known as the 'Vulgate', will also be considered. Although these versions are not early Old Testament text traditions, it is useful to examine them to discover what tradition they preserve and in what ways they stand in continuity to the texts and versions that precede them.

Greek Citations

Origen cites the LXX version of Isa. 6.9-10 *verbatim* in several places. He typically cites all or most of v. 9 and abbreviates v. 10: 'You shall indeed hear but never understand, and you shall indeed see but never perceive. For this people's heart has grown dull'[2] (cf. *Against Celsus* 2.8; *Homilies on Jeremiah* 14.12 [on Jer. 15.10-19]; 20.2 [on Jer. 20.7-12]). Sometimes his quotation is quite brief ('You shall indeed hear but never understand';[3] cf. *Commentary on John* 29 [on John 1.6]) or even a summary ('Unless you believe, you will never understand';[4] *Commentary on Matthew* 16.9 [on Mt. 20.29-30]). That he has in mind the whole passage is seen in the way he says 'and so forth' (καὶ τὰ ἑξῆς) at the end of the citation. The longer form of the Greek quotation is also found in the *Apostolic Constitutions* (5.16.4). Hippolytus paraphrases Mk 4.12, retains the ἵνα, but reverses the order of the hearing and seeing clauses in conformity with the LXX.[5]

Twice in his *Dialogue with Trypho* Justin Martyr cites Isa. 6.9-10 in a way that is quite free from the LXX. In 12.2 he says: 'For your ears are still blocked, your eyes have been hardened, and the heart has become fat'.[6] The presence of παχύνομαι makes it clear that Isa. 6.9-10 is the specific text in view. However, his quotation in *Dialogue* 33.1 ('But your ears have been blocked and your hearts have been hardened')[7] probably reflects the influence of John 12.40 where πωροῦν is used. Methodius also quotes Isa. 6.9-10 loosely,[8] but there is no reason to think that he has any version in mind other than the LXX.

There is one variation that does not appear to be based on the LXX. On one occasion Irenaeus quotes part of Isa. 6.10 in a way that closely parallels the Hebrew: 'Make the heart of this people fat, and make their ears dull and blind their eyes'.[9] This reading is interesting, because he is apparently following the Gospel of Matthew, which, of course, follows the LXX. (The presence of ἵνα, instead of ὅτι, would suggest Marcan influence as well; more on this below.)

Old Latin

The Old Latin version is based upon the LXX and not upon the Hebrew, as in the case of Jerome's translation (the Vulgate). E. Würthwein has noted that 'the Old Latin is a particularly important witness to the Septuagint text because it goes back to the period before the Septuagint recensions'.[10] The basic problem with the Old Latin version is that it is unknown whether there was originally one 'version from which the known forms are derived, or [whether] there were several independent versions'.[11] Another problem is the fragmentary preservation of the Old Latin. Much of it is to be reconstructed on the basis of quotations and, as noted in Chapter 3 above with respect to Theodoret's quotation of Symmachus, it is not always clear if variants in a given quotation are due to the existence of various Old Latin versions or simply faulty memory or deliberate paraphrase.

Most scholars are relatively certain that Tertullian and Cyprian were dependent on the Old Latin for their quotations of the Old Testament.[12] Both Tertullian and Cyprian cite Isa. 6.9-10, but there is enough variation in their respective quotations to make it difficult to tell if their variations are due to their use of different Old Latin versions or to their paraphrasing of one version. Since Tertullian cites Isa. 6.9-10 on more than one occasion with almost no variation, it is reasonable to assume in this case that his quotation is representative of the Old Latin, while Cyprian's quotation is either from another version or is paraphrastic. We shall examine Tertullian's citation of Isa. 6.9-10, comparing it with Cyprian's citation. The following quotation is taken from his work, *Against Marcion*:[13]

9 *Aure audietis et non audietis:*
   et oculis videbitis et non videbitis:
10 *Incrassatum est enim cor populi huius*
   et auribus graviter audierunt
   et oculos concluserunt,
   ne quando auribus audiant
   et oculis videant
   et corde coniciant
   et convertantur et sanem illos.

9 With (your) ear(s) you will listen and not hear
   and with (your) eyes you will look and not see:
10 For the heart of this people is dull
   and with (their) ears they have listened sluggishly
   and (their) eyes they have closed,
   lest with (their) ears they should hear
   and with (their) eyes they should see
   and with (their) heart they should understand
   and be converted and I heal them.

A few comments are necessary: (1) The opening line of v. 9 in Tertullian's quotation is similar to the LXX, though Cyprian's *intellegetis* is a closer equivalent. Tertullian's repetitive use of *videbitis* could possibly suggest his reliance on memory. The singular *aure* reflects ἀκοῇ of the LXX. (2) Tertullian's second line of v. 9 parallels his first line. We have *oculis* instead of the participle *videntes* as in the case of Cyprian's quotation. Both Latin quotations have the verbs of v. 9 in the future tense rather than as imperatives, as in the Hebrew. (3) Both quotations have *enim*, which would translate the

LXX's γάρ. Also, like the LXX, neither quotation contains an imperative in v. 10 as found in the MT, Targum, and 1QIsaiahᵃ. Tertullian uses the adjective *incrassatum* to describe the heart of the people (which could conceivably be a support for Cohen's suggestion that הֹשֹמֵן is an adjective).[14] Cyprian, however, uses the perfect *incrassavit*. (4) The next two lines are virtually identical in Tertullian and in Cyprian[15] and are close equivalents of the reading of the LXX. (5) Cyprian's *ne forte* is similar to Tertullian's *ne quando*, and either expression is a good translation of the LXX's μήποτε. (6) Whereas Cyprian uses *intellegere* (i.e., *intellegant*) again in v. 10, Tertullian uses the synonym *coniciant* ('should guess' or 'understand', i.e. in the sense of coming to the proper conclusion; the word literally means 'putting' or 'throwing something together'). (7) In the final line of v. 10, Tertullian and Cyprian again vary in vocabulary, with the former using *convertantur/sanem* and the latter *revertantur/curem*. The passive voice of the first verb of each pair agrees not with the LXX's ἐπιστρέψωσιν, but with Symmachus' ἐπιστράφη.

Clearly the Old Latin of Isa. 6.9-10 reflects the influence of the LXX and its recensions. In these texts it is apparent, as in the LXX, that the hardness of the heart of the people is viewed as a pre-existing condition, and not as a condition that the prophet is to bring about.

Vulgate

In 382 Pope Damascus I commissioned Jerome to prepare a reliable Latin translation of the Bible. This work became the official Bible of the church, and eventually became known as the 'Vulgate' (meaning 'common'). It was not, however, until the ninth century that Jerome's version finally displaced the popular Old Latin version. The reason for its slow acceptance was due in large measure to the reluctance of many of the church's theologians to depart from the Old Latin, which was dependent upon the LXX, regarded by many (e.g., Augustine) as divinely inspired. Jereome's insistence upon utilizing Origen's Hebrew text as the basis for the Latin Old Testament marks a milestone in the history of textual criticism.[16] Whereas the Old Latin is an important and early witness to the LXX, the Vulgate is a witness to the Hebrew text of the early centuries CE.

Isa. 6.9-10 in the Vulgate reads as follows:

9 *Et dixit: Vade, et dices populo huic:*
   Audite audientes, et nolite intellegere,
   et videte visionem, et nolite cognoscere.
10 *Excaeca cor populi huius,*
   et aures eius adgrava,
   et oculos eius claude,
   ne forte videat oculis suis,
   et auribus suis audiat,
   et corde suo intellegat,
   et convertatur, et sanem eum.[17]

9 And he said: 'Go, and you shall say to this people:
   "Hear indeed, and do not understand,
   and see the Vision, and do not learn".
10 Blind the heart of this people,
   and make its ears heavy,
   and shut its eyes,
   lest it should see with its eyes,
   and hear with its ears,
   and understand with its heart,
   and it be converted, and I heal it'.

Three comments are in order: (1) The presence of *visionem* seems odd in that the use of the participle *videntes*, while not making good Latin idiom, would provide a closer equivalent to the Hebrew infinitive absolute ראו (βλέποντες in the LXX), which in fact is used by Cyprian. In all probability Jerome's use of *visionem* is to be understood as an explicit reference to the vision described in the preceding verses of Isaiah 6. The Jews simply have not learned the truth despite the 'vision' of God's glory. It is quite probable that Jerome, under the influence of John 12.41 ('Isaiah... saw his glory'), understood Isa. 6.9-10 to be looking forward to the appearance of Christ, a manifestation of God's glory that produced obduracy, not faith, among the Jews.[18] It is likely that this is what lies behind the next variant to be considered.

(2) It is possible that *excaeca* ('make blind'), which is found instead of an equivalent to השׁמן ('make fat'), is nothing more than a stylistic variation, for Jerome does not translate a given word the same way every time. He uses *excaecare* to translate Rom. 11.7b: 'the rest, however, were blinded' (instead of 'hardened').[19] (The same variant

is found in the Latin translation of Origen's commentary on Romans, and in Augustine).[20] He uses cognate forms of this word to translate πώρωσις/πεπωρωμένη in Mk 3.5; 6.52; 8.17; but uses *obturare* to translate πωροῦν in 2 Cor. 3.14. However, when the septuagintal version of the quotation appears in Mt. 13.14-15 and Acts 28.26-27, in which παχύνομαι is found, a literal equivalent of the Hebrew, Jerome uses *incrassatus*. He uses *durus* and cognates to translate קשה/σκληρός (Prov. 28.14; Isa. 63.17; John 6.61). He uses *excaecare*, of course, to translate τυφλοῦν (John 12.40; 2 Cor. 4.4). I think that the real explanation for his translation of השמן lies here. Jerome's use of *excaecare* reflects the Christian idea of Jewish blindness to the significance of the 'vision' of the heavenly throne room, an idea first developed in John 12.37-41, and expressed by Jerome himself in his *Epistles* 18. His deliberate use of *excaecare* coheres with his use of *visio* in Isa. 6.9.

(3) The use of *excaeca* notwithstanding, Jerome's translation is quite literal (*adgravare*=הכבר; *claudere*=השע), attesting vocalization for hiphil imperatives in the Hebrew text of his time, rather than vocalization for indicative forms or, as Cohen suggested, adjectives. In this regard the Vulgate makes a most significant contribution to the question of the meaning of this particular Old Testament text. His translation provides an early and independent witness to the (hiphil) vocalization/pointing of the MT.[21]

Elsewhere in the Vulgate we find fairly literal renderings of the other obduracy texts. In a few places the LXX appears to have influenced Jerome, but on the whole, the severity of the obduracy passages is hardly lessened.[22]

Summary of Significance of the Latin Versions
The value of the Old Latin lies in the fact that it reflects, for the most part, Greek versions which in some cases antedate the LXX, and in the case of Isa. 6.9-10, preserves no new or startling tradition. The Vulgate, on the other hand, is useful in that it witnesses the hiphil vocalization of the Hebrew text, as it is now found in the pointing of the MT. Perhaps his reversion to the harsher reading and meaning of the Hebrew text reflects Jerome's thinking as a textual critic, more than his concern as a Christian. However, as a Christian, Jerome would not have had a problem with the harsh reading of the Hebrew text, as would perhaps a Jew. Therefore, it is possible that Christian

theology at that time (which was basically quite hostile toward the Jews, though Jerome himself was on good terms with them) provided enough incentive to part with the traditions of the Greek and Old Latin versions, and to re-establish the text along the harsher lines of the Hebrew text. This return to the harsher understanding of the text is underscored by the use of the words *visio* and *excaecare*, which serve to clarify Israel's contemporary (i.e., from the perspective of early Christians) blindness in her continued rejection of the Messiah.

B. *The Interpretation of Isaiah 6.9-10 in the Fathers*

Although the text of Isa. 6.9-10 is not cited in the writings popularly known as the 'Apostolic Fathers', there are some references to hardening that are worth noting. In the *Shepherd of Hermas* a severe warning is given to Christian apostates who 'have no salvation, because of the hardness of their hearts'.[23] Similarly in *1 Clement* the Christian is warned that 'it is better for man to confess his transgression than to harden his heart'.[24] Elsewhere in *1 Clement* the verb παχύνεσθαι occurs in a quotation from Deut. 32.15, in which the author warns the Corinthian Christians not to become fat and rebellious.[25] Later the author again reminds the brethren to avoid becoming 'stiff-necked', as the Israelites had been after their deliverance from Egypt.[26] The *Shepherd of Hermas* makes an interesting observation when it states that the Holy Spirit, being a gentle spirit, cannot dwell in a heart where there are evil spirits of 'hardness'.[27] In *Barnabas* the author polemicizes against unbelieving Jews, and cites Deut. 10.16 and Jer. 9.25-26 as scriptural proof that the Jew has a 'hard' and 'uncircumcised heart'.[28] In numerous other occurrences σκληρός is found meaning 'hard' or 'difficult'.[29]

The πωροῦν word group is represented only in the *Shepherd of Hermas*. In one instance the new convert needs divine help in order to gain understanding, since he has been hardened by his former evil deeds.[30] On another occasion *Hermas* sharply criticizes 'those who have the Lord on their lips, but their heart is hardened, and they are far from the Lord'.[31]

In the Christian passage on the life of Jesus in the *Sibylline Oracles* (1.324-386), the obduracy tradition, if not Isa. 6.9-10 itself, is alluded to:

And then Israel, intoxicated, *will not perceive nor yet will she hear,
afflicted with weak ears.* But when the raging wrath of the Most
High comes upon the Hebrews it *will also take faith away from
them,* because they did harm to the son of the heavenly God. Then
indeed Israel, with abominable lips and poisonous spittings, will
give this man blows. For food they will give him gall and for drink
unmixed vinegar, impiously, *smitten in breast and heart with an evil
craze, not seeing with their eyes, more blind than blind rats,* more
terrible than poisonous creeping beasts, *shackled with heavy sleep*
(1.360-371, emphasis mine).[32]

The allusion to Isa. 6.9-10, if indeed that specific text is in view, is
mediated by the gospel passages that quote and allude to it (Mt.
13.13-15; Mk 4.12; Lk. 8.10; John 12.40; Acts 28.26-27). The
reference to faith being taken away likely alludes to Mt. 13.12 (and
parallels). The references in ll. 370-71 to being 'more blind than
rats' and 'shackled with heavy sleep' may very well allude to Isa.
29.9-10: 'Blind yourselves and be blind. . . For the Lord has poured
over you a spirit of deep sleep, he has shut your eyes'. Finally, the
reference to being 'smitten . . . with an evil craze' (l. 369) could
allude to Deut. 28.28: 'The Lord will smite you with madness and
blindness and confusion of mind'.

In all of the references to the hardened heart, many of them based
upon an Old Testament quotation, Isa. 6.9-10 is never explicitly
cited, nor even clearly alluded to. However, this text is found
repeatedly in the Apologists and major theologians, and so the
following discussion shall be limited to this text alone.

In his polemic against the Jews, Justin Martyr (*c.* 100–*c.* 165)
explains why these people will not accept the new covenant in
Christ. He paraphrases Isa. 6.10, which he attributes to Jeremiah
(5.21, 23): 'For your ears are closed, your eyes are blind, and the
heart is hardened'.[33] In a different context, Irenaeus (*c.* 130–*c.* 200)
attempts to answer the Marcionite argument that God is the author
of sin, as is evidenced by his willingness to blind and harden men
such as Pharaoh. Irenaeus cites Mt. 13.11-16, but curiously does not
follow Matthew's LXX quotation of Isa. 6.9-10, but reverts back to the
causative Hebrew text, 'Make the heart of this people gross, and
make their ears dull', etc.[34] His explanation of why this is so is simple
enough: God hardens and blinds those who will not believe.
Therefore, such a text by no means makes God the author of sin.

Of all the apologists it is Tertullian (*c.* 160–*c.* 225) who most frequently appeals to Isa. 6.9-10 and its gospel versions. The vast majority of his quotations of Isa. 6.9-10 has to do with the explanation of why the Jews did not believe in Jesus, and accept him as the Messiah. This view is expressed persistently in his polemic against Marcion. Tertullian argues that

> it was demonstrated that they [the Jews], by their being deprived of those powers of knowledge and understanding and wisdom and prudence, would fail to know and understand that which was predicted, even Christ... when the people, like [the scribes and Pharisees], should hear with their ears and not understand Christ while he taught them, and see with their eyes and not perceive Christ, although he gave them signs. Similarly it is said elsewhere: 'Who is blind, but my servant? or deaf, but he who rules over them?' [Isa. 42.19].[35]

Tertullian goes on to cite Isa. 1.3: 'I have nourished and brought up sons, and they have rebelled against me. The ox knows his owner, and the ass his master's crib; but Israel does not know; my people does not consider'.[36] As far as Tertullian is concerned, the reason why Jesus spoke in parables was to confound the Jews, and thus fulfill the Isaianic prophecy. Tertullian expresses the idea as follows:

> But there is that direct mode of [Christ's] speaking to the people—'You shall hear with the ear, but you shall not understand'—which now claims notice as having furnished to Christ that frequent form of his earnest instruction: 'He who has ears to hear, let him hear'. ... first came, 'You shall hear with the ear, but shall not understand'; then followed, 'He who has ears to hear, let him hear'. For they wilfully refused to hear, although they had ears. He, however, was teaching them that it was the ears of the heart which were necessary; and with these the Creator said that they would not hear.[37]

Later Tertullian explains that in their refusing God's banquet invitation (cf. Lk. 14.12-14), the Jews have only been following a course of stubborn resistance to the divine will since the time that they asked Aaron to make gods for them (citing Exod. 32.1).[38] In another context he asks: 'When has the Jew not been a transgressor of the law; hearing with the ear, and not hearing?'[39] After disputing Marcion's punctuation of 2 Cor. 4.4, part of a passage where Paul develops his own obduracy theology, Tertullian has this to say of the Jews.

> Now it is these whom God had threatened for 'loving him with the
> lip, while their heart was far from him' [Isa. 29.13], in these angry
> words: 'You shall hear with your ears, and not understand; and see
> with your eyes, but not perceive' [Isa. 6.9]; and, 'If you will not
> believe, you shall not understand' [Isa. 7.9]; and again, 'I will take
> away the wisdom of their wise men, and bring to nought the
> understanding of their prudent ones' [Isa. 29.14].[40]

Tertullian's polemic reaches its most extreme expression in his
Apology. He argues that Jewish obduracy was God's will and was
even part of their punishment.

> It was the merited punishment of their sin not to understand the
> Lord's first advent: for if they had, they would have believed, they
> would have obtained salvation. They themselves read how it is
> written of them that they are deprived of wisdom and under-
> standing—of the use of eyes and ears. As, then, under the force of
> their pre-judgment, they had convinced themselves from his lowly
> guise that Christ was no more than a man.[41]

In fact, Tertullian asserts that the resurrected Lord did not go forth
into public gaze 'lest the wicked be delivered from their error'.[42] It
would appear that in Tertullian we are brought to the limits of the
idea of obduracy as a prevention from learning the truth and
repenting.[43]

In his work, *Against Celsus*, Origen (*c*. 185–*c*. 254) cites Isa. 6.9-10
to show that Jewish unbelief in Christ was foretold by the prophet.[44]
In two other places Origen struggles in his attempt to explain the
meaning of Mk 4.10-12 and parallels, particularly with respect to the
last phrase, 'lest they should be converted, and their sins be forgiven
them'.[45] He makes frequent reference to the Isaianic text in his
homilies and commentaries. Commenting on Jer. 15.13 ('Because of
your sins I will give your treasures as spoil'), Origen claims that God
'gave the treasures of that people [the Jews] to us' [Christians].
These treasures are 'the words of God taken from those people and
given to us'. (He then cites Mt. 21.43: 'The kingdom of God will be
taken away from you and given to a nation producing the fruits of
it'.) He adds: 'The knowledge [lit. mind] of the scriptures was taken
from them. . . they read and do not understand; for on account of
Christ is it fulfilled: "I said to that people: 'You will hear indeed. . . "'
etc.[46]

Cyprian (*c*. 200–258) cites Isa. 6.9-10, along with a host of other prophetic texts, to show that it had been foretold that the Jews would neither recognize nor receive their Messiah.[47] After paraphrasing Isa. 6.9, Methodius (*c.* 260–*c.* 312) queries: 'Can you see, O foolish Jew, how from the beginning of his discourse, the prophet declares confusion to you because of your unbelief?'[48] Commodian (third or fourth century) describes the Jewish heart as hard.[49] In another place he describes the Jews as habitually rebelling against the Lord, unwilling to hear or see, 'for the heart of this iniquitous people has become dull'.[50] A similar criticism of Jewish unbelief is found in *Didascalia Apostolorum.*[51]

Eusebius (*c.* 260–*c.* 340) applies Isa. 6.9-10 to the wicked, who are like the 'deaf adder that stops its ear and does not hear the voice of the charmers'.[52] In his commentary on Isa. 6.9-10 he states that the Jews are blind to the truth of the Christian gospel.[53] This theme is repeated in several places in his *Demonstration of the Gospel.*[54] Likewise, Athanasius (*c.* 296–373) understood Isa. 6.9-10 as a prophetic prediction of Jewish unbelief in Jesus.[55] Ambrose (*c.* 339–397) also cites and applies the text in a similar manner.[56]

In a homily on Isaiah 6, Jerome (*c.* 347–419 or 420) attempts to articulate a theology of obduracy by appealing to a series of related texts (e.g., Jer. 18; Ezek. 44.10-11; 2 Cor. 3.14-15).[57] He develops a sort of *Verdammnisgeschichte*, in which Israel is viewed as having suffered repeated acts of judgment by the hand of God for her persistent obduracy to divine truth. This history reaches its climax in the rejection of her Messiah. Elsewhere Jerome says that Isa. 6.9-10 was fulfilled when the Jews rejected the preaching of Paul and Barnabas in Acts (Acts 13.46-47; 28.25-28 are cited).[58] In the lengthy discussion that follows, Jerome cites several passages from John and Romans, concluding wth Jesus' lament in Mt. 23.37b: 'How often would I have gathered your children together as a hen gathers her brood under her wings, but you would not!' Similarly, in his commentary on Ezek. 12.1-2, a passage that is closely related to Isa. 6.9-10, Jerome says that the prophet's description of the Jewish people as having unseeing eyes is fulfilled in John 9.41: 'If you were blind, you would have no guilt; but now that you say, "We see", your guilt remains'.[59]

Chrysostom (*c.* 350–407) also believes that Isa. 6.9-10 was fulfilled in the Jewish rejection of Christ, but he disagrees with Tertullian by saying that it was not God's intention that the Jews be obdurate. Had it been God's will that the Jews not be converted, Jesus would have kept silent. Chrysostom does not intend, however, to be too charitable, for he believes that their blindness was and is the result of their own wickedness.[60] In speaking the words of Isa. 6.9-10, the prophet was 'describing their aggravated wickedness, and their determined defection from him'.[61] John Cassian (c. 360–435) likewise believes that Jewish blindness was 'freely chosen'. He cites Isa. 42.18-19 and 6.9-10 for evidence of his view.[62]

In his discussion of predestination, Augustine (354–430) argues that such a text as Isa. 6.9-10 makes it abundantly clear that the Jews were not predestined by God to perceive the truth of Jesus' messianic and divine identity. He reasons that 'by the predestination of grace' some people are not 'separated from the mass of perdition' and that 'in the same mass of ruin the Jews were left, because they could not believe such great and mighty works as were done in Christ' (he then cites John 12.37-41).[63] He goes on to say that none were as blind as the Jews, since the latter had not been predestined to have their stony heart removed. In commenting on John 12.37-41, Augustine says that because of his omniscience and foreknowledge God knew that the Jews would sin and reject Christ, but in no way were they compelled to do this.[64] Hence the prophet Isaiah uttered the words of 53.1 and 6.10. Alluding to the stupefaction of Isa. 29.10, Augustine says that this is what the Jews deserved, adding: 'for so God blinds and hardens, by abandoning and not assisting'.[65] He goes on to defend God's right (with phrases borrowed from Romans 9 and 11) to show mercy to some and to withhold mercy from others. In an interesting exegesis of God's 'passing'[66] before Moses (Exodus 33), Augustine believes that the hardening of the Jews is foreshadowed by God's act of covering Moses to prevent him from seeing his glory (which is Christ).[67] After the resurrection, the Jews, having been previously prevented from seeing the glory of Christ, can now see only the 'back parts' (which was all that Moses was allowed to see). In being prevented from seeing the full glory of Christ, the prophesy of Isa. 6.9-10 is fulfilled.[68] In his reply to Faustus the Manichaean, Augustine specifically addresses the question of why the Jews, whose prophecies Christians believe Christ had fulfilled, have not united themselves to Christians in common faith. He cites, by way of explanation, what he calls 'prophecies of unbelief' (Isa. 1.3; 65.2; 6.10//29.10) and argues that Jewish 'blindness is the just punishment of other secret sins known to God' (Rom. 1.28 is cited) and that 'their ignorance was the result of secret criminality'.[69] Augustine regarded Jews in general as obdurate, as is seen when he says that true religion is not to be sought 'in the confusion of pagans, nor in the rubbish of heretics, nor in the weariness of schismatics, nor in the hardness of Jews'.[70] In Cassiodorus (*c.* 485–*c.* 580) this interpretation takes an especially ugly turn.[71]

Caesarius of Arles (470–542) says that the giving of the manna on a Sunday, as opposed to a Sabbath, foreshadowed the gifts that the church would someday receive, gifts of which the Jews would be deprived. The manna that God continues to rain down upon Christians are the words of scripture, which the Jews are unable to appropriate.

> For this reason the unhappy Jews are to be deplored and bewailed, because they do not merit to receive manna as their fathers did. They never eat manna, because they are unable to eat what is small like a seed of coriander or white as snow. The unfortunate Jews find in the word of God nothing small, nothing fine, nothing spiritual, but everything rich and solid: 'For heavy is the heart of this people'.[72]

Although the text was sometimes appealed to for different reasons,[73] it would seem that the main function of Isa. 6.9-10 in the early fathers of the church was to explain why the Jews rejected Christ and why they continue to reject the Christian religion. For obvious reasons this rejection was an embarrassment to the church, especially in the first two or three centuries. Isa. 6.9-10 was understood as an explanation of Jewish rejection in at least three ways. These three applications overlap somewhat, and two or more may even appear in the same father. I have sketched these general groupings more as a summarizing aid, than as a specific assessment. First, this prophetic text demonstrates, it was believed, that the Jews were and are hardened for not believing in Christ, as foretold by the prophet Isaiah (so Justin Martyr, Origen, Cyprian, Athanasius, Ambrose, Chrysostom, Cassian). Secondly, Isa. 6.9-10 and other obduracy texts demonstrate that Jews are habitually obdurate to divine truth, so their rejection of Christ and the Christian message should occasion no surprise (so Eusebius, Methodius, Commodian, Jerome, Cassiodorus). Third, Isa. 6.9-10 and related texts demonstrate that the Jews were predestined to be obdurate and so were actually prevented from believing in Christ (so Tertullian, Augustine, Caesarius of Arles). The solution for the church was to view the Jewish rejection of Jesus as proof of the fulfillment of the scriptures.[74] The fathers were not, however, the originators of this idea, for it is rooted in Paul, in the Gospels, and possibly in Jesus himself.

C. *Isaiah 6.9-10 in Gnostic literature*

Isa. 6.10 is quoted twice in the Nag Hammadi Library (*Ap. John* [NHL II, *1*] 22.25-29; *Test. Truth* [NHL IX, *3* 48.8-13).[75] In both tractates the contexts are the same. The context is that of the typical Gnostic midrash on Genesis. Yahweh, the 'blind' and 'ignorant' god, did not wish Adam to eat of the Tree of Knowledge. Isa. 6.10 is cited as a text revealing the true malevolent nature of Yahweh. According to the *Apocryphon of John*, Yahweh brought a 'forgetfulness' over Adam, which was not 'sleep' in the literal sense (cf. Gen. 2.21), but a dullness of perception. To support this midrashic interpretation, the author cites Isaiah: 'For he said through the prophet, "I will make their hearts heavy that they may not pay attention and may not see"'. Likewise is Isa. 6.10 employed in the *Testimony of Truth*. Beginning with page 45 of the Coptic text there is developed a polemic against Yahweh (based upon the same kind of Genesis midrash). This author notes that Yahweh had 'envied' Adam for having eaten of the Tree of Knowledge (47.14-30). To support his case that this kind of god is 'malicious', he offers this paraphrase and comment:

'I will make their heart thick,
and I will cause their mind to become blind,
    that they may not know,
    nor comprehend the things that are said.'
But these things he has said to those
    who believe in him and serve him! (48.8-15).

A few other passages in Nag Hammadi might be mentioned briefly. In the *Apocryphon of James* (NHL I, *2*), the risen Christ tells his disciples: 'At first I spoke to you in parables and you did not understand; now I speak to you openly and you (still) do not perceive' (7.1-6). In language reminiscent of Mk 4.10-12 (and parallels) and John 16.29-30, the dullness of the disciples occasions the revelatory discourse that follows. The influence of Isa. 6.9-10 here is at best only indirect. In the *Apocalypse of Peter* (NHL VII, *3*), however, the Savior tells Peter: 'I have told you that these (people) are blind and deaf' (73.12-14; cf. 76.21-22). This passage clearly echoes the obduracy language of Isa. 6.9-10 and related materials. Although the literal reference is to (Jewish) 'scribes' and 'priests' (cf. 73.2-3), it is likely that rival Christian and gnostic groups are in view. The Jews are probably understood as the archetypes of obduracy to divine truth and so are used to characterize the author's opponents. In reporting a revelation of Christ, James the brother of Jesus tells his listeners that the risen Christ told him: 'Hear and understand — for a multitude, when they hear, will be slow-witted. But you, understand as I shall be able to tell you'.[76] This passage, unlike the others, is not polemical, but probably represents an exploitation of the Marcan parable idea in order to give a gnostic interpretation of Jesus' teaching. Finally, in *Authoritative Teaching* (NHL VI, *3*) the writer says that the 'matter strikes blows' at the eyes of the soul, 'wishing to make her blind' (27.28-29). Whether or not Isa. 6.9-10 itself is in view here,[77] the obduracy idea certainly is.

It is clear from the gnostic understanding and usage of Isa. 6.9-10, as also in the fathers, that this Old Testament text has assumed a very negative and pejorative connotation, particularly with respect to the Jews. In these traditions this application has indeed become pat. Marcion believed that the text proved that the God of the Old Testament was the author of sin, and gnostics, in keeping with their belief in a divided deity, saw in it evidence of Yahweh's insane jealousy. Although this conclusion with respect to Yahweh was completely unacceptable to mainstream Christian theology, the fathers agreed that the text pointed unmistakably to the reality and reason of Jewish obduracy.

Summary

Within Christian circles, Isa. 6.9-10 lent itself very conveniently for purposes of anti-Jewish polemic and apologetic, and it was exploited accordingly. For the New Testament and post-New Testament writers, the Isaianic text was used to explain the Jewish rejection of Jesus and the church's proclamation. Whereas the gospel writers appear to be divided over the question of Jesus' intention in speaking in parables, and so formulate their respective citations of Isa. 6.9-10 accordingly, the text gradually assumes a virtually fixed place in the developing dogmatic theology of the Patristic church. Although many of the Ante-Nicene fathers based an apologetic upon the text, as had the gospel writers before them, the Post-Nicene fathers, especially Augustine, utilize Isa. 6.9-10 as a proof text for purposes of systematic theology. In this case the text is seen as an important witness to God's sovereignty in a general sense, and to predestination more specifically. There seems to be little embarrassment with respect to the tradition that Jesus spoke parables to blind his hearers. Although usage of Isa. 6.9-10 increasingly had to do with predestination, the embarrassment occasioned by the Jewish rejection of Christ and Christianity, however, continued to be a major factor underlying the use of this text. Although applied in a different sense, Isa. 6.9-10 is still understood as a major witness to God's absolute sovereignty.

CONCLUSION

The Hebrew Tradition
It has been concluded that the original Hebrew text of Isa. 6.9-10 was
intended to convey the idea that it was God's purpose that his
prophet deepen Israel's obduracy. This idea is based upon the
conclusion that the verbs of v. 10 were originally hiphil imperatives,
as the MT points them. The prophet's word was a harsh word of
judgment intended to promote obduracy and to make the people ripe
for judgment. This severe word, however, is tempered by the hope of
a remnant and restoration, especially as seen in Second and Third
Isaiah. The final clause of 6.13, which introduces the positive idea of
the remnant as a 'holy seed', is likely an effort to relate Isaiah's
commission of judgment more closely to Isaiah's remnant idea.
(Nevertheless, Isa. 6.9-13b still stands as an unqualified word of
obduracy and judgment). The linkage of these two ideas mirrors the
theology of Isaiah in its canonical whole. Whereas First Isaiah speaks
mainly of judgment, informing Israel that her God was not tied to his
people and was not obligated to champion her every cause, Second
and Third Isaiah offer consolation and hope, reminding Israel of
God's love and faithfulness.

Versions
In the textual transmission of Isa. 6.9-10 there is observed a marked
tendency to move away from the harsh, telic understanding of the
Hebrew text. 1QIsaiah[a] is an independent witness to this trend (a
trend that is paralleled in the later versions of the Old Latin and
Peshitta as well as in the discussions of the Rabbis) in that the text is
understood as a warning to the godly and not as a word of judgment
to the unrepentant. In the other text traditions (LXX, Targum),
however, a more uniform tendency is to be observed. The notion that
the Lord would actually harden his own people and so prevent them

from repenting is apparently either unacceptable or unintelligible. In one way or another this idea has been circumvented. It has also been found that some of the early versions sought, in their own ways, to enhance the aspect of the righteous remnant. This latter activity is in all probability related to the former.

Related texts
It was observed that this same tendency is also to be found with respect to the related obduracy texts. There appears to be a consistent avoidance on the part of the LXX and the Targum to Isaiah to let stand unmodified the idea that Yahweh would harden his own people. Many of the textual variations were obviously self-serving in their attempts to domesticate God's attitude and activity.

It would appear, then, that the original tradition of Isaiah's message of judgment has undergone significant modification by means of haggadic concerns to contemporize scripture and to bring it into harmony with Jewish understanding of theology and history. With the exception of 1QIsaiah[a], which by means of a series of minor textual alterations has been transformed into an admonition to the faithful to take heed lest they fall prey to evil, the general approach was to 'soften' the Hebrew text by shifting the responsibility for the condition of obduracy away from the Lord to his people. God is no longer the agent of obduracy; the people themselves are. Rather than understanding the text of Isa. 6.9-10 as the *announcement* and *implementation* of judgment, the later text traditions have understood this text as an *explanation* of a pre-existing condition that necessitated, or unavoidably resulted in, judgment. This distinction at first glance may appear academic, if not irrelevant, but in terms of biblical theology it is significant. It takes faith to be able to affirm that God has not only decreed judgment, but has even rendered it certain by hardening the hearts of his own people. The tendency we have found in the later versions points to a reluctance to accept this kind of unqualified sovereignty. God judged Israel, but only because he *had* to do so due to Israel's sin, the later versions tell us. But Isaiah has claimed that God freely decreed judgment and did so by ruling out any opportunity for repentance. This idea the later traditions find difficult to accept. It would appear, then, that the monotheizing hermeneutic of the eighth-century prophet Isaiah, especially as it is expressed in Isa. 6.9-10, created a theological difficulty that the later versions sought to obviate.

Jesus and the New Testament

For Jesus and several New Testament writers Isa. 6.9-10, as an expression of the Old Testament obduracy idea, has played an important theological role. For them this text explained the mystery of the rejection of Jesus and the apostolic witness to him. The Gospel has been rejected, not simply because its hearers were dull, but because it was and continues to be God's will. The Jewish rejection of Jesus raised for the early Christian community the same sort of question raised in the minds of exiled Israel. To continue in faith one had to conclude that the debacle was the will of God. But this affirmation of faith also carried with it the belief that ultimately good would come of it.[1] In the case of Israel, there was the conviction that the exile was a purge from which a righteous remnant would emerge. In the case of the Church, there was the conviction that Jewish rejection and ostracism unwittingly furthered God's purposes in producing a new remnant of the faithful. The hermeneutic that underlies this text seems to be adopted more fully by Jesus and Paul than by the other New Testament writers. In both, the text is applied as a prophetic criticism to the community of the faithful. The faithful have not responded to the word of God, and that is because God has hardened their hearts. Jesus did not address 'outsiders' in the sense that he had in mind people outside of Israel (or the Church). He spoke as a prophet to the unbelieving and obdurate of his own people. If they will not repent and heed his teaching, they can expect judgment. So it is with Paul. In anguish he appeals to scripture to understand the unbelief of Israel, his own brethren, in his day (see Rom. 9.1-5). The only conclusion to which he can come is that the people of God are standing under the judgment of God. They are hardened because it is God's will.

With the rest of the New Testament writers, however, the perspective has shifted. Those who do not believe in Jesus are obdurate and in no sense are part of the 'people of God'. They stand outside the community. The word of Jesus, originally applied to God's people, is now applied to non-Christians. The shift is subtle, perhaps, but it is significant. The dynamic of the original context has been partly obscured. The interpretation has become more or less static. The text has ceased to be a prophetic criticism against the community itself.

Post-Biblical Writings
The prophetic thrust, especially the dynamic, of this passage is blunted, if not entirely lost, it seems to me, in the later writings of the rabbis and the fathers. With respect to the former, the text is moralized and applied in a way that has little to do with the original sense. With respect to the latter, although the text is understood as witnessing to God's sovereignty, as it should be, it becomes part of a larger philosophical/theological system concerned with predestination. There remains little sense of the text speaking to the community. Rather, the text is primarily understood as speaking about others. In the case of some gnostic interpretation, there is no appreciation for the theology of the text whatsoever. (And we should hardly be surprised, since most forms of Gnosticism rejected absolute monotheism.)

What then can be said in conclusion? The interpretation of Isa. 6.9-10 in early Jewish and Christian writings, it seems to me, witnesses the struggle to affirm God's unqualified sovereignty in all of life. At different stages in Judaism and Christianity, the vision of God is more clearly perceived than at other times. In the case of Judaism, if I may speak somewhat anachronistically, Isaiah the prophet had the most penetrating insight into the sovereignty of God. In the case of Christianity (and Judaism!), Jesus and Paul seem to have a deeper appreciation of God at work than do other early Christian theologians. Isa. 6.9-10 is a text that is shocking and disturbing, but that is how it should be, if it is to inform the people of God prophetically.

NOTES

Notes to Introduction

1. The first significant work which recognized this aspect of midrash and set the pace for midrashic studies since was that of R. Bloch, 'Midrash', *DBSup* 5 (1957), cols. 1263-81.

2. For examples see R. le Deaut, 'A Propos a Definition of Midrash', *Int* 25 (1971), pp. 262-82; idem, 'La tradition juive et l'exégèse chrétienne primitif', *RHPR* 1 (1971), pp. 31-50; idem, 'Un phénomène spontané de l'herméneutique juive ancienne: le "targumisme"', *Bib* 52 (1971), pp. 505-25; E.E. Ellis, 'Midrash, Targum and New Testament Quotations', *Neotestamentica et Semitica: Studies in Honour of Matthew Black* (ed. E.E. Ellis and M. Wilcox; Edinburgh: T & T Clark, 1969), pp. 61-69; idem, 'How the New Testament Uses the Old', *New Testament Interpretation: Essays on Principles and Methods* (ed. I.H. Marshall; Grand Rapids: Eerdmans, 1977), pp. 199-219; J.A. Sanders, 'From Isaiah 61 to Luke 4', *Christianity, Judaism, and Other Greco-Roman Cults* (Morton Smith Festschrift; ed. J. Neusner; Leiden: Brill, 1975), pp. 75-106. See the bibliographical article of M.P. Miller, 'Targum, Midrash and the Use of the Old Testament in the New Testament', *JSJ* 2 (1971), pp. 29-82; idem, 'Midrash', *IDBSup*, pp. 593-97.

3. See Miller, 'Midrash', pp. 594-95; and J.A. Sanders, 'Adaptable for Life: The Nature and Function of Canon', *Magnalia Dei: The Mighty Acts of God: Essays on the Bible and Archaeology in Memory of G.E. Wright* (ed. F.M. Cross; New York: Doubleday, 1976), pp. 31-60; repr. in J.A. Sanders, *From Sacred Story to Sacred Text: Canon as Paradigm* (Philadelphia: Fortress, 1987), pp. 11-39. There is, of course, much debate over exactly what must be present in a text before it can be called an instance of 'midrash', for other views see A.G. Wright, *The Literary Genre Midrash*, (Staten Island: Alba House, 1967); G. Porton, 'Defining Midrash', *The Study of Ancient Judaism* (ed. J. Neusner; New York: Ktav, 1981), pp. 55-92; J. Neusner, *What is Midrash?* (Guides to Biblical Scholarship; Philadelphia: Fortress, 1987).

4. G. Vermes, *Scripture and Tradition in Judaism* (SPB 4; Leiden: Brill, 1973), p. 229. Seen in this light even pesher exegesis as practiced at Qumran, and the allegorical exegesis as practiced by Philo of Alexandria, share this common ingredient with midrash and so might be considered distinctive variations of midrashic exegesis. See also D. Patte, *Early Jewish Hermeneutic in Palestine* (SBLDS 22; Missoula: Scholars, 1975), pp. 122-25.

5. See J.A. Sanders' review of R.E. Brown, *The Birth of the Messiah: A Commentary on the Infancy Narratives in Matthew and Luke* (New York: Doubleday, 1977) in *USQR* 33 (1978), pp. 193-96. Sanders (p. 196) states: 'It would be more accurate to say that the purpose of midrash was to call on scripture to interpret contemporary life and history. When the ancients believed that what was happening to them was part of God's plan, and that God was acting in their day, they reported that belief and those events in scriptural terms. They engaged in re-signification of scripture in order to understand themselves, and what was happening to them. There was a two-way process: their context was signified by scripture and scripture was re-signified in its high adaptability to speak to many contexts'.

6. See the recent study by M. Fishbane, 'Revelation and Tradition: Aspects of Inner-Biblical Exegesis', *JBL* 99 (1980), pp. 343-61; idem, *Biblical Interpretation in Ancient Israel* (New York: Oxford University Press, 1985). Other studies would include G. Vermes, 'Bible and Midrash: Early Old Testament Exegesis', *The Cambridge History of the Bible* (ed. P.R. Ackroyd and C.F. Evans; Cambridge: Cambridge University Press, 1970), pp. 199-231; B.S. Childs, 'Midrash and the Old Testament', *Understanding the Sacred Text* (M. Enslin Festschift; ed. J. Reumann; Valley Forge: Judson, 1972), pp. 47-59.

7. A recent example of this effort is seen in G.L. Archer and G.C. Chirichigno, *Old Testament Quotations in the New Testament: A Complete Survey* (Chicago: Moody, 1983).

8. P. Borgen, *Bread from Heaven: An Exegetical Study of the Concept of Manna in the Gospel of John and the Writings of Philo* (NovTSup 10; Leiden: Brill, 1965); W.A. Meeks, *The Prophet-King: Moses Traditions and the Johannine Christology* (NovTSup 14; Leiden: Brill, 1967); D.M. Hay, *Glory at the Right Hand: Psalm 110 in Early Christianity* (SBLMS 18; Nashville: Abingdon, 1973); J. Schaberg, *The Father, the Son, and the Holy Spirit: The Triadic Phrase in Matthew 28:19b* (SBLDS 61; Chico: Scholars, 1981); K.R. Snodgrass, *The Parable of the Wicked Tenants: An Inquiry into Parable Interpretation* (WUNT 27; Tübingen: Mohr [Siebeck], 1983); M. Callaway, *Sing, O Barren One: A Study in Comparative Midrash* (SBLDS 91; Atlanta: Scholars, 1986).

9. Neither R.N. Longenecker (*Biblical Exegesis in the Apostolic Period* [Grand Rapids: Eerdmans, 1975]) nor H. Shires (*Finding the Old Testament in the New* [Philadelphia: Westminster, 1974]) probes in any detail beyond the observation and categorization of explicit and allusive quotations.

10. Luke–Acts yields several important examples of this phenomenon. Large sections (e.g. Luke 7–10, 22–24; Acts 1–9) of the two-volume work appear to be in various ways drawing upon the Elijah/Elisha narratives of 1 Kings 17–21 and 2 Kings 1–8. See T.L. Brodie, *Luke the Literary Interpreter: Luke–Acts as a Systematic Rewriting and Updating of the Elijah–*

Elisha Narrative in 1 and 2 Kings (dissertation; Rome: Angelicum University, 1981). Another large section of the Gospel (9.51-18.14, the so-called 'central section') appears to parallel Deuteronomy 1-26 (see C.F. Evans, 'The Central Section of St. Luke's Gospel', *Studies in the Gospels: Essays in Memory of R.H. Lightfoot*, ed. D.E. Nineham (Oxford: Blackwell, 1957), pp. 37-53, and J.A. Sanders, 'The Ethic of Election in Luke's Great Banquet Parable', *Essays in Old Testament Ethics: J. Philip Hyatt In Memoriam*, eds. J.L. Crenshaw and J.T. Willis (New York: Ktav, 1974), pp. 247-71. Virtually every chapter in Luke's gospel gives evidence of literary and theological interaction with the Greek Old Testament; for example, see D.P. Moessner, 'Luke 9.1-50: Luke's Preview of the Journey of the Prophet like Moses of Deuteronomy', *JBL* 102 (1983), pp. 575-605.

I have no intention of debating the definition of midrash. However, the reader is entitled to know at least what I assume, even if I make no attempt to demonstrate it. I believe that midrash is essentially the activity of searching sacred tradition (whether pre-canonical sacred tradition, or the stabilized sacred tradition of the canon) for guidance and understanding in a new context in life (see John 5.39). However, this search is not simply a Jewish equivalent for consulting a crystal ball. It is a quest for continuity, the continuity of the past with the present. That is, does the present experience of the community stand in continuity with the sacred past? This continuity was established in a variety of ways: early Christianity underscored its continuity with scripture through prophecy and fulfilment; Qumran believed that scripture contained mysteries, mysteries which explained what would happen to them; Philo believed that scripture contained allegories, allegories that should foster a synthesis of Jewish religion with Hellenistic philosophies; and rabbinic Judaism believed that through careful study one could unpack the oral tradition within scripture, a tradition that went all the way back to Sinai. Exegesis in the modern sense often is not concerned with continuity. What did the passage originally mean? is what we usually ask. But the midrashist asks how the Passage explains his situation and how it offers guidance, while assuring him that his experience is 'biblical', that is, part of God's activity among and in behalf of his people.

Is there midrash in the New Testament? I believe that there are midrashic elements within some of the New Testament writings. Indeed there are some passages which approximate rabbinic midrash (e.g. Gal. 3.16; 4.21-31). However, there is no book in the New Testament that should be regarded as a literary example of midrash, either broadly defined, or narrowly defined. Recently it has been claimed by some that one or more of the Gospels are midrashim. I believe that these claims rest upon a hopelessly distorted view of midrash, both as method and as genre. These claims do not represent a scholarly consensus, nor do I think that they ever will. More compelling is the claim that the Gospels are in places cognate to midrash (and targum).

See B.D. Chilton, *Targumic Approaches to the Gospels* (Studies in Judaism; New York: University Press of America 1986), pp. 1-14.

11. See the helpful introductory statement in Callaway, *Sing, O Barren One*, pp. 1-12.

12. 'Stage' seems to imply certain fixed points on a line (or 'trajectory', as J.M. Robinson puts it). In the case of the present study such a trajectory, i.e., a development of an idea in which there seem to be a *terminus a quo* and a *terminus ad quem*, does seem to emerge. This aspect, however, is not fundamental to a study in comparative midrash. Whether or not there is an 'outcome' is not important, however, interesting it might be. What is important, rather, is the observation of the various ways in which an authoritative tradition may function in respective communities of faith. To use the terminology of J.A. Sanders (cf. 'Hermeneutics', *IDBSup*, p. 404), this study traces the history of a 'stabilized' text which finds itself 'adapted' in various historical contexts.

13. See his *Torah and Canon* (Philadelphia: Fortress, 1972); idem, 'The Bible as Canon', *Christian Century* (1981), pp. 1250-55; idem, *Canon and Community* (Philadelphia: Fortress, 1985); idem, *From Sacred Story to Sacred Text: Canon as Paradigm*.

14. See his *Introduction to the Old Testament as Scripture* (Philadelphia: Fortress, 1979), pp. 46-83, and *The New Testament as Canon: An Introduction* (Philadelphia: Fortress, 1985). Childs reviews Sanders (*Torah and Canon*) in 'A Call to Canonical Criticism', *Int* 27 (1973), pp. 88-91. Sanders discusses Childs' understanding of what constitutes 'canon' (the latter limits the concept to the finished product) in 'Canonical Context and Canonical Criticism', *HBT* 2 (1980), pp. 173-97, to which Childs replies, pp. 203-204.

15. Less satisfactory is the approach of J. Barr, *Holy Scripture: Canon, Authority, Criticism* (Oxford: Oxford University/Philadelphia: Westminster, 1983).

16. He states ('Hermeneutics', p. 404): 'That process itself is as canonical as the traditions which emerged out of it'. See also his 'Text and Canon: Concepts and Methods', *JBL* 98 (1979), pp. 5-29.

17. As, for example, F. Hesse, *Das Verstockungsproblem im Alten Testament* (BZAW 74; Berlin: Töpelmann, 1955), or more recently R.R. Wilson, 'The Hardening of Pharaoh's Heart', *CBQ* 41 (1979), pp. 18-36.

Notes to Chapter 1

1. Portions of this section are taken from my study, 'The Text of Isaiah 6.9-10', *ZAW* 94 (1982), pp. 415-18.

2. W.H. Brownlee (*The Meaning of the Qumran Scrolls for the Bible* [New York: Oxford University Press, 1964], p. 186) refers to the MT of Isa. 6.9-10

as the 'doubtless(ly) original text'. Brownlee offers no explanation for his judgment, perhaps because he believes it to be obvious enough. It is reasonable to assume, then, that the MT represents at least the earliest, if not original, extant tradition, and that the other text traditions, to the extent that they differ from it, represent variations of the Hebrew as it is now preserved in the MT. This assumption is reasonable in light of two considerations: (1) The text of 1QIsaiah[a] provides an early witness to the MT, and its own differences are readily accounted for, as will be shown later. (2) As is usual in the practice of textual criticism, the reading which is deemed original is that reading which best accounts for the variants. As will be shown below, the MT best accounts for the variants found in the other versions.

3. In a footnote the NEB suggests the possibility that the two apodoses of v. 9 may be interrogative, i.e. '. . . but how will you understand?' That אל can be so construed is doubtful. Moreover, there is no evidence of such an understanding in any of the other versions.

4. Every occurrence of 'their' is literally 'its'.

5. Lit. 'it'.

6. Lit. 'and its heart understand'.

7. E. Kautzsch, *Gesenius' Hebrew Grammar* (Oxford: Clarendon, 1910) §136b (p. 442).

8. Kautzsch, §113r (p. 343): 'hear ye continually'; see also E.J. Young, *The Book of Isaiah, Volume I: Chapters I–XVIII* (NIC; Grand Rapids: Eerdmans, 1965), p. 256, n. 42 and J.D.W. Watts, *Isaiah 1–33* (WBC 24; Waco: Word, 1985), p. 69.

9. See H. Wildberger, *Jesaja 1–12* (BKAT 10/1; Neukirchen-Vluyn: Neukirchener Verlag, 1972), p. 255.

10. Young, *Isaiah. . . I–XVIII*, p. 256, n. 42.

11. The interrogative suggested in a note in the NEB is unlikely.

12. Of course, the hiphil (as well as the pi'el) at times may denote more of a permissive idea than that of the causative (see 1 Kgs 2.6; 2 Chr. 34.11, RSV; on the permissive pi'el see Kautzsch, *Hebrew Grammar*, §52g [p. 141]). Nevertheless, the fact that the permissive and causative ideas are expressed by the same form would indicate that in the Hebrew mind the distinction is not great; for in either case it is the stem that indicates responsibility.

13. A. Cohen, 'השע, הכבר, השמן', *BM* 50/3 (1972), pp. 360-61. The quote is from the English summary on p. 379. As will be noted below, the Old Latin does in fact use an adjective corresponding to השמן even though the LXX, upon which the Old Latin is probably based, has the verb ἐπαχύνθη.

14. O. Kaiser, *Isaiah 1–12* (OTL; Philadelphia: Westminster, 1972),p. 72. Watts (*Isaiah 1–33*, p. 75) states: 'The MT, however, sees the messenger playing an active part in hardening and dulling so that repentance will not take place, now that the decision to destroy has been taken'. M. Buber (*Bücher der Kündung: Das Buch Jeschajahu* [Köln: Hegner, 1958], p. 26),

however, translates: 'sonst könnte es mit seinen Augen sehn' ('otherwise it could see with its eyes'), which strikes me as an attempt to mitigate the severity of the text. Luther translates, 'dass sie nicht sehen mit ihren Augen', which could imply either result or purpose. In Wildberger (*Jesaja 1-12*, 231) the text reads: 'damit es mit seinen Augen nicht sieht', which implies purpose.

15. Wildberger, *Jesaja 1-12*, p. 233. On the use of ל in this context see Kautzsch, *Hebrew Grammar*, §119s (p. 381).

16. Note the contrast with Jeremiah: 'Ah, Lord God! Behold, I do not know how to speak, for I am only a youth' (1.6; cf. 20.9). Note the similarities with the accounts of Moses (Exod. 3.11; 4.10), Gideon (Judg. 6.15), and Solomon (1 Kgs 3.7). See Kaiser, *Isaiah 1-12*, p. 82.

17. S.H. Blank ('Traces of Prophetic Agony in Isaiah', *HUCA* 27 [1956], pp. 81-92) suggests that Isaiah's 'How long?' parallels the cries of desperation in the Psalter: 'Return, O Lord! How long? Have pity on thy servants!' (90.13; cf. 74.10; 79.5; 89.46; see also the similar cries in Amos 7.25; Hab. 1.2; Ezek. 9.8; 11.13).

18. Wildberger, *Jesaja 1-12*, pp. 239-40; Watts, *Isaiah 1-33*, p. 73. C. Whitley ('The Call and Mission of Isaiah', *JNES* 18 [1959], pp. 38-48) believes that the entire chapter is post-exilic.

19. K. Marti, *Das Buch Jesaja* (Tübingen: Mohr, 1900), xviii, pp. 67-71.

20. Kaiser, *Isaiah 1-12*, p. 84; R. Knierim, 'The Vocation of Isaiah', *VT* 18 (1968), pp. 47-68.

21. Kaiser (*Isaiah 1-12*, n. b) cites more than a dozen scholars who regard these verses as original. Although vv. 12-13ab originally may not have been part of the call narrative, they are probably Isaianic. (Kaiser [p. 84] calls these verses 'a fragment of a genuine saying of Isaiah'). The issue is significant, for the verses not only add to the theme of destruction and exile, but v. 13 introduces the idea of a remnant (i.e., the 'tenth'), though in a negative, destructive sense; see also P. Graham, 'The Remnant Motif in Isaiah', *RestQ* 19 [1976], pp. 217-28, esp. p. 219.

22. The clause is omitted in the texts of J. Ziegler, *Septuaginta: Vetus Testamentum Graecum: Isaias* (vol. 14; Göttingen: Vandenhoeck & Ruprecht, 1939) and A. Rahlfs, *Septuaginta* (Stuttgart: Württem, 1935). Aquila and Symmachus retain it, while Origen and Theodotion mark it off with asterisks. The clause is also found in 1QIsaiah[a].

23. See J.A. Emerton, 'The Translation and Interpretation of Isaiah vi. 13', *Interpreting the Bible: Essays in Honour of E.I.J. Rosenthal* (ed. J.A. Emerton and S.C. Reif; UCOP 32; Cambridge: University Press, 1982), pp. 85-118. B. Duhm (*Das Buch Jesaja* [Göttingen: Vandenhoeck & Ruprecht, 1968[5]] p. 69) and V. Herntrich (*Der Prophet Jesaja: Kapitel 1-12* [ATD 17; Göttingen: Vandenhoeck & Ruprecht, 1950] p. 110), as well as many others, regard 6.13c as a later scribal gloss.

24. Kittel also explains its omission from the LXX as an instance of homoioteleuton. The error, of course, may have resulted not in transcribing the Greek, but in the translation of the Hebrew into Greek.

25. Marti, *Das Buch Jesaja*, pp. 68-71. W. Metzger ('Der Horizon der Gnade in der Berufungsvision Jesajas', *ZAW* 93 [1981], pp. 281-84) argues that the remnant idea in Isaiah was originally ambiguous, pointing both to severe judgment and to grace. However, the description of the seed as 'holy' involves no ambiguity.

26. The expression is likely proverbial (cf. Amos 5.3); Kaiser, *Isaiah 1-12*, p. 84.

27. Kaiser (*Isaiah 1-12*, p. 4) states: 'There is no reflection here on the possibility that God's rejection may conceal a hidden affirmative, and that his judgment is a purification of his congregation. See also E. Jenni, 'Jesajas Berufung in der neueren Forschung', *TZ* 15 (1959), pp. 321-39, esp. p. 339.

28. On the difficulties of this part of v. 13 see Emerton, 'Isaiah vi. 13', esp. 105-15. Blank ('Traces of Prophetic Agony', p. 86, n. 12) suggests that following v. 13ab ('. . . a stump remains') the original text implied: 'And it in turn is burned as fuel'.

29. A later tradent may have seen in this verse a hint of a remnant. Emerton ('Isaiah vi. 13', p. 115) states: 'The later writer saw that the mention of the stumps left open the possibility of survival and hope for the future'. In the Targum this idea is developed much more elaborately: 'so the exiles of Israel shall be gathered together, and shall return to their land; for a holy seed is their plant' (trans. by J.F. Stenning, *The Targum of Isaiah* [Oxford: Clarendon, 1949], p. 22). There is also in 1QIsa[a] 6.8-10 (6.13) some interesting features, but more will be said about this in Ch. 2.

30. P. Ruben ('A Proposed New Method of Textual Criticism', *AJSL* 51 [1934], pp. 30-45, esp. 40-42), J.M. Ward (*Amos & Isaiah: Prophets of the Word of God* [Nashville: Abingdon, 1969] pp. 159-61), and G.W. Ahlström ('Isaiah VI. 13', *JSS* 19 [1974], pp. 169-72), among others, have concluded that the clause is original. Compare the similar image in 11.1a.

31. Marti, *Das Buch Jesaja*, p. 67; Herntrich, *Der Prophet Jesaja*, pp. 107-9; Th. C. Vriezen, 'Prophecy and Eschatology', VTSup 1 (1953), pp. 199-229, esp. p. 210; Jenni, 'Jesajas Berufung', pp. 335-39; J. Lindblom, *Prophecy in Ancient Israel* (Philadelphia: Fortress, 1962), pp. 186-87; F. Montagnini, 'La Vocazione di Isaia', *BeO* (1964), pp. 163-72, esp. pp. 67-71; G. von Rad, *The Message of the Prophets* (London: SCM, 1965), pp. 122-26, esp. p. 125; G. Fohrer, 'Wandlungen Jesajas', in *Festschrift für Wilhelm Eilers* (ed. G. Wiessner; Wiesbaden: Harrassowitz, 1967), pp. 58-71, esp. pp. 61-63; J.M. Schmidt, 'Gedanken zum Verstockungsauftrag Jesajas (Jes. 6)', *VT* 21 (1971), pp. 68-90, esp. pp. 89-90; O.H. Steck, 'Bemerkungen zu Jesaja 6', *BZ* 16 (1972), pp. 188-206; Knierim, 'Vocation of Isaiah', p. 59; Kaiser, *Isaiah 1-12*, p. 82-83; K. Nielsen, 'Is 6.1-8.18 as Dramatic Writing', *ST* 40 (1986),

pp. 1-16, esp. pp. 10-11; J.N. Oswalt, *The Book of Isaiah: Chapters 1-39* (NIC: Grand Rapids: Eerdmans, 1986), p. 188.

32. M. Kaplan, 'Isaiah 6.1-11', *JBL* 45 (1926), pp. 251-59; Hesse, *Das Verstockungsproblem im Alten Testament* (BZAW 74; Berlin: Töpelmann, 1955), p. 84; J. Love, 'The Call of Isaiah', *Int* 11 (1957), pp. 282-96; C. Kuhl, *The Prophets of Israel* (Edinburgh: Oliver & Boyd, 1960), p. 79; R.P. Carroll, 'Ancient Israelite Prophecy and Dissonance Theory', *Numen* 24 (1977), pp. 135-51, esp. p. 144; R. Kilian, 'Der Verstockungsauftrag Jesajas', in *Bausteine biblischer Theologie* (G.J. Botterweck Festschrift; ed. H.-J. Fabry; BBB 50; Bonn: Hanstein, 1977), pp. 209-25; A. Schoors, 'Isaiah, Minister of Royal Anointment', *OTS* 20 (1977), pp. 85-107; C. Hardmeier, 'Jesajas Verkündigungsabsicht und Jahwes Verstockungsauftrag in Jes', in *Die Botschaft und die Boten* (H.W. Wolff Festschrift; ed. J. Jeremias and L. Perlitt; Neukirchen-Vluyn: Neukirchener Verlag, 1981), pp. 235-51. According to S.H. Blank (*Prophetic Faith in Isaiah* [New York: Harper & Row, 1958], p. 4): 'Taken literally as God's word the verse [Isa. 6.10] is bad theology. But, taken as a prophet's anguished comment on his failure, it is good pyschology'. More recently, H. Hoffmann (*Die Intention der Verkündigung Jesajas* [Berlin: de Gruyter, 1974], pp. 77-80) has concluded that the prophet did not preach a message of obduracy until 701 BCE.

33. A. Heschel, *The Prophets* (New York: Harper & Row, 1969), pp. 89-90.

34. Whitley, 'The Call and Mission of Isaiah', pp. 38-48; Kaiser, *Isaiah 1-12* (OTL; Philadelphia: Westminster, 1983²), pp. 120-21. This view is rightly rejected by Knierim ('Vocation of Isaiah', p. 47, n. 1) and others, e.g. Jenni, 'Jesajas Berufung', pp. 321-22.

35. N. Habel ('The Form and Significance of the Call Narratives', *ZAW* 77 [1965], pp. 297-323, esp. pp. 309-14) tries to show that the passage parallels the call of Moses in Exodus, and so must be a call narrative. See also R.H. Pfeiffer, *Introduction to the Old Testament* (New York: Harper & Row, 1941), p. 429; I. Engnell, *The Call of Isaiah* (UUÅ 1949:4; Uppsala: Lundequistska; Leipzig: Harrassowitz, 1949), p. 26; F. Horst, 'Die Visionsschilderungen der alttestamentlichen Propheten', *EvT* 20 (1969), pp. 193-205; E.J. Kissane, *The Book of Isaiah* (vol. 1; Dublin: Browne and Nolan, 1960), p. 69; T.T. Crabtree, 'The Prophetic Call—A Dialogue with God', *SWJT* 4 (1961), pp. 33-35; Lindblom, *Prophecy*, p. 189; von Rad, *Message of the Prophets*, p. 122; Wildberger, *Jesaja 1-12*, p. 241. Based on a misreading of the text, many Medieval interpreters believed that Isaiah had been a prophet prior to the vision of ch. 6.

Scholars have suggested a variety of specific occasions in which Isaiah may have received his vision. The enthronement festival (for Jotham) is suggested by Schoors, 'Isaiah, the Minister of Royal Anointment?', pp. 85-107; and W. Vischer, *Die Immanuel-Botschaft im Rahmen des königlichen Zionsfestes*

(*Theologische Studien* 45; Zollikon-Zürich: Evangelischer Verlag, 1955). Some scholars have suggested that the vision should be seen against the New Year's Day autumn festival in which Yahweh appears 'issuing decrees and making assessment of his people'; cf. J.H. Eaton, *Vision in Worship* (London: SPCK, 1981), pp. 49-50; earlier S. Mowinckel, *He that Cometh* (New York: Abingdon, 1956), pp. 80-87, esp. p. 84, n. 1. However, R.E. Clements (*Isaiah 1-39* [NCB; London: Marshall, Morgan & Scott, 1980], p. 73) holds such a specific identification in reserve. None has won a consensus, and Knierim ('Vocation of Isaiah', p. 54) doubts that a festival is in mind at all. Knierim is probably right, for there is no specific element that compels us to see a festival as the setting. The opening words, 'In the year that King Uzziah died', are probably intended to underscore the passing of a peaceful and prosperous era. Judah must now have faith in Israel's true King, not the faithless kings who follow Uzziah (such as his grandson Ahaz).

36. Knierim, 'Vocation of Isaiah', p. 57; so also Watts, *Isaiah 1-33*, p. 70; W. Zimmerli, *Ezekiel* 1 (Philadelphia: Fortress, 1979), p. 98-100; K. Koch, *The Prophets* (Philadelphia: Fortress, 1983), p. 113; and Ward, *Amos & Isaiah*, p. 145. Knierim (p. 59) believes that two literary *Gattungen*, that of the prophetic call and that of a special commission of judgment are combined in Isaiah 6.

37. Knierim, 'Vocation of Isaiah', p. 55. The parallels between Isaiah and 1 Kings have been studied in detail by H.-P. Müller, 'Glauben und Bleiben: Zur Denkschrift Jesajas Kapitel vi-viii 18', *VTSup* 26 (1974), pp. 25-54, esp. pp. 25-32; see also J.A. Montgomery, *A Critical and Exegetical Commentary on the Books of Kings* (ICC; New York: Scribner's, 1951), p. 338; J. Gray, *I & II Kings* (OTL; Philadelphia: Westminster, 1963), p. 402; and Wildberger, *Jesaja 1-12*, pp. 235, 239-41. A few of the parallels between Isaiah and Amos are noted by a A. Weiser, *Die Profetie des Amos* (BZAW 53; Giessen: Töpelmann, 1929), pp. 41-42; and J.L Mays, *Amos* (OTL; Philadelphia: Westminster, 1969), pp. 152-53.

38. Knierim, 'Vocation of Isaiah', p. 59: 'Thus he [Isaiah] hears... that Yahweh needs a messenger in order to initiate His action... Isaiah... becomes the preparer and first executioner of the judgment'; Steck, 'Bemerkung zu Jesaja 6', p. 206: '[Die] Verstockung des Volkes von Anfang an [war] Jahwes Werk... verankert in jenem Ereignis [i.e., the Syro-Ephraimite war] als Beschluss Jahwes und als Auftrag Jesajas'; and Watts, *Isaiah 1-33*, p. 72: Isaiah 6 'stands in a tradition in which God reveals (and in some measure defends) his decisions to bring judgment'.

39. For further discussion see Hoffmann, *Die Intention der Verkündigung Jesajas*, pp. 37-59, 81-125.

40. von Rad, *Message of the Prophets*, pp. 123-24.

41. von Rad, *Message of the Prophets*, p. 124.

42. E.C. Kingsbury, 'The Prophets and the Council of Yahweh', *JBL* 83

(1964), pp. 279-86, esp. pp. 284-85. Schoors ('Isaiah, the Minister of Royal Anointment?', pp. 85-107) finds parallels with similar Mesopotamian traditions of Numushda.

43. A.F. Key, 'The Magical Background of Isaiah 6.9-13', *JBL* 86 (1967), pp. 198-204. Key (p. 201) discusses the ancient concept that the prophetic word had magical power, in that it has the power to bring about the prophesied event itself: 'To speak the prophetic word of destruction is "to take a positive hand in the destructive event—to release, in the very proclamation of doom, the power to produce the debacle"' (he quotes B.D. Napier, *IDB* III, p. 912).

44. So von Rad, *Message of the Prophets*, p. 125.

45. See Ward, *Amos & Isaiah*, p. 154. B. Hollenbach ('Lest They Should Turn and Be Forgiven: Irony', *BT* 34 [1983], pp. 312-21) has rightly noted the presence of irony in Isaiah's commission, but he fails to take adequately into account the very serious nature of the decision of judgment reached by the heavenly council.

46. See J.A. Sanders, *Torah and Canon* (Philadelphia: Fortress, 1972), pp. 9-15.

47. This fact is well known; see Sanders, *Torah and Canon* pp. 56-57; Th. C. Vriezen, 'Essentials of the Theology of Isaiah', *Israel's Prophetic Heritage* (James Muilenburg Festschrift: ed. B.W. Anderson and W. Harrelson; New York: Harper & Row, 1962), pp. 128-46, esp. pp. 128-31. If Isa. 10.24-26 derives from the eighth-century prophet, then this passage would represent one unambiguous reference to the Exodus. Vriezen (p. 129, n. 1) regards 11.16 and 4.5 as non-Isaianic: 'Reminiscences of historical traditions we find only in the mention of such names as Sodom and Gomorrah (1.9; 3.9)' and 'in the allusion to the story of Gideon (9.3; [10.26?])'. Vriezen also points out (p. 129, n. 2) that 'Abraham is mentioned only in a later passage (29.22)' and that references to 'Jacob' (e.g. in chs. 2, 8, 10, 27, 29) refer not to the patriarch himself, but to Israel. Mosaic traditions are restricted to Second Isaiah (see 48.20-22; 50.5; 63.10-14). Perhaps it is no wonder that Second Isaiah brings in Mosaic and other Pentateuchal traditions. Whereas royal theology (i.e. Davidic traditions) involved the prophet mediating between God and the king (the apparent function of the eighth-century prophet Isaiah), in the context of the Mosaic covenant the prophet mediated between God and the people. After the Babylonian conquest Israel had no king, and hence royal theology became less relevant (or perhaps we should say royal theology took on new meaning). Second Isaiah reaffirms, however, the hermeneutic of First Isaiah (cf. 6.5) when Yahweh is called the 'King of Jacob' (cf. 41.21). The theology of Second Isaiah will be treated below.

48. See Sanders' discussion (*Torah and Canon*, pp. 78-79) of the prophetic hermeneutic when Israel's sacred tradition is cited or alluded to.

49. Portions of the discussion that follows are taken from my studies, 'On

Isaiah's Use of Israel's Sacred Tradition', *BZ* 30 (1986), pp. 92-99, and 'An Interpretation of Isa. 8.11-15 Unemended', *ZAW* 97 (1985), pp. 112-13.

50. These texts associate David with emerging messianic expectation. Vriezen ('Theology of Isaiah', p. 130) sees 11.1 as a later messianic prophecy after the house of David has collapsed.

51. Vriezen, 'Theology of Isaiah', pp. 130-31.

52. See the discussion of Kaiser, *Isaiah 13-39* (OTL; Philadelphia: Westminster, 1974), pp. 253-54; and J.J.M. Roberts, 'Yahweh's Foundation in Zion (Isa. 28.16)', *JBL* 106 (1987), pp. 27-45.

53. Blank, 'Traces of Prophetic Agony', pp. 81-92.

54. K. Budde, *Jesaja's Erleben: Eine gemeinverständliche Auslegung der Denkschrift des Propheten (Kap. 6.1-9.6)* (Gotha: Klotz, 1928); Steck, 'Bemerkungen zu Jesaja 6', pp. 188-206; idem, 'Rettung und Verstockung: Exegetische Bemerkungen zu Jesaja 7.3-9', *EvT* 33 (1973), pp. 77-90; idem, 'Beiträge zum Verständnis von Jesaja 7.10-17 und 8.1-4', *TZ* 29 (1973), pp. 161-78; T. Lescow, 'Jesajas Denkschrift aus der Zeit des syrisch-ephraimitischen Krieges', *ZAW* 85 (1973), pp. 315-33; Müller, 'Glauben und Bleiben', pp. 25-54; J. Schreiner, 'Zur Textgestalt von Jes 6 und 7.1-17', *BZ* 22 (1978), pp. 92-97; Nielsen, 'Is 6.1-8.18', pp. 1-16; for a different view of this section see J. Lindblom, *A Study on the Immanuel Section in Isaiah* (Lund: Gleerup, 1958). Most extend the report to 8.18, some to 8.23, others to 9.6[7].

Not all scholars include ch. 6, since the prophet's vision took place in the year of Uzziah's death, which would be the year of Jotham's installation, not that of his son Ahaz who would later be concerned with the Syro-Ephraimite war. Therefore, ch. 6 cannot strictly speaking be a part of a 'report' of what took place during this period. Its linkage with chs. 7-8 is literary and theological, though in exactly what sense is the subject of scholarly debate; see L.J. Liebreich, 'The Position of Chapter Six in the Book of Isaiah', *HUCA* 25 (1954), pp. 37-40. Liebreich has argued that Isaiah 6 provides a proper introduction to chs. 7-8, in which there are messages about two human kings who have formed the Syro-Ephraimite alliance against Ahaz. In contrast, Isaiah 6 affirms Yahweh's kingship and sets the stage for the advent of a righteous king (9.1-7). Other studies that are concerned with the literary unity of this section include L.G. Rignell, 'Das Immanuelszeichen: Einige Gesichtspunkte zu Is 7', *ST* 11 (1957), pp. 99-110; R.P. Carroll, 'Inner Tradition Shifts in Meaning in Isa. 1-11', *ExpTim* 89 (1978), pp. 301-304; and T.L. Brodie, 'The Children and the Prince: The Structure, Nature and Date of Isaiah 6-12', *BTB* 9 (1979), pp. 27-31. In its present canonical context, this unit welds history and theology together, establishing the core around which the major literary components of Isaiah came to be gathered.

55. See Nielsen, 'Is 6.1-8.18', p. 12.

56. T. Bird, 'Who is the Boy in Isa. 7.16?' *CBQ* 6 (1944), pp. 435-43; N.K. Gottwald, 'Immanuel as the Prophet's Son', *VT* 8 (1958), pp. 36-47; Kuhl, *The Prophets of Israel*, p. 78; H. Wolf, 'A Solution to the Immanuel Prophecy in Isaiah 7.14–8.22', *JBL* 91 (1972), pp. 449-56. It has also been held, of course, that Immanuel refers to a child of King Ahaz; so Mowinckel, *He that Cometh*, pp. 110-12; E. Hammershaimb, 'The Immanuel Sign', *ST* 3 (1949-51), pp. 124-42; J. Scullion, 'An Approach to the Understanding of Isa. 7.16-17', *JBL* 87 (1968), pp. 288-300. For a discussion of the problems with both of these interpretations see Kaiser, *Isaiah 1-12* (1983²), pp. 157-59; for his own solution see pp. 159-72.

57. Steck, 'Bemerkungen zu Jesaja 6', pp. 198-206; idem, 'Beiträge zum Verständnis von Jesaja 7.10-17 und 8.1-4', p. 161; Nielsen, 'Is 6.1–8.18', pp. 12-13.

58. Vischer, *Die Immanuel-Botschaft*, pp. 12-16; Jenni, 'Jesajas Berufung', pp. 330-35; Knierim, 'Vocation of Isaiah', pp. 48-57.

59. Knierim, 'Vocation of Isaiah', p. 49; W.J. Dumbrell, 'Worship and Isaiah 6', *RTR* 43 (1984), pp. 1-8, esp. pp. 1-2 and 5.

60. Dumbrell, 'Worship and Isaiah 6', p. 2. See also H. Cazelles, 'La vocation d'Isaïe (ch. 6) et les rites royaux', *Homenaje à Juan Prado* (eds. A.A. Verdes and E.J.A. Hernandez; Madrid: Consejo Superior de Investigaciones Científicos, 1975) pp. 89-108.

61. On the priestly pronouncement of 'unclean' (טמא) with reference to a leper see Lev. 13.3.

62. See Liebreich, 'Chapter Six in the Book of Isaiah', pp. 37-40.

63. Vischer, *Die Immanuel-Botzchaft*, p. 15; Kaiser, *Isaiah 1-12* (1972), p. 74; see further discussion in *Isaiah 1-12* (1982²), pp. 124-26, esp. n. 36; Knierim, 'Vocation of Isaiah', pp. 51-52.

64. Kaiser, *Isaiah 1-12* (1972), p. 76; H. Wildberger, *Jesaja, das Buch der Prophet und seine Botschaft* (BKAT 10/3; Neukirchen-Vluyn: Neukirchener Verlag, 1982), pp. 1646-47.

65. The reference to Uzziah, which is otherwise unnecessary, is to impress upon the reader the relevance of the vision in the preceding chapter.

66. In an attempt to catch the play in English, Watts (*Isaiah 1-33*, p. 93) translates: 'If you do not firm up, you will not be confirmed'.

S.H. Blank ('Immanuel and Which Isaiah?', *JNES* 13 [1954], pp. 83-86) has interpreted v. 9 differently: 'If you are in doubt, ask a sign. . . ' (p. 84). He also suggests that v. 13 belongs to vv. 17-25 and that, therefore, vv. 1-16, not composed by Isaiah, constitute 'unclouded promise' (p. 84; see also Blank, *Prophetic Faith in Isaiah*, pp. 9-33). Similarly other scholars argue that the signs of chs. 7-8 originally were either wholly positive or wholly negative, and so the chapters are emended accordingly. There may be some validity in these arguments, but since all three signs apparently contain a mixture of positive and negative elements, likely reflecting the 'if/then' warning of 7.9, I believe that it is prudent to try to make sense of the chapters as they stand. Moreover, Roberts ('Yahweh's foundation in Zion', pp. 27-45) is correct when he says, 'threat and promise are often mixed in Isaiah's oracles (1.19-20; 1.21-26; 7.7-9; 29.1-8; 31.4-9)'.

67. Vischer, *Die Immanuel-Botschaft*, pp. 18-19.

68. See Lescow, 'Jesajas Denkschrift', pp. 315-31. For more on אמן in the hiphil see R. Smend, 'Zur Geschichte von האמין', VTSup 16 (1967), pp. 284-90; and Müller, 'Glauben und Bleiben', pp. 32-38.

69. von Rad, *Message of the Prophets*, p. 27.

70. So also Kaiser, *Isaiah 1-12*, pp. 18-19. Watts (*Isaiah 1-33*, pp. 13, 23) translates: 'Community of faithfulness'.

71. Kaiser, *Isaiah 1-12* (1983²), p. 45.

72. As proposed by J. Vermeylen, *Du Prophète Isaïe à l'apocalyptique: Isaïe i-xxxv, miroir d'un demimillénaire d'expérience religieuse en Israël* (EtB; vol. 1; Paris: Gabalda, 1977), p. 90 (cited by Kaiser, *Isaiah 1-12* [1983²], p. 45, n. 33).

73. For a discussion of the theology and policy of Israel's 'official' theologians (i.e., royal advisors, priests, and [false] prophets) see Sanders, *Torah and Canon*, pp. 85-90.

74. Vischer, *Die Immanuel-Botschaft*, p. 20; Oswalt, *Isaiah*, p. 209.

75. Vischer (*Die Immanuel-Botschaft*, pp. 21-23) thinks that the name 'Immanuel' may allude to 2 Sam. 7.9 ('I have been with you wherever you went'); 1 Kgs 11.38 ('I will be with you'); Ps. 89.21 ('my hand shall ever abide with him').

76. Oswalt, *Isaiah*, p. 213.

77. Herntrich, *Der Prophet Jesaja*, pp. 129-30; Gottwald, 'Immanuel', pp. 46-47.

78. The clause is better translated: 'as though someone took me by the hand so that he might turn me away from walking in the way of this people' (Watts, *Isaiah 1-33*, p. 119).

79. G.R. Driver ('Two Misunderstood Passages of the Old Testament', *JTS* 6 [1955], pp. 82-87) emends the text to read: 'You shall not call a difficulty... It is the Lord of hosts whom you will find difficult'. His solution is followed by Kaiser, *Isaiah 1-12* (1972), pp. 117-18; Wildberger, *Jesaja 1-12*, pp. 334-41; Steck, 'Bemerkungen zu Jesaja 6', p. 201. Cf. the NEB. I believe that the emendation is unnecessary (see Evans, 'An Interpretation of Isa. 8, 11-15 Unemended', pp. 112-13; Oswalt, *Isaiah*, pp. 233-34; and Nielsen, 'Is 6.1-8.18', p. 3). E.J. Young (*The Book of Isaiah, Volume II: Chapter XIX-XXXIX* [NIC; Grand Rapids: Eerdmans, 1969] p. 310 and 310, n. 27), who also sees no need to emend the text, concludes that קֶשֶׁר refers to what the people were saying about Isaiah's efforts to dissuade Ahaz from making an alliance with Assyria for protection against the Syro-Ephraimite league. The people were accusing Isaiah of 'treason', of

advocating a suicidal foreign policy and a false theology. But in what sense does Isaiah's warning that his disciples not call his policy and theology 'treason' stand over against the injunction of v. 13 to 'sanctify the Lord'? Here Young fails to show adequately the contrast that must exist between vv. 12 and 13 (see Young, *Isaiah. . . I–XVIII*, p. 311).

80. In the prophetic tradition there is evidence that קֶשֶׁר may sometimes carry a religious connotation. An instructive example may be cited from Jeremiah: 'Again the Lord said to me, "There is a revolt [קֶשֶׁר] among the men of Judah and the inhabitants of Jerusalem. They have turned back to the iniquities of their forefathers, who refused to hear my words; they have gone after other gods to serve them; the house of Israel and the house of Judah have broken my covenant which I made with their fathers"' (11.9-10, RSV). In this context קֶשֶׁר very clearly connotes in a negative sense religious as well as political treason. Vischer (*Die Immanuel-Botschaft*, p. 30) refers to Absalom's treason in 2 Sam. 15.12.

81. In this context the idea of the sanctuary as a place of refuge and safety is probably in view (assuming that מקדש is not a gloss, as thought by W. Eichrodt, *Der Heilige in Israel: Jesaja 1-12* [Stuttgart: Calwer, 1960], p. 101, and others, or a misreading for מוקש ['snare'], as supposed by B. Duhm, *Das Buch Jesaja*, p. 84, and others).

82. The Assyrian king boasts that he captured 46 of king Hezekiah's fortified cities (see Pritchard, *ANET*, p. 288).

83. See the colorful translation offered by G.R. Driver, '"Another Little Drink"—Isaiah 28.1-22', *Words and Meanings* (D.W. Thomas Festschrift; ed. P.R. Ackroyd and B. Lindars; Cambridge: University Press, 1968), pp. 47-67, esp. pp. 61-63.

84. See Vriezen, 'Theology of Isaiah', pp. 131-38.

85. Vriezen ('Theology of Isaiah', p. 130) states: 'In his preaching, the judgment remains the point at issue. This is the paramount fact for Isaiah. At the beginning of his ministry there is, in my estimation, no possibility of the restoration either of the nation as a whole or of a remnant thereof'.

86. It is difficult to say, but the subject may refer either to the drunken prophet (as teacher) or to the Lord speaking through his true prophet. Watts (*Isaiah 1-33*, p. 363) thinks the former, in the sense that they are so unqualified because of their drunkenness they would be unable to teach children the alphabet. Kaiser (*Isaiah 13-39*, p. 245) thinks the latter, in the sense that the prophet portrays his efforts to instruct the priest and prophets as if they were children. Driver ('Another Little Drink', p. 64) thinks that the drunken prophets have mocked Isaiah and asked if he supposes himself to be teaching infants.

87. See Young, *Isaiah. . . XIX–XXXIX*, p. 280; W.W. Hallo, 'Isaiah 28.9-13 and the Ugaritic Abecedaries', *JBL* 77 (1958), pp. 324-38.

88. Kaiser, *Isaiah 13–39*, p. 250.

89. Sanders, *Torah and Canon*, pp. 72-73.

90. Both the qal infinitive and the nominal construct are מוֹת. 'Moth' could refer to either an Egyptian or a Canaanite deity; see Watts, *Isaiah 1–33*, p. 369.

91. B.S. Childs (*Isaiah and the Assyrian Crisis* [SBT 3; second series; London: SCM, 1967], pp. 28-31, 65) has argued on form-critical grounds that 28.16-17a, though likely from Isaiah, is likely not original to this passage. Roberts ('Yahweh's Foundation in Zion', p. 38) disagrees, arguing that v. 16 is the central verse in 28.14-22.

92. Roberts, 'Yahweh's Foundation in Zion', pp. 39-43. Great stones of quality had been used to construct the temple (1 Kgs 5.31; 7.9-12). Because Yahweh resided in Jerusalem (Isa. 8.18), the city could not be shaken (Pss. 48.9; 87.1, 5).

93. In 2 Sam. 5.22 the site is called the 'valley of Rephaim', while it is called 'Gibeon' in 1 Chr. 14.16. Driver ('Another Little Drink', p. 65), Kissane (*Isaiah*, p. 308), and Watts (*Isaiah 1–33*, p. 371) assume that the reference is to David, while Kaiser (*Isaiah 13–39*, p. 255) thinks the reference is to Joshua. I am inclined, with some hesitation, to think that the reference is to Joshua (1) because Isaiah refers to Gibeon, rather than Rephaim, the older tradition; and (2) because the references to the Lord 'trembling' or 'quaking' [רגז] in v. 21 and to the hailstones in v. 17 parallel the episode in Joshua more closely than that in 2 Samuel. Targum Jonathan also takes it as a reference to Joshua. Of course, it is quite possible that both episodes, linked by their common geography, are in mind.

94. Watts, *Isaiah 1–33*, p. 381.

95. The idea of a stone being laid in Zion may allude ironically, and in an altogether different sense, to the siege stones that were lying about inside the city walls. The irony is that whereas one would naturally suppose that military defeat meant destruction and the end, in this case it is actually the laying of a new foundation and a new beginning.

96. The 'stone' in 28.16 probably alludes to the stone of 8.14; see Watts, *Isaiah 1–33*, p. 372.

97. J. Jensen, 'Weal and Woe in Isaiah: Consistency and Continuity', *CBQ* 43 (1981), pp. 167-87.

98. G. Fohrer, 'Die Struktur der alttestamentlichen Eschatologie', *Studien zur alttestamentlichen Prophetie (1949-1965)* (BZAW 99; Berlin: Töpelmann, 1967), pp. 32-58; idem, *Die Propheten des Alten Testaments* (2 vols.; Gütersloh: Mohn, 1974-76) I, p. 16; IV, pp. 10-12. Earlier Blank ('Traces of Prophetic Agony', pp. 86-92) had concluded that Isaiah entertained no thought of a remnant. To arrive at this conclusion Blank not only must eliminate every passage that speaks of a remnant, but he begs the question when he accuses Isaiah of being 'irrational' in writing down his testimony for

future generations (see 8.16; 30.8) which the prophet knows will not exist.

99. Fohrer, 'Prophetie und Geschichte', *TLZ* 89 (1964), cols. 481-600; Jensen, 'Weal and Woe', p. 68.

100. Jensen, 'Weal and Woe', p. 168.

101. Jensen, 'Weal and Woe', p. 170; cf. J.P. Hyatt, *Prophetic Religion* (New York: Abingdon-Cokesbury, 1947), p. 97. It is questionable on form-critical grounds; see Sanders, *Torah and Canon*, p. 75.

102. Jensen, 'Weal and Woe', p. 173. In n. 23 Jensen notes that regarding this passage Fohrer admits to the presence of 'eine gewisse Hoffnung' (*Das Buch Jesaja I* [Zürich/Stuttgart: Zwingli, 1966²], pp. 44-45) which sees the judgment as purificatory, but he (Fohrer) considers it 'einmalig'; see also Fohrer, *Studien zur alttestamentlichen Propheten* (Berlin: Töpelmann, 1967), pp. 155-56. For more on Isa. 1.24-26 see Kaiser, *Isaiah 1-12* (1972), pp. 20-21; Eichrodt, *Der Heilige in Israel*, pp. 36-37.

103. The word is נֶאֱמָנָה and it may be an allusion to 2 Sam. 7.16. See discussion on 7.1-17 above.

104. Jensen ('Weal and Woe', p. 174) notes that most commentators have taken the phrase 'as at first' and 'as in the beginning' as referring to the time of David, a period of time which came to be idealized. With approval he cites Fohrer, *Das Buch Jesaja I*, p. 44.

105. Jensen, 'Weal and Woe', p. 174.

106. Childs (*Isaiah and the Assyrian Crisis*, p. 65) regards vv. 16-17a as unquestionably authentic and originally an oracle of promise.

107. J.W. Whedbee, *Isaiah and Wisdom* (New York: Abingdon, 1971), p. 141, n. 69. The 'stump of Jesse' (11.1) probably refers to the reduced and weakened kingdom, which in the time of Ahaz is no more than a vassal to Assyria. It is not necessary to conclude, as Kaiser (*Isaiah 1-12* [1983²], p. 254), that the whole of Isa. 11.1-5 is post-exilic.

108. These passages are completely in keeping with Isaiah's criticism of Ahaz and his advisors. In stark contrast to these faithless, corrupt, and undiscerning leaders, stands the faithful and righteous king whom Isaiah believes, in keeping with his covenant with David, God will raise up.

109. See also Jensen's recent study, 'Yahweh's Plan in Isaiah and in the Rest of the Old Testament', *CBQ* 48 (1986), pp. 443-55, esp. pp. 445-46.

110. Vriezen ('Theology of Isaiah', p. 133) states: 'in his preaching, the judgment remains the point at issue. This is the paramount fact for Isaiah. At the beginning of his ministry there is, in my estimation, no possibility of restoration either of the nation as a whole or of a remnant thereof'. Childs also has stated (*Introduction to the Old Testament as Scripture* [Philadelphia: Fortress, 1979], p. 327): 'Historically First Isaiah spoke mainly of judgment to pre-exilic Israel'.

111. G.F. Hasel, *The Remnant: The History and Theology of the Remnant Idea from Genesis to Isaiah* (AUM 5; Berrien Springs: Andrews University

Press, 1972), pp. 217ff.; see also the survey of Graham, 'The Remnant Motif in Isaiah', pp. 217-28.

112. Hasel (*The Remnant*, p. 243) states: 'Isaiah's cleansing experience "symbolizes Yahweh's cleansing and forgiveness of Israel"' (citing W. Harrelson, *Interpreting the Old Testament* [New York: Holt, Rinehart, and Winston, 1963], p. 232).

113. Hasel, *The Remnant*, pp. 238-40. He (pp. 239-40) states: 'The remnant motif is here used in a negative sense to illustrate the magnitude of the disaster which will come over "this people"'.

114. Hasel, *The Remnant*, pp. 236-43.

115. Hasel, *The Remnant*, pp. 250-57; cf. Kaiser, *Isaiah 1-12* (1972), p. 19.

116. Hasel, *The Remnant*, p. 253. Kaiser (*Isaiah 1-12* [1972], p. 20) states: 'Here again, it is clear that according to biblical belief, God's judgment is not simply a punishment. It is a division between the devout and the godless. The destruction of the godless is followed by the renewal of the congregation. . . ' It was noted above that Jensen cites this passage as one that points to the hope of restoration.

117. Hasel, *The Remnant*, pp. 257-70. As to the question of authenticity see Hasel, pp. 258-60, nn. 156-59.

118. Hasel, *The Remnant*, pp. 270-301.

119. Hasel, *The Remnant*, pp. 276-77.

120. See Hasel, *The Remnant*, pp. 276-77 nn. 226-30 for the bibliography in support of the various possibilities.

121. Hasel, 'Linguistic Considerations Regarding the Translation of Isaiah's "Shear-jashub"', *AUSS* 9 (1971), pp. 36-46; idem, *The Remnant*, p. 274.

122. See Hasel, *The Remnant*, pp. 279-80.

123. Hasel, *The Remnant*, p. 280. So also Metzger (see n. 25 above). Isa. 6.13c was likely added to ch. 6 to link the commission of judgment to Isaiah's theology of restoration and remnant. It would, of course, allude to 4.3. Such an editorial/exegetical act, in my view, is in keeping with Isaiah's overall theology, when once we recognize the presence of a futuristic hope in the prophecy of the eighth-century prophet.

124. S.H. Blank, 'The Current Misinterpretation of Isaiah's *She'ar Yashub*', *JBL* 67 (1948), pp. 211-15; idem, 'Traces of Prophetic Agony', pp. 87-88. Blank believes that the name of Isaiah's son is authentic, but that its interpretation in ch. 7 and in 10.20-22 reflects the later idea of a remnant, an idea that Blank doubts existed in the prophet's preaching. For reasons already given, I cannot accept Blank's conclusions.

125. See Hasel, *The Remnant*, p. 281, n. 247. J. Day's recent study ('Shear-Jashub (Isaiah VII 3) and "The Remnant of Wrath" (Psalm LXXVI 11),' *VT* 31 [1981] pp. 76-78) is not persuasive. It is better to interpret the

'remnant' idea in the context of Isaiah itself than to appeal to Zion Psalms (with which the prophet usually did not agree). In Isaiah the remnant is Israel (or Judah), and so in the case of Shear-Jashub's name it is not likely that reference is being made to a remnant of Jerusalem's enemies.

126. Hasel (*The Remnant*, p. 281) has borrowed this expression from J. Lindblom, *The Immanuel Section*, p. 10. See further Hasel, *The Remnant*, p. 281, n. 249.

127. Hasel, *The Remnant*, pp. 282-83.

128. Hasel (*The Remnant*, p. 287) states: 'Faith alone will be the *criterium distinctionis* between the surviving remnant and the perishing masses'.

129. See Hasel's discussion, *The Remnant*, pp. 288-98. Hasel notes that A.E. Skemp ('"Immanuel" and "Suffering Servant of Yahweh", a suggestion', *EvT* 44 [1932], pp. 44-45) had suggested that 'Immanuel' was not an individual, but a cipher for the remnant itself.

130. Hasel, *The Remnant*, p. 298-301.

131. See Hasel, *The Remnant*, p. 301, nn. 321 and 322.

132. Hasel, *The Remnant*, p. 304, n. 332.

133. Hasel, *The Remnant*, pp. 311-12.

134. Hasel, *The Remnant*, pp. 313-14.

135. Hasel (*The Remnant*, p. 320, n. 394) cites Wolff, Eichrodt, Kaiser, and Fohrer, among others, who have concluded that 10.20-23 is post-exilic.

136. Hasel, *The Remnant*, pp. 331-34. Although the 'two invasions' theory is not without its supporters (e.g. Bright, Wright, Gray, and Harrelson), recently it has been sharply criticized by Childs, *Isaiah and the Assyrian Crisis*, and R.E. Clements, *Isaiah and the Deliverance of Jerusalem* (JSOTSup 13; Sheffield: JSOT, 1980). Childs believes that there is inadequate evidence for advancing a second invasion, and Clements believes that 2 Kgs 18.17-19.37 (the 'second' invasion) represents later reflections on Isa. 10.5-15 (perhaps during the Josianic era). Nevertheless, most scholars do accept the oracle as coming shortly after the time of the Assyrian invasion of Judah.

137. Hasel, *The Remnant*, pp. 339-40.

138. Hasel, *The Remnant*, p. 339.

139. Hasel, *The Remnant*, pp. 345-47.

140. Jensen apparently has not seen Hasel's work.

141. Ward (*Amos & Isaiah*, p. 154) has reached a similar conclusion: 'Isaiah's commission was to harden the hearts of the people of Israel in order to bring about the fall of the nation and thus enable a genuine renewal of their life under God to take place'.

142. So also Ward, *Amos & Isaiah*, p. 158: 'Isaiah's task was rather to be an agent of this radical healing and during the process to bear witness to what was taking place in the hope that it would be morally redemptive and not simply destructive'.

143. Childs, *Introduction*, pp. 325-34. Other scholars who have stressed the literary and theological unity of Isaiah and have attempted to relate its major literary components would include L.J. Liebreich, 'The Compilation of the Book of Isaiah', *JQR* 46 (1955-56), pp. 259-77, and 47 (1956-57), pp. 114-38; J. Becker, *Isaias—der Prophet und sein Buch* (SB 30; Stuttgart: Katholisches Bibelwerk, 1968); P. Ackroyd, 'Isaiah I-XII: Presentation of a Prophet', *VTSup* 29 (1978), pp. 16-48; R.E. Clements, *Isaiah 1-39*; idem, 'The Unity of the Book of Isaiah', *Int* 36 (1982), pp. 117-29; J. Eaton, 'The Isaiah Tradition', *Israel's Prophetic Tradition* (Peter Ackroyd Festschrift; eds. R. Coggins, A. Philips, and M. Knibb; Cambridge: Cambridge University Press, 1982), pp. 58-76; C.A. Evans, 'On the Unity and Parallel Stucture of Isaiah', *VT* 38 (1988), pp. 129-47; and M.A. Sweeney, *Isaiah 1-4 and the Post-Exilic Understanding of the Isaianic Tradition* (BZAW 171; Berlin and New York: de Gruyter, 1988), pp. 27-99.

144. Childs, *Introduction*, pp. 325-26.

145. Childs, *Introduction*, p. 327. Sanders ('Canonical Context and Canonical Criticism', *HBT* 2 [1980], pp. 180-81) views Childs's interpretation favorably.

146. Brownlee, *Meaning*, pp. 247-59. Childs is apparently unaware of Brownlee's analysis.

147. Actually, the space between chs. 33 and 34 (i.e., cols. 27 and 28) is found at the bottom of col. 27; cf. P. Kahle, *Die hebräischen Handschriften aus der Höhle* (Stuttgart: Kohlhammner, 1951), pp. 72-73, cited by Brownlee, *Meaning*, pp. 247. Three blank lines point to a division between books; cf. K.H. Richards, 'A Note on the Bisection of Isaiah', *RevQ* 18 (1964), pp. 257-58. The MT has a mid-point marginal note at 33.20.

148. C.C. Torrey, *The Second Isaiah* (New York: Scribner's, 1928), pp. 93-54, 279-301.

149. Brownlee, 'The Manuscripts of Isaiah from which DSIᵃ was copied', *BASOR* 127 (1952), pp. 16-21.

150. See Brownlee's outline in *Meaning*, pp. 247-49.

151. Brownlee, *Meaning*, pp. 249-50, 255. Possible examples of pre-exilic oracles in Second Isaiah would include 56.9-57.13 and 58.1-9.

152. Brownlee (*Meaning*, pp. 259) states: ' . . . in the clarification of the message of the total work, corresponding parts of each book (insofar as truly parallel) need to be expounded together'. For an assessment of Brownlee's proposed two-volume outline of Isaiah see Evans, 'On the Unity and Parallel Structure of Isaiah'.

153. Brownlee, *Meaning*, p. 255. Although his arrangement differs, Brownlee's sensitivity to the literary and theological unity of the Book of Isaiah anticipates certain features of canonical criticism.

154. Duhm, *Das Buch Jesaja*, p. 64; among others.

155. Oswalt, *Isaiah*, pp. 172-73.

156. Liebreich ('The Position of Chapter Six', p. 40) has suggested that the chapter concludes the preceding section, while introducing, at the same time, the following section. Ackroyd ('Isaiah I-XII', pp. 16-48) has recently suggested that ch. 6 is the central part of chs. 1-12, a section concerned with the dual themes of judgment and salvation.

157. Nielsen, 'Is. 6.1-8.18', p.14.

158. J. Jensen, *The Use of Torah by Isaiah: His Debate with the Wisdom Tradition* (CBQMS 3; Washington: Catholic Biblical Association, 1973); Whedbee, *Isaiah and Wisdom*.

159. For discussion of Isaiah 1 and wisdom elements, see Jensen, *Use of Torah*, pp. 68-84.

160. See Kaiser, *Isaiah 13-39*, pp. 271-72.

161. Schmidt, 'Gedanken zum Verstockungsauftrag Jesajas', p. 89.

162. The Hebrew is second person singular.

163. C. Westermann (*Isaiah 40-66* [OTL; Philadelphia: Westminster, 1969], p. 110), in light of the reading of the Vulgate (*nisi ad quem nuncios meos misi*), suggests the rendering: 'Who is deaf but the one to whom I sent my messengers'. If this emendation is accepted, then the problem of understanding in what sense is Yahweh's servant a 'messenger' is resolved. Yahweh's servant is regarded as deaf, for he has failed to listen to Yahweh's messengers (i.e., the prophets). Although Westermann's suggestion apparently simplifies the meaning of the verse, it is based upon flimsy textual grounds and should be regarded with reservation.

164. Westermann, *Isaiah 40-66*, pp. 108-11.

165. Westermann, *Isaiah 40-66*, p. 121.

166. Compare also the expression, 'my people' (denoting endearment, 40.1), with 'this people' (denoting contempt, 6.9); cf. C.R. North, *The Second Isaiah: Introduction, Translation and Commentary to Chapters XL-LV* (Oxford: Clarendon, 1964), p. 72; E.J. Young, *The Book of Isaiah, Volume III: Chapters XL-LXVI* (NIC; Grand Rapids: Eerdmans, 1972), p. 18.

167. Westermann, *Isaiah 40-66*, p. 394.

168. In a study published some years ago F. Hesse (*Das Verstockungsproblem*) attempted to trace, along *heilsgeschichtliche* lines, the history of the idea of 'obduracy' in the literature and theology of Israel. He provides a well ordered and thorough treatment of the relevant vocabulary of obduracy (e.g. אמץ ['to be strong'], קשה ['to be hard'], קשח ['to be hard'], חזק ['to be firm'], שמן ['to be fat'], לבב ערלת ['uncircumcised heart'], קשה ערף ['hard in neck'], ערלת לבם ['closing of their heart']; New Testament equivalents would include πωροῦν, σκληρύνειν, σκληρός, παχύνειν, πώρωσις, σκληρότης, σκληροτράχηλος, and σκληροκαρδία) and attempts to trace out an historical development of the idea (cf. pp. 6-70). Hesse finds three distinctive

stages within this history. First, the concept of obduracy is ascribed to non-Israelites who have come into contact with Israel (pp. 33-34). Pharaoh would be the example *par excellence* in this category. The king of Sihon would be another example. The second stage is to be traced in the prophetic literature in which the concept of obduracy is applied to the nation of Israel (*als Volksganzes*) which was regarded in some of the prophetic tradition as being in a condition of *massa perditionis* (pp. 35-37). The third and final stage emerges in post-exilic literature where the language of obduracy was applied to individual Israelites who were considered apostate in contrast to the obedient and righteous (pp. 37-40). Although not singling out Hesse's study B.S. Childs, in an excursus on the hardening of Pharaoh (*The Book of Exodus: A Critical, Theological Commentary* [OTL; Philadelphia: Westminster, 1974], pp. 170-75), concludes that 'efforts to illuminate the concept of hardness. . . have been less than satisfactory' (p. 170). Part of the problem lies in the fact that it is not always certain at what date an obduracy text should be assigned. Later tradents may be picking up texts or traditions which may, for instance, be classified as belonging to the first stage. It is not always clear as to what literary strand a given text is to be assigned. For example, Hesse (p. 45) assigns Exod. 8.32 to J in which Pharoah himself has hardened his heart, but Childs (p. 172) assigns the text to P, a later tradition which should fall into Hesse's third category, reflecting the period when Israel's theology was completely monotheized (as opposed to the J period). I am inclined to agree with Childs. The obduracy tradition does not appear to follow any clear line of development.

169. R.P. Carroll (*Jeremiah* [OTL; Philadelphia: Westminster, 1986], p. 187) thinks that the critical reference to 'this people' in Jer. 5.23 may be an allusion to the same expression in Isa. 6.9-10.

170. In 4.23, reminiscent of Gen. 1.2, the earth is described as תהו ובהו ('formless' and 'void'). J. Bright (*Jeremiah* [AB 21; Garden City: Doubleday, 1965], p. 33) states: 'It is as if the earth had been "uncreated"'.

171. R.K. Harrison, *Jeremiah and Lamentations: An Introduction and Commentary* (London: Tyndale, 1973), p. 77; and W.L. Holladay, *Jeremiah 1* (Hermeneia; Philadelphia: Fortress, 1986), pp. 195-96.

172. Zimmerli (*Ezekiel*, pp. 269-70) says that Ezek. 12.1-2 stands in the Isaianic succession, and (p. 138) 'strongly recalls Isa. 6.9f', while W.H. Brownlee (*Ezekiel 1-19* [WBC 28; Waco: Word, 1986], p. 171) comments that the people are like those encountered by Isaiah.

173. J.B. Taylor, *Ezekiel: An Introduction and Commentary* (London: Tyndale, 1969), pp. 114-15; Zimmerli, *Ezekiel*, pp. 172, 270-71.

174. W. Eichrodt (*Ezekiel* [OTL; Philadelphia: Fortress, 1970], p. 66) thinks that Ezek. 3.6 alludes to Isa. 28.11: '. . . by men of strange lips and with an alien tongue the Lord will speak to this people'.

175. Zimmerli (*Ezekiel*, 138) notes that although Ezekiel borrows many words and ideas from Isaiah, 'with Ezekiel, however, the hardening of the people is already an established fact... No room is left therefore for the Isaianic concept of the hardening being brought about by the prophet's preaching'. So also Eichrodt (*Ezekiel*, p. 149-50) who contrasts hardening in Isaiah as the consequence of preaching with hardening in Ezekiel as the pre-existing condition of the people: 'The exiles have, apparently, lost the faculty to perceive what God is saying and doing'.

176. J. Baldwin, *Haggai, Zechariah, Malachi: An Introduction and Commentary* (London: Tyndale, 1972), p. 147.

177. R.L. Smith, *Micah–Malachi* (WBC 32; Waco: Word, 1984), p. 227; D.L. Petersen, *Haggai and Zechariah 1–8* (OTL; Philadelphia: Westminster, 1984), pp. 292-93. Petersen (p. 290) states: 'Zechariah is utilizing material found elsewhere in the prophetic corpus'.

178. Lit. the people have made their hearts as hard as a 'diamond' (שמיר, RSV translates 'adamant'; cf. Ezek. 3.9).

179. Cf. G. von Rad, *Deuteronomy* (OTL; Philadelphia: Westminster, 1966), p. 179.

180. R.K. Harrison and G.T. Manley ('Deuteronomy', *The New Bible Commentary: Revised* [ed. D. Guthrie, J.A. Motyer, *et al.*; Grand Rapids: Eerdmans, 1970], p. 225) put it aptly: 'In attributing such incapabilities to God, the Hebrew lawgiver is merely following OT traditions generally in relating everything to Him as the ultimate source or ground of being'.

Notes to Chapter 2

1. Portions of this chapter are taken from my studies, 'The Text of Isaiah 6.9-10', *ZAW* 94 (1982), pp. 415-18, and '1QIsaiah[a] and the Absence of Prophetic Critique at Qumran', *RevQ* 11 (1984) pp. 537-42.

2. See M.P. Horgan, *Pesharim: Qumran Interpretations of Biblical Books* (CBQMS 8; Washington: Catholic Biblical Association, 1979).

3. For 'remnant' idea see 1QH 6.8-10; 14.1-7; 1QM 14.7-9; in 1QS 8.5; 11.8; CD 1.7 the community is called 'an everlasting planting'; in 1QS 8.7 the community calls itself the 'precious corner-stone', alluding to Isa. 28.16; in 1QH 6.25-27 we have a midrash on Isa. 28.16-17 in which the community sees itself as a solid building made of tested stones. In 4QpIsa[a] 1.26-29, Isa. 10.21-22 ('a remnant will return, a remnant of Jacob, to the mighty God') is interpreted; T.H. Gaster (*The Dead Sea Scriptures* [Garden City: Doubleday, 1976[3]], p. 305) restores the pesher as follows: '[This remnant of Is]rael denotes [the congregation of the elect(?),] the godly champions of righteousness'. His reconstruction, however, may be a bit too daring (see Horgan, *Pesharim*, pp. 73-74). Also in 1QH 6.8: 'Thou wilt raise a reviving for Thy

people and grant to Thine inheritance a remnant, and refine them, to purge them of guilt' (Gaster, *Dead Sea Scriptures*, p. 167). The allusion is to Ezra 9.8-9 (see also 1QH 14.1).

4. There are less significant variants that have to do with spelling, e.g., the insertion of ו for certain vowels.

5. W.H. Brownlee, *The Meaning of the Qumran Scrolls for the Bible* (New York: Oxford University, 1964), p. 186: 'Singly each one of these errors can be explained as accidental, but when viewed collectively they impress one as a deliberate reshaping of the text'.

6. These would appear to be the only reasonable options.

7. F.J. Morrow, *The Text of Isaiah at Qumran* (unpublished dissertation; Washington: Catholic University of American, 1973), p. 27. So also G. Vermes (*The Dead Sea Scrolls in English* [New York: Penquin, 1975²], p. 172) who translates, 'my heart is dismayed'.

8. Brownlee, *The Meaning of the Qumran Scrolls*, pp. 186-87.

9. The use of שׁמם in Jer. 2.12-13 is instructive: 'Be appalled [שׁמו], O heavens, at this, be shocked, be utterly desolate, says the Lord, for my people have committed two evils: they have forsaken me. . . ' Here שׁמם is used in the context of being appalled at Israel's sin, which is quite similar to its meaning in 1QIsaiahᵃ.

10. Brownlee, *The Meaning of the Qumran Scrolls*, p. 186. The italicized words are the variants.

11. Brownlee, *The Meaning of the Qumran Scrolls*, p. 186.

12. Brownlee, *The Meaning of the Qumran Scrolls*, p. 186.

13. Brownlee, *The Meaning of the Qumran Scrolls*, p. 186.

14. Brownlee, *The Meaning of the Qumran Scrolls*, p. 187. M. Mansoor (*The Thanksgiving Hymns* [Leiden: Brill, 1961], 148, n. 6) links the text to Isa. 6.10. Compare also the reading of 1QH 18.20, where שׁשם probably has a positive sense.

15. Brownlee, *The Meaning of the Qumran Scrolls*, p. 187.

16. Brownlee, *The Meaning of the Qumran Scrolls*, p. 187.

17. Brownlee, *The Meaning of the Qumran Scrolls*, p. 187.

18. 4QpIsaᵇ 3.8-9 appears to contain commentary on Isa. 6.9, but the text is not preserved well enough to be of much help; see Horgan, *Pesharim*, p. 89, 93. Although the commentary is lost, judging by their other *pesharim*, it is likely that the men of Qumran felt that Isa. 6.9 (and perhaps the rest of the passage) had some futuristic, or even contemporary application.

19. W.H. Brownlee, 'The Text of Isaiah VI 13 in the Light of DSIᵃ, '*VT* 1 (1951), pp. 296-98; S. Iwry, 'Massebah and Bamah in 1QIsaiahᵃ 6.13', *JBL* 76 (1957), pp. 225-32; J. Sawyer, 'The Qumran Reading of Isaiah 6.13', *ASTI* 3 (1964), pp. 111-13; U. Worschech, 'The Problem of Isaiah 6.13', *AUSS* 12 (1974), pp. 126-38; J.A. Emerton, 'The Translation and Interpretation of Isaiah vi. 13', *Interpreting the Hebrew Bible: Essays in Honour of E.I.J.*

190

To See and Not Perceive

Rosenthal (ed. J.A. Emerton and S.C. Reif; UCOP 32; Cambridge: Cambridge University Press, 1982), pp. 85-118.

20. See Sawyer, 'The Qumran Reading', pp. 111-13.

21. Sawyer, 'The Qumran Reading', p. 112.

22. Sawyer, 'The Qumran Reading', p. 112. He notes that במה has this meaning in Judg. 16.5, 6.

23. Brownlee, *The Meaning of the Qumran Scrolls*, p. 239.

24. Brownlee (*The Meaning of the Qumran Scrolls*, p. 238) translates the difficult verse as follows: 'And if there be yet a tenth in it, it in turn shall be for burning, as a terebinth when it is thrown down, and as an oak by the sacred column of a high place'.

25. The Vulgate reads, *quae expandit ramos suos* ('which expands its branches'), a reading which may attest משלחת (see BH).

26. Brownlee, *The Meaning of the Qumran Scrolls*, p. 239. The dash in his translation corresponds with the space in the Isaiah Scroll. See the Isaiah Targum. Emerton ('Isaiah vi. 13', p. 115) translates the last part: 'like a terebinth and like an oak which are cast down from their stumps; in them the holy seed comes from its stump'.

27. In col. 6 of a piece he calls the 'Prayer for Intercession' (4QDibHam) Gaster (*Dead Sea Scriptures*, p. 275) translates a portion: '[yet didst thou not abjure] Thy Covenant, neither [reject us, to wipe out] the seed of Israel'. Also in col. 5 (p. 276): 'yet, despite all of this, Thou didst not reject the seed of Jacob, neither contemn Israel, to make an end of them, and abjure Thy Covenant with them'. Judging by the larger context, it seems clear that the 'seed' of Israel and Jacob refers to the eschatological community. The idea here is completely in accord with the general idea of 'remnant' (see n. 3 above).

28. This has been observed by J.A. Sanders, 'The Ethic of Election in Luke's Great Banquet Parable', *Essays in Old Testament Ethics: J. Philip Hyatt, In Memoriam* (ed. J.L. Crenshaw and J.T. Willis; New York: Ktav, 1974), pp. 247-71, esp. p. 253; idem, 'From Isaiah 61 to Luke 4', *Christianity, Judaism and Other Greco-Roman Cults* (Morton Smith Festschrift; ed. J. Neusner; Leiden: Brill, 1975), pp. 75-106; and Evans (see n. 1 above).

29. The phrase בלכתם בשרירות לבם, is probably derived from Jer. 13.10: ההלכים בשררות לבם (cf. Jer. 23.17). In 1.13, Hos. 4.16 is quoted: 'Like a stubborn heifer, Israel was stubborn'. The translations are from Gaster, *Dead Sea Scriptures*.

30. Gaster, *Dead Sea Scriptures*, pp. 271-78.

31. Gaster, *Dead Sea Scriptures*, p. 273.

Notes to Chapter 3

1. R.W. Klein, *Textual Criticism of the Old Testament: The Septuagint after Qumran* (Philadelphia: Fortress, 1974).

2. I.L. Seeligmann, *The Septuagint Version of Isaiah: A Discussion of Its Problems* (Leiden: Brill, 1948), pp. 3-4.

3. Seeligmann, *The Septuagint Version of Isaiah*, pp. 48-49.

4. Portions of this section are taken from my study, 'The Text of Isaiah 6.9-10', *ZAW* 94 (1982), pp. 415-18.

5. A and C read ἀκούσητε.

6. εἴδητε is read only by א and the Vulgate's Latin equivalent *cognoscere*, and is based upon ידע of the Hebrew.

7. Symmachus reads ἐλιπάνθη (from λιπαίνειν which means 'to anoint', 'to enrich', or 'to make fat' [cf. Deut. 32.15]), and so is basically synonymous with παχύνεσθαι, cf. J. Ziegler, *Septuaginta: Vetus Testamentum Graecum: Isaias* (Vol. 14; Göttingen: Vandenhoeck & Ruprecht, 1939), p. 144.

8. The first αὐτῶν is omitted in the original reading of א and in the citations of Matthew (13.14-15) and Acts (28.26-27), while the second αὐτῶν is omitted in B, 393, and Origen's LXX.

9. ἐπιστρέψουσιν is read by א.

10. ἰάσωμαι is supported by the Vulgate and no doubt reflects an effort to bring the mood into conformity.

11. Seeligmann (*The Septuagint Version of Isaiah*, p. 55) notes that the Greek translator 'endeavored to obtain the same effect by adding to the conjugated verb either a *nomen actionis* in the dative, or a declined participle of the verb in question'. Both forms occur side by side in the LXX's rendering of Isa. 6.9.

12. It is possible that the Greek futures could have the imperative force (as in the Decalogue). However, in view of the alterations in v. 10, these verbs are probably no more than predictive futures.

13. παχύνεσθαι is derived from παχύς meaning 'thick', 'fat', and 'firm', and is a suitable word for the underlying Hebrew word. See K.L. Schmidt and M.A. Schmidt, *TDNT* V, p. 1025.

14. Seeligmann, *The Septuagint Version of Isaiah*, p. 55.

15. Seeligmann, *The Septuagint Version of Isaiah*, p. 55.

16. Seeligmann, *The Septuagint Version of Isaiah*, p. 55. He also states (p. 56): '[The translator] often sacrifices grammatical accuracy to his own stylistic text-formulation. He deals pretty arbitrarily with gender and mood of the verb, with person and number'. See also J. Ziegler, *Untersuchungen zur LXX des Buch Isaias* (Münster: Aschendorff, 1934), pp. 108-109.

17. Ziegler (*Untersuchungen*, p. 108) suggests that the translator may have been influenced by Deut. 32.15 (where ἐπαχύνθη appears). According to I. Engnell (*The Call of Isaiah* [Uppsala: Lundequistska; Leipzig: Harrassowitz,

1949] 11) the LXX translator rendered the verbs of v. 10 as indicatives because he had an unvocalized Hebrew text before him. The use of γάρ, as well as the changes in v. 9, suggests, however, that more lies behind the LXX at this point than the unvocalized Hebrew.

18. Seeligmann, *The Septuagint Version of Isaiah*, pp. 63-64.

19. In v. 13 a few textual variants may be mentioned. A reads ἐκσπάσθη (ἐκσπᾶν, 'to draw out' or 'to throw out') for ἐκπέση (ἐκπίπτειν, 'to fall'). The reading of ἐκσπάσθη supports the reading מְשֻׁלְכֶת in the Hebrew text, and could represent an attempt to smooth out the meaning B, L, and C read ἐκ for ἀπό.

20. E. Würthwein, *The Text of the Old Testament* (Grand Rapids: Eerdmans, 1979), p. 180.

21. B. Lifschitz, 'Greek Documents from the Cave of Horror', *IEJ* 12 (1962), pp. 201-207.

22. D. Barthélemy, 'Redécouverte d'un chaînon manquant de l'histoire de la Septante', *RB* 60 (1953), pp. 18-29; idem, *Les Devanciers d'Aquila* (VTSup 10; Leiden: Brill, 1962), pp. 163-78.

23. C.H. Roberts is cited by Würthwein, p. 180; P. Kahle, 'Problems of the Septuagint', *Studia Patristica I* (TU 63; Berlin: Akademie, 1957), p. 332. Barthélemy (*Les Devanciers*, p. 168) now holds to a mid-first century CE date.

24. E. Vogt ('Fragmenta prophetarum minorum deserti Juda', *Bib* 34 [1953], pp. 423-26) also sees the scroll as a recension.

25. A.C. Sundberg, *The Old Testament of the Early Church* (HTS 20; Cambridge: Harvard University, 1964), p. 91.

26. The fragment is from the *Hexapla* as cited by Theodoret, cf. F. Field, *Origensis Hexapla* (Hildesheim: Olms, 1964), II, p. 441. Caution must be exercised here because it is difficult to tell how much of the variation is due to Theodoret and how much is due to Symmachus. See also Ziegler, *Septuaginta*, p. 144.

27. The Old Latin and Targum read plural. There are other uncertainties as to the original reading of vv. 19-20; see C. Westermann, *Isaiah 40-66* (OTL; Philadelphia: Westminster, 1969), pp. 110-11. The translator may have wished to distinguish between the messianic Servant and Israel (cf. 54.17; 56.6; 63.17; 65.8, 9, 13-15; 66.14).

Notes to Chapter 4

1. There is some evidence that some Targums may have existed in written form much earlier. W.H. Brownlee ('The Habakkuk Midrash and the Targum of Jonathan', *JJS* 7 [1956], pp. 169-86) has concluded that 1QpHabakkuk presupposed a Targumic Habakkuk tradition. Naturally, the

discovery of a Targum to Job at Qumran (11QtgJob) provides dramatic evidence. A. Diez-Macho ('The Recently Discovered Palestinian Targum: Its Antiquity and Relationship with Other Targums', *Congress Volume: Papers Read at the Third Congress of the International Organization for the Study of the Old Testament, Oxford, 31 August to 5 September, 1959* [VTSup 7; Leiden: Brill, 1960], pp. 224-45) has also concluded that at least one Palestinian Targum can be dated in the second century CE. M. Miller ('Targum, Midrash, and the Use of the Old Testament in the New Testament', *JSJ* 2 [1972], pp. 29-82) believes that a consensus of scholarship has begun to emerge which understands 'that by means of a comparative historical approach, i.e. comparing material not easily dated with materials whose early date is established (e.g., the Pseudepigrapha, the New Testament, Philo, Josephus, Qumran, Ps.-Philo), an early date for much of the PT [Palestinian Targum] can be established' (p. 31). Useful examples are to be had in M. McNamara, *Targum and Testament: Aramaic Paraphrases of the Hebrew Bible: A Light on the New Testament* (Shannon: Irish University, 1972); idem, *The New Testament and the Palestinian Targum to the Pentateuch* (AnBib 27a; Rome: Pontifical Biblical Institute, 1978); B.D. Chilton, *The Glory of Israel: The Theology and Provenience of the Isaiah Targum* (JSOTSup 23; Sheffield: JSOT, 1983); and idem, *A Galilean Rabbi and His Bible: Jesus' Use of the Interpreted Scripture of His Time* (GNS 8; Wilmington: Glazier, 1984). Note the caution, however, offered by A.D. York, 'The Dating of Targumic Literature', *JSJ* 5 (1974), pp. 49-62. York argues that whereas there is some good evidence for the early dating of some of the Targumic tradition, with the New Testament itself providing some of the best evidence, care needs to be exercised, for some of this tradition is quite late. Nevertheless, the Targumic material can often yield important and early traditions. See Chilton, *A Galilean Rabbi*, pp. 40-47.

2. J.F. Stenning, *The Targum of Isaiah* (Oxford: Clarendon, 1949), pp. xii-xiii. He also notes (p. xiv) that the aim of the Targumist is 'to modify the language of the prophet where it seemed inconsistent with the traditional view of the plain meaning of the text'.

3. Portions of this section are taken from my study, 'The Text of Isaiah 6.9-10', *ZAW* 94 (1982), pp. 415-18.

4. The text is from A. Sperber, *The Bible in Aramaic* (Leiden: Brill, 1962) III, p. 13. The text that Stenning has used differs in a few places with respect to spelling. A few insignificant variants are to be found in Kimhi, the Antwerp Polyglot Bible (1569), and the First and Second Rabbinic Bibles (i.e., the Bomberg editions of 1515 and 1524).

5. Kimhi reads וחזון מחזי for וחזון מחזא. The Antwerp Polyglot Bible (1569) reads מחזון for מחזא.

6. The First and Second Rabbinic Bibles (i.e., the Bomberg editions of 1515 and 1524) read וחזור.

7. The First and Second Rabbinic Bibles read עמעם (from עמם) which in the *geminatum* (pilpel) form means 'to obscure' or 'to make dim'. As Sperber and Stenning do, Lagarde reads the verb טמם (but without י), which in the *geminatum* (pilpel) means 'to close' or 'to block'. טמם appears to be a technical term with medical reference and, so far as can be determined, is not used in Rabbinic literature with reference to the eyes or to sight. However, note the interesting reading in *b. Pesah.* 42a: '[Avoid. . . the] Babylonian porridge which blocks [מטמטם] the heart, closes the eyes, and weakens the body'. עמם, however, is commonly used with reference to eyes and sight, e.g., *Sipre Numbers*, ed. H.S. Horrowitz, p. 12; *J. Roš Haš.* 3.1. Therefore, its appearance in some of the manuscripts and versions would probably be an instance of a *lectio facilior*.

8. *Codex Reuchlinianus*, Ms. p. 116 of the Montefiore Library, the First and Second Rabbinic Bibles, and the Antwerp Polyglot Bible read ובאורניהון.

9. Chilton (*A Galilean Rabbi*, p. 93) notes that ד 'cannot possibly mean "in order that" at this point in the Targum'.

10. It is possible, of course, that the Targumist has in mind the entire nation, understood as a people 'who hear'. . . But in view of his tendency to shift criticism onto Israel's enemies, and to enhance Israel's righteousness and her future glory, it is probable that the Targumist understands the description of obduracy as applying to many, but not to all.

11. Translation from B.D. Chilton, *The Isaiah Targum* (The Aramaic Bible 11; Wilmington: Glazier, 1987), pp. 20, 83. The emphasis is Chilton's, showing where the targum differs from the MT.

12. See *Mekilta de-Rabbi Ishmael, Baḥodesh* 1 (on Exod. 19.2); *b. Roš. Haš.* 17b; *b. Meg.* 17b; *y. Ber.* 2.3; *Seder Elijah Rabbah* 16 (pp. 82-83). These passages are discussed in Ch. 11, section B.

13. See Chilton, *The Glory of Israel*, pp. 28-33.

14. Chilton, *Isaiah Targum*, pp. 57-58.

15. Chilton, (*The Glory of Israel*, pp. 54-56) notes that this is one text among several that are understood as teaching that prophecy ceased in Israel when the Shekinah departed. God has removed his prophets and his teachers of Torah (see *Tg.* Isa. 8.16, 20).

16. Chilton, *Isaiah Targum*, pp. 82-83.

17. See Chilton, *The Glory of Israel*, pp. 37-43, esp. pp. 39-40.

18. Chilton, *Isaiah Targum*, p. 84.

19. Chilton, *The Glory of Israel*, p. 29.

20. Chilton, *Isaiah Targum*, p. 88.

21. Chilton, *Isaiah Targum*, p. 122.

22. This tendency on the part of the Isaiah Targumist is all the more noteworthy when it is observed that the Aramaic translations of the other obduracy texts follow the Hebrew quite closely (Deut. 29.3; Jer. 5.21, 23; Ezek. 12.2; Zech. 7.11-12).

23. This same tendency is found in 52.13–53.12 where the Targumist is careful to divorce the Servant of Yahweh (expressly identified as the 'Messiah') from the judgments inflicted upon him.

24. See Chilton, *The Glory of Israel*, pp. 110-11.

Notes to Chapter 5

1. M.P. Miller ('Targum, Midrash, and the Use of the Old Testament in the New Testament', *JSJ* 2 [1971], pp. 29-82) has noted that Baumstark and Kahle have advanced the thesis that 'the Peshitta is dependent (at least for the Pentateuch) on a Palestinian Targum' (p. 31). M. Black ('The Problem of O.T. Quotations in the Gospels', *JMUEOS* 23 [1942], p. 4) states that 'the original Aramaic Targum which had influenced the Gospel writers, had been in part actually preserved in the Old Syriac texts'.

2. F.C. Burkitt (*Early Eastern Christianity* [New York: Dutton, 1904], pp. 71-73) concluded that the Peshitta may be dated to the first century. Burkitt may be a little overly confident, but the possibility that the Syriac tradition may actually yield some early and distinctive tradition ought at least be entertained.

3. Our text is based upon the text of Ambrosianus in M. Ceriani, *Translatio Syra Pescitto Veteris Testamenti ex Codex Ambrosiano II* (Milan: Impensis Bibliothecae Ambrosianie, 1876-83). The Syriac text of Isaiah 6 is also to be found in I. Engnell, *The Call of Isaiah* (UUÅ 1949:4; Uppsala: Lundesquistska, 1949), pp. 8-10, and S.P. Brock, *Isaiah* (Vetus Testamentum Syriace 3/1; Leiden: Brill, 1987), p. 11, who also lists a few minor variants.

4. G.M. Lamsa (*The Holy Bible from Ancient Eastern Manuscripts* [Nashville: Holman, 1957] p. 704) translates: 'darkened'.

5. Lamsa (*The Holy Bible from Ancient Eastern Manuscripts*, p. 704) translates, 'so that they may not see with their eyes'.

6. W. Baars, *New Syro-Hexaplaric Texts: Edited, Commented upon and Compared with the Septuagint* (Leiden: Brill, 1968), p. 92. Engnell (*The Call of Isaiah*, p. 11) thinks that the first three verbs of v. 10 (*'t'by*, *'wwr*, and *š'*) are perfect because the translator had an unvocalized Hebrew text before him. Engnell, however, has underestimated the extent of the LXX's influence (see comments below).

7. B.D. Chilton (*A Galilean Rabbi and His Bible: Jesus' Use of the Interpreted Scripture of His Time* [GNS 8; Wilmington: Glazier, 1984], p. 91) thinks that the similarity is due to the influence of the New Testament on the Peshitta.

Notes to Chapter 6

1. That Paul has in mind Scripture is clear enough from the introductory formula, ἀλλὰ καθὼς γέγραπται.

2. C.K. Barrett (*A Commentary on the First Epistle to the Corinthians* [HNTC; New York: Harper & Row, 1968], p. 73) cites LXX Isa. 64.3.

3. Barrett (*First Epistle to the Corinthians*, p. 73) suggests this passage, though admitting to uncertainty. G.D. Fee (*The First Epistle to the Corinthians* [NIC; Grand Rapids: Eerdmans, 1987, p. 108) cites LXX Isa. 64.3; 65.16. A.T. Robertson and A. Plummer (*A Critical and Exegetical Commentary on the First Epistle of St. Paul to the Corinthians* [ICC; Edinburgh: T & T Clark, 1914, p. 40) cite Isa. 65.17 and Jer. 3.16. All that these passages have to commend them is the prepositional phrase, ἐπὶ (τὴν) καρδίαν (עַל־לֵב) (see also its use in Acts 7.23). Neither Old Testament passage clarifies Paul's thinking. P. Prigent's suggestion ('Ce que l'oeil n'a pas vu, 1 Cor. 2, 9. Histoire et préhistoire d'une citation', *TZ* 14 [1958], pp. 416-29, esp. p. 425) that Ps. 31.20, along with Isa. 64.3, underlies the quotation hardly accounts for the contents of the quotation.

4. See E. von Nordheim, 'Das Zitat des Paulus in 1 Kor. 2, 9, und seine Beziehung zum koptischen Testament Jakobs', *ZNW* 65 (1974), pp. 112-20; A. Feuillet, 'L'énigme de I Cor., II, 9. Contribution à l'étude des sources de la christologie paulinienne', *RB* 70 (1963), pp. 52-74; K. Berger, 'Zur Diskussion über die Herkunft von I Kor. II.9', *NTS* (1977-78), pp. 270-83. Berger finds parallels in the Ethiopic *Apocalypse of Ezra*, the Syriac *Apocalypse of Daniel*, the *Apocalpyse of Pseudo-Hippolytus*, the *Apocalypse of Peter*, the Arabic *Gospel of Pseudo-John*, the Ethiopic *Apocalypse of Mary*, and the *Letter of Pseudo-Titus*. Origen (*Commentary on Matthew* 117 [on Mt. 27.9]) suggested the *Secrets of the Prophet Elijah*. Jerome (*Commentary on Isaiah* 17 [on Isa. 64.4]) says that the passage occurs in the *Apocalypse of Elijah* and the *Ascension of Isaiah*. At 11.34 in some mss. of the *Ascension* a close parallel to 1 Cor. 2.9 does occur. However, chs. 5-11 of this apocryphal work represent later Christian material, and so can scarcely be Paul's source. The *Apocalypse of Elijah* is a first-century Jewish work that has been greatly expanded and embellished by Christian writers well into the fourth century, and so it too is of dubious value. In any case, no parallel to 1 Cor. 2.9 is to be found in the extant fragments published by J.H. Charlesworth, *Old Testament Pseudepigrapha* (vol. 1; Garden City: Doubleday, 1983), pp. 735-53. Although the *Gospel of Thomas* in part derives from the first century, log. 17 (NHL II, 2, 36.5-9), which parallels 1 Cor. 2.9 closely, is in all likelihood dependent on Paul and perhaps also on 1 John 1.1b ('what our hands touched') as well.

5. So H.St.J. Thackeray, *The Relation of St. Paul to Contemporary Jewish Thought* (London: Macmillan, 1900), pp. 243-45. Similarly M. Philonenko

('Quod oculus non vidit, I Cor. 2, 9', *TZ* [1959], pp. 51-52) concludes that the presence of this quotation in *Biblical Antiquities* provides evidence that this tradition existed in the first century. He rightly argues, moreover, that Paul is not dependent upon Pseudo-Philo. Prigent ('Ce que l'oeil n'a pas vu', pp. 416-29) plausibly suggests that this tradition took shape in the liturgy of the synagogue, a suggestion that receives some support by the continuing appearance of similar tradition in rabbinic literature (see Str-B 3.328). The Latin version reads: *ex eo quod oculus non vidit nec auris audivit, et in cor hominis non ascendit*; see G. Kisch, *Pseudo-Philo's Liber Antiquitatum Biblicarum* (Notre Dame: University of Notre Dame, 1949), p. 188. The missing final line, 'for those who love him' is found in the Hebrew fragments of *Biblical Antiquities* preserved in the *Chronicles of Jerahmeel* 57.23: לאוהבי. The pronominal suffix is in the first person, however, since in this context God is himself speaking; see D.J. Harrington, *The Hebrew Fragments of Pseudo-Philo* (Texts and Translations 3; Pseudipigrapha Series 3; Missoula; Society of Biblical Literature, 1974), p. 50.

    6. H. Conzelmann (*1 Corinthians* [Hermeneia; Philadelphia: Fortress, 1975], pp. 63-64) points out that Paul's quotation reflects ideas at Qumran (e.g. 1QH 1.21; 12.12-14; 1QS 11.13).

    7. Compare also in John the similar idea of inability to receive or know the Spirit (14.17).

    8. Barrett, *A Commentary on the Second Epistle to the Corinthians* (HNTC; New York: Harper & Row, 1973), p. 120; see also B. Lindars, *New Testament Apologetic* (Philadelphia: Westminster; London: SCM, 1961), pp. 159-63.

    9. Paul's phrase in v. 14 reads, ἄχρι γὰρ τῆς σήμερον, differing from what is found in the LXX: ἕως τῆς ἡμέρας ταύτης. However, the phrase in v. 15 is somewhat closer: ἕως σήμερον. V.P. Furnish (*II Corinthians* [AB 32A; Garden City: Doubleday, 1984], p. 208) believes that Paul has in mind Deut. 29.3.

    10. Furnish, *II Corinthians*, pp. 207-208. He notes that Paul also uses the nominal cognate, πώρωσις, in Rom. 11.25.

    11. Furnish, *II Corinthians*, p. 208.

    12. See Furnish, *II Corinthians*, p. 233-34.

    13. M.J. McNamara (*The New Testament and the Palestinian Targum to the Pentateuch* [AnBib 27a; Rome: Pontifical Biblical Institute, 1978], pp. 168-81, and *Targum and Testament* [Shannon: Irish University, 1972], p. 111) has shown that Paul's exegesis of Exodus 33-34 here in 2 Corinthians has much in common with that reflected in the Palestinian Targum.

    14. Käsemann, *Commentary on Romans* (Grand Rapids: Eerdmans, 1978), pp. 256-321.

    15. See O. Schmitz, 'Verstockung', *RGG* V, p. 1574; and J. Munck, *Christ & Israel: An Interpretation of Romans 9-11* (Philadelphia: Fortress, 1967), pp. 14-22.

16. This sacred tradition is formally recognized and catalogued in the introduction to the section in terms of the essential ingredients of Judaism, all of which are evidence of Israel's election (cf. vv. 4-5): υἱοθεσία (בני בכרי; Exod. 4.22); δόξα (כבוד; Exod. 40.34-35); διαθῆκαι καὶ ἐπαγγελία (בריתים from Abraham to Moses); νομοθεσία (תורה; Deut. 4.44); λατρεία (עבודה; Exod. 12.25-26); οἱ πατέρες (אבות; Exod. 3.13, 15); χριστός (משיח; 2 Sam. 22.51).

17. See the recent studies of R.R. Wilson, 'The Hardening of Pharaoh's Heart', *CBQ* 41 (1979), pp. 18-36; P.E. Dinter, 'Paul and the Prophet Isaiah', *BTB* 13 (1983), pp. 48-52; G.K. Beale, 'An Exegetical and Theological Consideration of the Hardening of Pharaoh's Heart in Exodus 4-14', *TrinJ* 5 (1984), pp. 129-54; W.R. Stegner, 'Romans 9.6-29—A Midrash', *JSNT* 22 (1984), pp. 37-52; and J.W. Aageson, 'Scripture and Structure in the Development of the Argument in Romans 9-11', *CBQ* 48 (1986), pp. 265-89.

18. LXX Exod. 7.3 reads: 'I will harden [σκληρύειν] Pharaoh's heart' (see also Exod. 4.21; 7.22; 8.15 [8.19, RSV]; 9.12, 35; 10.1, 20, 27; 11.10; 14.8 where σκληρύνειν is used in reference to Pharaoh, and Deut. 2.30 where it is used with reference to King Sihon). H.J. Schoeps (*Paul: The Theology of the Apostle in the Light of Jewish Religious History* [Philadelphia: Westminster, 1961]) has noted that in the Jewish writings of the New Testament era such predestinarian doctrines cannot be found.

19. So Käsemann, *Romans*, p. 270.

20. There is a rough parallel here with Isaiah's theology. As was argued above in Ch. 1, Isaiah believed that the obdurate condition of the people would lead to judgment and destruction, after which there would emerge a righteous remnant. Similarly, in Paul's thinking because of Israel's obduracy a remnant will emerge. See Dinter, 'Paul and the Prophet Isaiah', pp. 48, 51, 52.

21. Recall their significance in Isaiah's theology (se Ch. 1 above).

22. In the New Testament Jesus is identified as the 'stone which the builders rejected' (Ps. 118.22 [LXX 117.22]; see Mk 12.10-11; see Mk 12.10-11 par.). In 1 Pet. 2.6-8 this Old Testament reference is found sandwiched between citations of Isa. 28.16 and 8.14 (see also *Barn.* 6.2-4).

23. Dinter ('Paul and the Prophet Isaiah', p. 19) agrees: 'Although Paul's text draws directly from the Greek Bible that he knew so well, he was in fact reaching back to the meaning of the Hebrew text of the prophet'. The targumic reading differs greatly and appears to have exercised no direct influence on Paul's version.

24. Käsemann (*Romans*, pp. 278-79) states that Paul's interpretation runs in the opposite sense of the first part of the quotation (Isa. 28.16a). On the contrary, there is no doubt that Paul would have accepted Isa. 28.16 as it stands, for surely he would view Christ as the costly, tested corner-stone laid

in Zion by God. But he also understood that stone in terms of Isa. 8.14, that is, as a stone of stumbling and as a rock of offense. For some (believers) Christ is the precious foundation of salvation, while for others (unbelievers) Christ is a stumbling-block.

25. In at least one text at Qumran (cf. 1QH 6.26-27) the eschatological community identifies itself with the building founded on the costly stone. The targum replaces 'stone' with the 'strong, mighty, and terrible king'. Although the Messiah is sometimes referred to as king (see 11.1; 41.25; 66.7), the reference in 28.16 is not to the Messiah, but to one of the Roman emperors.

26. This is especially noticeable in 8.18 in the targum: 'signs and portents will be... upon Israel, that if they see and repent, the decree which was decreed against them... will be void'; translation from B.D. Chilton, *The Isaiah Targum* (The Aramaic Bible 11; Wilmington: Glazier, 1987), p. 20.

27. See Dinter, 'Paul and the Prophet Isaiah', p. 50; and E.P. Sanders, *Paul and Palestinian Judaism: A Comparison of Patterns of Religion* (London: SCM, 1977), p. 483 n. 36. The idea of 'stumbling' is tied closely to the obduracy theme.

28. Their zeal that is 'not according to knowledge' is another expression of obduracy.

29. Käsemann, *Romans*, p. 284; idem, *Perspectives on Paul* (Philadelphia: Fortress, 1971), pp. 155-66.

30. Dinter ('Paul and the Prophet Isaiah', p. 48) argues that Paul identifies himself with the Servant of Isaiah.

31. Both Paul and the LXX refer to the λεῖμμα.

32. The voice may be an instance of the 'divine passive'; C.E.B. Cranfield, *The Epistle to the Romans* (ICC; Edinburgh: T & T Clark, 1979), p. 549; M. Black, *Romans* (NCB; London: Oliphants, 1973), p. 142.

33. So B. Lindars, *New Testament Apologetic*, pp. 159, 161, 164; Dinter, 'Paul and the Prophet Isaiah', pp. 48-52; E.E. Ellis, *Paul's Use of the Old Testament* (Edinburgh: T & T Clark, 1957), p. 84 n. 4; and Munck, *Christ & Israel*, p. 114.

34. Dinter ('Paul and the Prophet Isaiah', p. 50) makes a point out of the fact that Paul does not actually quote Isa. 6.9-10, but instead draws upon a number of other related texts. However, the significance of his explanation at this point is obscure. Whether God hardens the heart or pours out a spirit of stupor, the result is the same. In either case it is, as Dinter himself has described it, part of the 'tradition of divine stupefaction'.

35. Dinter ('Paul and the Prophet Isaiah', p. 50) is surely mistaken when he suggests the θήρα is derived from LXX Isa. 8.14, for the word does not appear in this passage. (παγίς ['snare'], however, does occur in all three).

36. Dinter ('Paul and the Prophet Isaiah', p. 51) has tried to show that the reference to the 'table' ('feast' RSV] is meant to recall the false prophets'

tables of vomit and excrement (Isa. 28.7-8; 29.10). He believes that these 'tables' would have been taken to refer to the reading tables in the synagogue from which the scrolls of the Old Testament were read. Because the religious leaders are blind to the gospel, their reading table has become a snare and a trap. The suggestion is ingenious and may be correct; see also Black, *Romans*, p. 142; and Cranfield, *Romans* pp. 551-52.

37. See E.P. Sanders, *Paul and Palestinian Judaism*, p. 447. In this cluster of texts the three divisions of Tanach are represented, which probably signifies Paul's attempt to marshal the total witness of Scripture; cf. Käsemann, *Romans*, p. 301, and Schoeps, *Paul*, p. 241.

38. In 'Paul and the Hermeneutics of "True Prophecy". A Study of Romans 9-11', *Bib* 65 (1984), pp. 560-70, I have tried to show that the manner of Paul's application of Scripture to his own generation is similar to the hermeneutics of prophetic criticism employed by the canonical prophets of the Old Testament. Dinter ('Paul and the Prophet Isaiah', p. 52) has rightly said: 'Paul's understanding of God's continuing activity was *prophetic* and dynamic. God could, as in the days of Isaiah, do a "new thing"'. See also Aageson, 'Scripture and Structure', pp. 265-89.

39. Paul's strongly monotheistic hermeneutic finds expression in Rom. 3.29-30: 'Or is God the God of Jews only? Is he not the God of the Gentiles also? Yes, of Gentiles also, since God is one. . . ' (RSV). To this sentiment the Rabbis came to reply: 'I am God over all who come into the world, but my name have I united only with you. I am not called the God of the Gentiles but God of Israel' (*Exod. Rab.* 29.4 [on 20.1]; cf. Schoeps, *Paul*, p. 249).

Notes to Chapter 7

1. Matthew's formal citation of the LXX is evidence that the Marcan paraphrase was understood as indeed a specific reference to Isa. 6.10 by at least one early Christian.

2. M. Black, *An Aramaic Approach to the Gospels and Acts* (Oxford: Clarendon, 1967³), p. 214.

3. This reading is also found in the Peshitta, but as argued above in Ch. 5, the Peshitta is dependent on the Targum at this point, perhaps even on Mark itself.

4. E.g., T.W. Manson, *The Teaching of Jesus* (Cambridge: University Press, 1948), pp. 77-78; W. Grundmann, *Das Evangelium nach Markus* (THKNT 2; Berlin: Evangelische Verlagsanstalt, 1959), p. 92; J. Gnilka, *Die Verstockung Israels: Isaias 6, 9-10 in der Theologie der Synoptiker* (SANT 3; Munich: Kösel, 1961), p. 16; Black, *An Aramaic Approach*, pp. 214-15; E. Schweizer, *The Good News according to St. Mark* (Atlanta: John Knox, 1970), pp. 92-93; J. Jeremias, *The Parables of Jesus* (New York: Scribner's,

1971), p. 15; W.L. Lane, *The Gospel according to Mark* (NIC; Grand Rapids: Eerdmans, 1974), p. 158; H. Anderson, *The Gospel of Mark* (NCB; London: Marshall, Morgan & Scott, 1976), p. 131; and B.D. Chilton, *A Galilean Rabbi and His Bible: Jesus' Use of the Interpreted Scripture of his Time* (GNS 8; Wilmington: Glazier, 1984), pp. 91-93, 96. A notable exception is F. Hesse, *Das Verstockungsproblem im Alten Testament* (BZAW 74; Berlin: Töpelmann, 1955), p. 64. For the distinctive reading of the Targum see Ch. 4 above.

5. Manson, *The Teaching of Jesus*, pp. 74-81. So also C.C. Torrey (cited by V. Taylor, *The Gospel according to St. Mark* [London: Macmillan, 1966²], p. 257).

6. Manson, *The Teaching of Jesus*, p. 76. See also F. Hauck, *TDNT* 5, pp. 744-61.

7. Manson, *The Teaching of Jesus*, p. 77.

8. Manson, *The Teaching of Jesus*, pp. 77-78. See the discussion above in Ch. 4.

9. Manson, *The Teaching of Jesus*, pp. 78-79.

10. Manson, *The Teaching of Jesus*, pp. 79-80.

11. Chilton (*A Galilean Rabbi*, p. 93) states: 'Whoever rendered the Aramaic saying from its original language into Greek (whether Mark, or as is more likely, a predecessor) certainly had more difficult constructions to contend with, and could never have succeeded if this particle, which cannot possibly mean 'in order that' at this point in the Targum, proved too difficult for him correctly to understand'.

12. M.-J Lagrange, *Évangile selon Saint Marc* (Paris: Gabalda, 1929), p. 99. More recent scholars who hold this view would include J.W. Doeve, *Jewish Hermeneutics in the Synoptic Gospels and Acts* (Assen: Van Gorcum, 1954), p. 163; W. Marxsen, 'Redaktionsgeschichtliche Erklärung der sogenannten Parabeltheorie des Markus', *ZTK* 52 (1955), pp. 255-71. Marxsen (p. 269) states: 'Eine Abbreviatur für ἵνα πληρωθῇ[ist]'. Marxsen believes that the logion does allow room for the possibility of repentance. See E.F. Siegman, 'Teaching in Parables (Mk 4, 10-12; Lk. 8, 9-10; Mt. 13, 10-15)', *CBQ* 23 (1961), pp. 161-81, esp. 176; G.K. Falusi, 'Jesus' use of Parables in Mark with Special Reference to Mark 4.10-12', *IJT* 31 (1982), pp. 35-46, esp. 41. J.R. Kirkland ('The Earliest Understanding of Jesus' Use of Parables: Mark IV 10-12 in Context', *NovT* 19 [1977], pp. 1-21) overstates the case when he refers to this position (pp. 6-7) as 'the most widely accepted view'. To document this claim he cites Siegman (p. 176 n. 40), but Siegman notes only the work of Lagrange.

13. Lagrange, *Marc*, p. 99, i.e., in the sense that Matthew has retained the fuller version.

14. Jeremias, *Parables*, p. 17. Jeremias does not, however, cite Lagrange.

15. I sympathize with C.H. Peisker ('Konsekutives ἵνα in Markus 4.12',

ZNW 59 [1968], pp. 126-27) who complains of Jeremias' position: 'Damit ist die Verstockung Absicht Gottes, und nicht Jesu!' Such a distinction does appear to be dubious.

16. Jeremias, *Parables*, p. 17 n. 24.

17. Jeremias, *Parables*, p. 17, and n. 26. Also see the discussion above in Ch. 2.

18. C.E. Carlston (*The Parables of the Triple Tradition* [Philadelphia: Fortress, 1975], pp. 106-108) finds the grammatical and lexical evidence for this meaning of μήποτε unconvincing. I doubt if in this case the rabbinic understanding represents an early tradition.

19. B. Metzger, 'The Formulas Introducing Quotations of Scripture in the NT and the Mishnah', *JBL* 70 (1951), pp. 297-307, esp. p. 306.

20. Metzger, 'Formulas', pp. 306-307.

21. T.A. Burkill, *Mysterious Revelation: An Examination of the Philosophy of St. Mark's Gospel* (Ithaca: Cornell, 1963), p. 112. Burkill defends this position by noting that 'from such passages as John 8.56 and Mt. 25.9 it is argued that these translations are linguistically permissible; also St. Matthew may have understood St. Mark's ἵνα in a causal sense, since in 13.13 he replaces it with ὅτι'. See idem, 'Cryptology of Parables in St. Mark's Gospel', *NovT* 1 (1956), pp. 246-62; and idem, *New Light on the Earliest Gospel* (Ithaca: Cornell, 1972), pp. 3-8. See also H. Windisch, 'Die Verstockungsidee in Mc. 4.12 und das Kausale ἵνα der späteren Koine', *ZNW* 26 (1927), pp. 203-209.

22. C.F.D. Moule, 'Mark 4.1-20 Yet Once More', *Neotestamentica et Semitica* (M. Black Festschrift; ed. E.E. Ellis and M. Wilcox; Edinburgh: T & T Clark, 1969), pp. 95-112, esp. 101. The idea is quite similar to later Rabbinic exegesis.

23. Peisker, 'Konsekutives ἵνα', p. 127. However, למען can also be either telic or causal.

24. Peisker, 'Konsekutives ἵνα', p. 127. A. Suhl (*Die Funktion der alttestamentlichen Zitate und Anspielungen im Markusevangelium* [Gütersloh: Mohn, 1965], p. 149) states: 'Das ἵνα dürfte *konsekutiv* zu verstehen sein' (emphasis his).

25. Anderson, *Mark*, p. 131.

26. According to Chilton (*A Galilean Rabbi*, p. 95): '4.12 appears to be a characterization of those who refuse to see and hear, and not to reflect a deliberate banishment of the "outsiders"'. And again (p. 97): "They are like those of whom Isaiah spoke", is the complaint, without any claim that they must be that way, or that God intends them to have such an attitude'. Of all the studies in this category, Chilton's has the most to commend it (see pp. 91-98).

27. See Taylor (*St. Mark*, p. 257), who cites C.J. Cadoux.

28. J.A. Fitzmyer (*Luke I-IX* [AB 28; Garden City: Doubleday, 1981]

p. 709) notes that Luke's omission of the clause 'is an argument in favor of the final interpretation'. Matthew omits Mark's μήποτε clause, but includes, of course, the clause in his formal LXX quotation. However, the clause in the context of the LXX quotation has a different meaning.

29. Schweizer, *Mark*, pp. 92-94; Grundmann, *Markus*, p. 92.

30. Taylor, *St. Mark*. p. 257.

31. A.M. Ambrozic, 'Mark's Concept of the Parable', *CBQ* 29 (1967), pp. 220-27. He concludes (p. 227): 'Mark's primary concern in regard to the parables is not understanding as opposed to ignorance, but the favorable, or unfavorable, effect produced by God in men by means of the parables'; E. Stauffer, *TDNT*, III, p. 327.

32. W. Manson, 'The Purpose of Parables: A Re-Examination of St. Mark iv. 10-12', *ExpTim* 68 (1957), pp. 133-34.

33. Black, *An Aramaic Approach*, pp. 213-14. Black is referring, of course, to T.W. Manson, *The Teaching of Jesus*.

34. D. Daube, *The New Testament and Rabbinic Judaism* (London: Athlone, 1956), p. 149. Also. R. Pesch (*Das Markusevangelium* [Freiburg: Herder und Herder, 1976], p. 237) states: 'Das Verstockungslogion hat Markus eingefügt, weil es nicht nur *ad vocem* παραβολή ἀκούειν und τοῖς ἔξω. . . passte, sondern weil es den Gedanken der Scheidung der Hörerschaft vertiefen, schärfen interpretieren konnte'.

35. H.C. Kee (*Community of the New Age: Studies in Mark's Gospel* [Philadelphia: Westminster, 1977], p. 58) states: 'That the inability to perceive is the intended outcome rather than merely a chance result is clear from the final line of the quotation, μήποτε ἐπιστρέψωσιν καὶ ἀφεθῇ αὐτοῖς'.

36. G.R. Beasley-Murray, *Jesus and the Kingdom of God* (Grand Rapids: Eerdmans, 1986), p. 106.

37. J. Marcus, *The Mystery of the Kingdom of God* (SBLDS 90; Atlanta: Scholars, 1986), pp. 119-21; idem, 'Mark 4.10-12 and Marcan Epistemology', *JBL* 103 (1984), pp. 557-74.

38. Taylor (*St. Mark*, p. 257) believes that these Q sayings reflect what Mark has attempted in 4.11-12.

39. B. Lindars (*New Testament Apologetic* [Philadelphia: Westminster, 1961], pp. 159-60) thinks that it likely represents 'one of the forms in which the text was current at an early time'.

40. So F. Eakin ('Spiritual Obduracy and Parable Purpose', *The Use of the Old Testament in the New and Other Essays* [W.F. Stinespring Festschrift; ed. J. Efird; Durham: Duke, 1972], pp. 87-107) who believes that Mark intended the logion to have telic meaning in order to explain the rejection and death of Jesus.

41. Mark's meaning, therefore, is quite similar to that of the original prophetic utterance. W.L. Holladay (*Isaiah: Scroll of a Prophetic Heritage*

[Grand Rapids: Eerdmans, 1978], p. 36) has remarked: 'The adoption of the Isaiah passage in the Gospel of Mark shows that Isaiah and the New Testament community held a common perception of how God works'.

42. Jeremias, *Parables*, pp. 16-18; Schweizer, *Mark*, p. 93; Pesch, *Markusevangelium* p. 239; Chilton, *A Galilean Rabbi*, p. 96.

43. W. Marxsen ('Redaktionsgeschichtliche Erklärung', p. 264 n. 1) states: 'Markus hat das Logion aus der Tradition übernommen, nicht jedoch selbst geschaffen'.

44. According to Marxsen ('Redaktionsgeschichtliche Erklärung', p. 264): 'Wir können also feststellen, dass von der Verwendung der Begriffe bei Markus her gesehen keine irrtümliche Interpolation vorlag. . .'

45. Marxsen, 'Redaktionsgeschichtliche Erklärung', p. 264. I am inclined to agree with this aspect of Marxsen's study (more on this below).

46. The evangelist probably changed the singular 'parable' into the plural in order to draw a closer connection to the logion's reference to 'parables'.

47. See Gnilka, *Die Verstockung Israels*, pp. 24-25; and W. Kelber, *The Kingdom in Mark: A New Place and a New Time* (Philadelphia: Fortress, 1974), pp. 32-33. See discussion below for more on the vocabulary of the logion.

48. See W. Wrede, *The Messianic Secret* (Cambridge: James Clark, 1971), pp. 22, 57, 61, 211.

49. The term, 'outsiders', refers, contrary to Kelber (*The Kingdom in Mark*, pp. 25-26, 30-31), to unbelievers (so Grundmann, *Markus*, p. 92; Black, *An Aramaic Approach*, pp. 76-77).

50. The word 'secret' (μυστήριον) is derived from Jewish apocalyptic (=רז in Dan. 2.27-28, etc.), and probably originally referred to the belief that the kingdom was present in Jesus. In the interpretation of the parable, the 'secret of the kingdom' is referred to as 'the word' (i.e., the 'seed' that was sown), an expression deriving from early Christian preaching. See R.E. Brown, *The Semitic Background of the Term "Mystery" in the New Testament* (Philadelphia: Fortress, 1968).

51. It might be objected that whereas the logion has in view only two groups of people, the parable has in view four types of soil, and therefore the parallel breaks down. However, there are really only two types of people in the parable: those who are not fruitful (represented by the first three types of soil) and those who are (represented by the last type of soil).

52. I have suggested this interpretation in my studies, 'A Note on the Function of Isaiah VI, 9-10 in Mark IV', *RB* 88 (1981), pp. 234-35, and 'The Isaianic Background of Mark 4.1-20', *CBQ* 47 (1985), pp. 464-68. J.W. Bowker ('Mystery and Parable: Mark iv. 1-20', *JTS* 25 [1974], pp. 300-17) has in fact argued that Mk 4.1-20 is a midrash on the 'holy seed' of Isa. 6.13c. Perhaps it is, but since the phrase, 'holy seed', does not actually occur, one probably should hesitate to describe Mk 4.1-20 as a midrash on Isa. 6.13. The

passage does have midrashic elements, and may intend to allude to the 'seed' of Isaiah 6, but that is about all that can be said. I think that the same applies in the case of M. Gertner ('Midrashim in the NT', *JSS* 7 [1962], pp. 267-92), who has suggested that Mk 4.1-20 is a midrash on Jer. 4.3: 'For thus says the Lord to the men of Judah and to the inhabitants of Jerusalem: "Break up your fallow ground, and sow not among thorns"'.

53. Marcus, *The Mystery of the Kingdom of God*, p. 147; idem, 'Mark 4.10-12', pp. 567-70.

54. T.J. Weeden, *Mark: Traditions in Conflict* (Philadelphia: Fortress, 1971).

55. F. Watson ('The Social Function of Mark's Secrecy Theme', *JSNT* 24 [1985], pp. 49-69, esp. pp. 54-60) argues correctly that the Marcan obduracy idea, especially as it is seen in 4.11-12, is part of the evangelist's secrecy/ predestination theology. However, Watson fails to note that the disciples themselves are obdurate and so hardly function in the gospel as exemplars for the Marcan congregation. They are 'insiders' according to 4.11-12, but 'outsiders' according to 6.52 and 8.17-19.

56. Marcus, *The Mystery of the Kingdom of God*, p. 147. Marcus notes (p. 147, n. 88) that ἵνα is used in Mk 9.12 and 14.49 in reference to Jesus' intention to die.

57. Marcus, *The Mystery of the Kingdom of God*, pp. 147-51; idem, 'Mark 4.10-12', pp. 573-74.

58. C.H. Dodd, *The Parables of the Kingdom* (London: Nisbet, 1935), pp. 13-14. The seven vocabulary items are μυστήριον, οἱ ἔξω, πρόσκαιρος, ἀπάτη, ἐπιθυμία, διωγμός, and θλῖψις. Dodd's objections weigh more heavily against the parable's explanation than they do against the logion itself. Moreover, his vocabulary evidence is not as impressive as at first glance it may appear. Lane (*Mark*, p. 156 n. 24) observes: 'Two of Dodd's seven works, διωγμός and θλῖψις, recur in Mk. 10.30; 13.19, 24; οἱ ἔξω as a phrase occurs only here, but in Mk. 3.32, ἔξω has been used of Jesus' mother and brothers in a passage which contrasts their unbelief with the true belief of those seated before Jesus within the house (τοὺς περὶ αὐτόν, corresponding to οἱ περὶ αὐτόν of the disciples in Mk. 4.10)'.

59. R. Bultmann (*The History of the Synoptic Tradition* [Oxford: Blackwell, 1963], p. 325, n. 1) states: 'In my view Mk. 4.10-12 is an editorial formulation of Mark. . . concealing the transition which in Mark's sources had led on from the similitude of the Sower to its interpretation' (see also p. 199). This may explain one of the reasons why Mark put the logion here (see the other reasons discussed above), but such a reason in itself cannot rule out the possiblity of authenticity.

60. F.C. Grant, *The Gospel according to St. Mark* (New York: Abingdon, 1951), p. 636. C.E.B. Cranfield (*The Gospel according to Saint Mark* [Cambridge: University Press, 1963], p. 154) comes to the opposite conclusion.

61. F. Hauck, pp. 757-58; G. Haufe, 'Erwägungen zum Ursprung der sogenannten Parabeltheorie Markus 4, 11-12', *EvT* 32 (1972), pp. 413-21. But if the logion originally had nothing to do with parables, this observations becomes irrelevant.

62. Manson, *Teaching of Jesus*, pp. 75-80.

63. Jeremias, *Parables*, pp. 17-18.

64. Jeremias, *Parables*, pp. 15-17. So also J.M. Robinson, 'On the *Gattung* of Mark (and John)', *Jesus and Man's Hope* (ed. D.G. Buttrick and J.M. Bald; Pittsburgh: Pittsburgh Theological Seminary, 1970), pp. 111-12; idem, 'The Literary Composition of Mark', *L'Evangile selon Marc: Tradition et Rédaction* (ed. M. Sabbe; Gembloux: Louvain University, 1974), pp. 18-19; idem, 'Gnosticism and the New Testament', *Gnosis* (H. Jonas Festschrift; ed. B. Aland; Göttingen: Vandenhoeck & Ruprecht, 1978), pp. 134-42. In these various studies Robinson has shown how in gnostic literature all of Jesus' pre-Easter teachings and activities were regarded as 'parabolic', i.e., enigmatic, and in need of interpretation.

65. J. Gnilka, *Die Verstockung Israels*, pp. 26-27, 198-205. See also idem, *Das Evangelium nach Markus* (EKKNT; Zürich: Benziger, 1978), I, pp. 162-72.

66. Kirkland, 'The Earliest Understanding of Jesus' Use of Parables', pp. 1-2.

67. Kirkland, 'The Earliest Understanding of Jesus' Use of Parables', pp. 20-21. In support of this view he cites (p. 15 n. 57) the example of Clement of Alexandria in *Stromateis* where it is claimed that Jesus taught in mysteries. I think, however, that Kirkland has not adequately taken into consideration the logion's relationship to the Marcan secrecy theme. On the whole, it seems much more likely that although Jesus may have appealed to the Old Testament obduracy tradition, it is Mark, rather than Jesus, who is responsible for the secrecy idea.

68. Taylor, *St. Mark*, p. 257.

69. Siegman, 'Teaching in Parables', pp. 161-63. J.A. Baird ('A Pragmatic Approach to Parable Exegesis: Some New Evidence on Mark 4.11, pp. 33-34', *JBL* 76 [1957], p. 206) concluded that 'the principle enunciated in Mark 4.11, 33-34 was indeed the practice of Jesus'.

70. E.P. Gould, *A Critical and Exegetical Commentary on the Gospel according St. Mark* (ICC; Edinburgh: T & T Clark, 1896), pp. 71-74; T.W. Manson, *The Teaching of Jesus*, pp. 74-81; N. Perrin, *The Kingdom of God in the Teaching of Jesus* (Philadelphia: Fortress, 1963), p. 132; Lane, *Mark*, pp. 156-57; Chilton, *A Galilean Rabbi*, p. 98; Beasley-Murray, *Jesus and the Kingdom*, pp. 106-107; Fitzmyer, *Luke I–IX*, p. 707.

71. Beasley-Murray (*Jesus and the Kingdom*, p. 105) states: '*All* that Jesus says and does in relation to the kingdom of God is an enigma to those whose eyes have not been opened to the significance of his mission' (emphasis his).

72. Bowker, 'Mystery and Parable', pp. 311-13. Bowker provides examples from rabbinic literature where the concept of 'mystery' is involved in the interpretation of scripture, and where rabbis use 'parables' in their dialogues with 'outsiders', that is, with Romans and *minim*. He points out that these various dialogues, like Mk 4.1-20, often begin with a parable, are followed by a question, and then are explained. The rabbinic sources used by Bowker are, of course, post-70 CE and, therefore, may not necessarily reflect practices of pre-70 Palestine.

73. One might invoke the criterion of dissimilarity in this case, for there is little in the gospels or in other Christian writings that depict Jesus as a fiery prophet. Fitzmyer (*Luke I-IX*, pp. 464, 473-74) believes that the tradition is early.

74. Fitzmyer (*The Gospel according to Luke X-XXIV* [AB 28A; Garden City: Doubleday, 1985], p. 994) believes that this saying likely reflects Jesus' thinking.

75. Taking a different view, Chilton (*A Galilean Rabbi*, p. 98) concludes: 'It would appear on reflection that Jesus rebuked his hearers for a dull-wittedness akin to that described in the Targum they used in their synagogues because he was frustrated by their response to his teaching, and wished to shame them into a more positive appreciation of his message'. If Mark's ἵνα is to be taken in the sense of result, as Chilton so understands (see discussion above), then his interpretation is as likely as any. However, Chilton's historical picture is still plausible even if the ἵνα is telic.

76. Eakin, 'Spirtual Obduracy and Parable Purpose', p. 101. Beasley-Murray (*Jesus and the Kingdom*, p. 106) states: 'Just as in Isaiah's day the hardening of the nation had been qualified by the creation of an obedient remnant, so in Jesus' day the blindness of the people was qualified by the calling of a remnant of believing disciples'. And again (p. 107): 'It is most plausibly conjectured that Jesus made the statement at the end of his Galilean ministry, when it had become apparent that the majority of the people had rejected his proclamation'. Likewise Fitzmyer (*Luke I-IX*, p. 707) comments that 'there is no genuine reason why Jesus himself could not have used the words of Isaiah to explain the lack of success that often attended his preaching'. See Jeremias, *Parables*, p. 18; Gnilka, *Die Verstockung*, pp. 204-205.

77. I am making use of Chilton's categories (see *A Galilean Rabbi*, p. 70).

78. C.A. Moore ('Mark 4.12: More Like the Irony of Micaiah than Isaiah', *A Light unto My Path* [J.M. Myers Festschrift; ed. H.N. Bream, R.D. Heim, and C.A. Moore; GTS 4; Philadelphia: Temple, 1974], pp. 335-44) has argued that Jesus intended his reference to Isa. 6.9-10 to be ironic and not judgmental, much in the same spirit as in the case when Micaiah warned King Ahab (1 Kgs 22.15). Mark, Moore avers, fails to perceive the irony, and

for this reason Matthew and Luke, who are dependent upon Mark, find it necessary to soften Mark's 'hardening theory' of parables. In response I should point out that the presence of irony (or sarcasm) does not rule out judgment. The judgmental nature of the message of the prophets is scarcely tempered by their frequent use of irony, hyperbole, metaphor, and other figures of speech. In any case, the appeal to Micaiah strikes me as farfetched.

B. Hollenbach ('Lest They Should Turn and Be Forgiven: Irony', *BT* 34 [1983], pp. 312-32) tries to show that neither Jesus nor Mark meant the saying in Mk 4.11-12 to be taken in any other sense than ironic. While we cannot know for certain with respect to Jesus (in which case what was said with regard to Moore obtains), it is clear that the evangelist Mark understands the logion as teaching that obduracy was the intention of the parables. As discussed above, such an understanding of the parables is only part of Mark's larger secrecy/predestination scheme. Hollenbach's study at many points rests upon naive and unfounded assumptions.

79. Much of the discussion seems to assume that Mark is either combatting or reinterpreting some sort of 'divine man' christology; see E. Schweizer, 'Towards a Christology of Mark?', *God's Christ and His People* (Nils Alstrup Dahl Festschrift; ed. J. Jervell and W.A. Meeks; Oslo: Universitetsforlaget, 1977), pp. 29-42.

Notes to Chapter 8

1. There are several variants in the manuscript tradition. The text cited above is read by ℵ B* C K L W X Δ Π, several miniscules, and versions. Miniscule 1365 has replaced the οὐ/οὐδέ negatives with the μή/μηδέ negatives, but retains the indicative mood. Δ Θ, various lectionaries, several Italian and Syrian versions, and a few fathers read ἵνα βλέποντες μὴ βλέπωσιν καὶ ἀκούοντες μὴ ἀκούωσιν καὶ μὴ συνιῶσιν μήποτε ἐπιστρέψωσιν. This variant appears to be influenced by Mark's version. Finally, two Italian and two Coptic versions read ἵνα βλέποντες μὴ βλέπωσιν καὶ ἀκούοντες μὴ ἀκούωσιν οὐδὲ συνιῶσιν. The appearance of ἵνα here would reflect the influence of either Mark or Luke or both.

2. D inserts Isa. 6.9a: Πορεύθητι καὶ εἰπὲ [LXX: εἰπὸν] τῷ λαῷ τούτῳ. Finally, Δ and several miniscules read ἰάσομαι.

3. C.E. Carlston (*The Parables of the Triple Tradition* [Philadelphia: Fortress, 1975], pp. 4-5) exaggerates when he claims that the Matthean Jesus does not answer the question of his disciples.

4. Carlston, *Triple Tradition*, pp. 4-5.

5. R.H. Gundry, *Matthew: A Commentary on His Literary and Theological Art* (Grand Rapids: Eerdmans, 1982), p. 255.

6. Carlston, *Triple Tradition*, p. 5. H. Conzelmann's view (*The Theology of St Luke* [New York: Harper & Row, 1961], p. 103) that the plural number suggests 'a timeless secrecy to which there corresponds an equally timeless disclosure of the mysteries thanks to gnosis' is unfounded.

7. Gundry, *Matthew*, p. 255.

8. Carlston, (*Triple Tradition*, p. 5, n. 3) thinks that Matthew's ἐκεῖνοι is scarcely softer than Mark's οἱ ἔξω. On the contrary, since the expression, 'outsiders', referred to unbelievers (or non-Israelites), often connoting a derogatory sense, its deletion by Matthew in all probability is an attempt to be less offensive. See W. Grundmann, *Das Evangelium nach Markus* (THKNT 2; Berlin: Evangelische Verlaganstalt, 1959), p. 92; M. Black, *An Aramaic Approach to the Gospels and Acts* (Oxford: Clarendon, 1967³), pp. 176-77.

9. See B. van Elderen, 'The Purpose of Parables according to Matthew 13.10-17', *New Dimensions in New Testament Study* (ed. R.N. Longenecker and M.C. Tenney; Grand Rapids: Zondervan, 1974), pp. 180-90, esp. pp. 185-86.

10. E. Schweizer (*The Good News according to Matthew* [Atlanta: John Knox, 1975], p. 299) states: 'The hardness of men's hearts is therefore not in accordance with God's purpose; on the contrary, Jesus speaks in parables because their hearts are already hardened'. Carlston (*Triple Tradition*, p. 7) states: 'The Markan "hardening theory" is softened almost into nonexistence'.

11. D. Hill, *The Gospel of Matthew* (NCB: London: Oliphants, 1972), p. 227.

12. Schweizer, *Matthew*, p. 299.

13. Note the emphatic 'you' at the beginning of v. 16.

14. The beatitude, especially as we have it preserved in Luke 10.24 ('many prophets and kings desired to see what you see'), may be based on Isa. 52.15: 'So shall he startle many nations; kings shall shut their mouths because of him; for that which has not been told them they shall see, and that which they have not heard they shall understand'.

15. Schweizer, *Matthew*, pp. 299-300; J. Gnilka, *Die Verstockung Israels: Isaias 6.9-10 in der Theologie der Synoptiker* (SANT 3; Munich: Kösel, 1961), pp. 94-102.

16. For more on the text of the quotation and its background see Gundry, *Matthew*, pp. 270-71; idem, *The Use of the Old Testament in St. Matthew's Gospel* (NovTSup 18; Leiden: Brill, 1967), pp. 118-19. R.N. Longenecker (*Biblical Exegesis in the Apostolic Period* [Grand Rapids: Eerdmans, 1975], p. 72) cites this quotation as an instance of pesher interpretation.

17. Gundry (*Matthew*, p. 227) explains that Matthew has omitted this part of Mark because of his deletion of the reference to the silence of the Pharisees. But the argument could just as easily be turned around: Matthew

deleted the reference to silence because he had elected to omit the reference to Jesus' anger.

18. Schweizer (*Matthew*, p. 321) correctly avers: 'Peter is being used once more to illustrate the meaning of discipleship'. See also Gundry, *Matthew*, pp. 298-300.

19. Jesus' language clearly echoes the language of the Old Testament obduracy texts (see discussion in Ch. 7 above).

20. See Gundry, *Matthew*, pp. 326-27.

Notes to Chapter 9

1. D and W read ἴδωσιν.

2. D. Wenham, 'The Synoptic Problem Revisited: Some New Suggestions about the Composition of Mark 4.1-34', *TynBul* 23 (1972), pp. 3-38.

3. See I.H. Marshall, 'Tradition and Theology in Luke (8.5-15)', *TynBul* 20 (1969), pp. 56-75, esp. p. 63.

4. So Marshall, *The Gospel of Luke: A Commentary on the Greek Text* (NIGTC; Grand Rapids: Eerdmans, 1978), p. 322; and J.A. Fitzmyer, *The Gospel according to Luke I–IX* (AB 28; Garden City: Doubleday, 1981), pp. 707-708. Contrary to H. Conzelmann (*The Theology of St. Luke* [New York: Harper & Row, 1961], p. 103), the words have nothing to do with gnosticism.

5. Some scholars have described Luke's portraits of the 'crowds' and other non-disciples as 'impressed unbelievers'; see J. Nolland, 'Impressed Unbelievers as Witnesses to Christ (Luke 4.22a)', *JBL* 98 (1979), pp. 219-29; C.H. Giblin, *The Destruction of Jerusalem according to Luke's Gospel* (AnBib 107; Rome: Pontifical Biblical Institute, 1985), pp. 26-28, 50-55.

6. J. Gnilka, *Die Verstockung Israels: Isaias 6.9-10 in der Theologie der Synoptiker* (SANT 3; Munich: Kösel, 1961), p. 124; W.C. Robinson, 'On Preaching the Word of God', *Studies in Luke–Acts* (ed. L.E. Keck and J.L. Martyn; New York: Abingdon, 1966), pp. 131-38.

7. So Fitzmyer, *Luke I–IV*, p. 708.

8. Recall the description of the man devoted to study in Sir. 39.1-5, parts of which read, 'he will preserve the discourse of notable men and penetrate the subtleties of parables [παραβολαί]; he will seek out the hidden meanings of proverbs and be at home with the obscurities of parables [παραβολαί]' (vv. 2-3). Note also the later words of the risen Lord: '"O foolish men, and slow of heart to believe all that the prophets have spoken. . ." And. . . he interpreted to them in all the scriptures the things concerning himself' (Lk. 24.26-27).

9. Fitzmyer (*Luke I–IX*, p. 709), who prefers the final sense for other reasons, also notes that Luke's omission of the μήποτε clause 'is an argument

in favor of the final interpretation of *hina*'.

10. C.E. Carlston (*The Parables of the Triple Tradition* [Philadelphia: Fortress, 1975], p. 57) states: '[Luke] either does not fully understand or does not share (or both) Mark's view that the *purpose* of Jesus' person and ministry is to harden men's hearts'.

11. Fitzmyer (*Luke I-IX*, p. 712) cites this interesting passage from 2 Esdras (=4 Ezra) 8.41-44: 'Just as a farmer sows many seeds upon the ground and plants a host of seedlings, yet not all that were sown will be saved nor all that were planted will take root, so too not all of those who have been sown in the world will be saved'.

12. Fitzmyer (*Luke I-IX*, p. 709) agrees, and states: '[Luke] adds a similar, less offensive, clause to the interpretation of the first group of hearers in the interpretation of the parable'.

13. Whereas in Luke's version Jesus says, 'those who hear the word of God and do it', Mark's version reads simply, 'whoever does the will of God'. The appearance of 'hear' in Luke draws this unit into closer harmony with what precedes.

14. At the very least, vv. 19-21 belong to the context of 8.4-21, in which Luke develops the theme of 'preaching and accepting the word of God' (see Fitzmyer, *Luke I-IX*, p. 699).

15. Δ Θ and a few other mss add the omitted Marcan material.

16. Fitzmyer (*Luke I-IX*, p. 192) has noted that Luke evidences a 'tendency to suppress the marks of human emotion, even vehemence, that are found in the Marcan gospel at times'.

17. See Fitzmyer, *Luke I-IX*, pp. 604-605.

18. Consider the following sample: (1) In Mark's version of the stilling of the storm (4.35-41), Jesus asks his disciples, 'Why are you afraid? Have you no faith?' (v. 40). In the Lucan version (8.22-25), however, Jesus asks his disciples, 'Where is your faith?' (v. 25a). The Lucan version implies no more than a momentary lapse. (2) In Mark's version of the healing of the woman with the hemorrhage (5.24b-34), the disciples respond to Jesus' question about being touched in a manner that borders derision, 'You see the crowd pressing around you, and yet you say, "Who touched me?"' (v. 31). In Luke, however, the disciples simply comment, 'Master, the multitudes surround you and press upon you!' (v. 45b). (3) Mark's account of Peter's rebuke (8.32-33) is omitted in Luke. (4) In Lk. 10.21-24 (Q material), Jesus blesses his disciples. (5) In Lk. 17.5 the disciples enjoin Jesus, 'Increase our faith!' (compare parallel material in Q and in Mark). (6) In Lk. 19.37-39 it is the disciples of Jesus who rejoice and cry out, 'Blessed is the king', while in Mk 11.9 it is simply 'those ahead' and 'those behind'. (7) In Lk. 22.3-4 we are told that Satan entered Judas to betray Jesus. Mark 14.10-11 says nothing of Satan's involvement. (8) Only in Luke does Jesus tell Simon Peter that he has prayed for him that his 'faith might not fail' (22.31-32). In Mk 14.27,

however, Jesus tells his disciples. 'You will all fall away'. (9) In Lk. 22.45 the
disciples sleep while Jesus prays because of 'sorrow', and not, as Mk 14.37-41
implies, for lack of concern. (10) Luke omits reference to the disciples' flight
after Jesus' arrest (compare Mk 14.50 and Lk. 22.54). (11) In the Lucan
account of the third denial, Peter does not curse (compare Mk 14.71 and Lk.
22.60).

19. Recent works that view Luke as anti-Semitic include R.R. Ruether,
Faith and Fratricide: The Theological Roots of anti-Semitism (New York:
Seabury, 1974), pp. 86-93; S. Sandmel *Anti-Semitism in the New Testament?*
[Philadelphia: Fortress, 1978], pp. 77-89; L. Gaston, 'Anti-Judaism and the
Passion in Luke and Acts', in *Anti-Judaism in Early Christianity* (ed.
P. Richardson; Waterloo: Wilfrid Laurier University, 1986), pp. 127-64.

Recent works that do not view Luke as anti-Semitic include J. Jervell,
Luke and the People of God: A New Look at Luke–Acts (Minneapolis:
Augsburg, 1972), E. Franklin, *Christ the Lord: A Study in the Purpose and
Purpose and Theology of Luke–Acts* (Philadelphia: Westminster, 1975); D.L.
Tiede, *Prophecy and History in Luke–Acts* (Philadelphia: Fortress, 1980),
Luke I-IX; idem, *Luke X-XXIV* (AB 28A; Garden City: Doubleday, 1985);
R.C. Tannehill, 'Israel in Luke–*Acts: A Tragic Story*', *JBL* 104 (1985),
pp. 69-85; J.B. Tyson, *The Death of Jesus in Luke–Acts* (Columbia:
University of South Carolina, 1986); and R.L. Brawley, *Luke–Acts and the
Jews: Conflict, Apology, and Conciliation* (SBLMS 33; Atlanta: Scholars,
1987).

20. J.T. Sanders, 'The Parable of the Pounds and Lucan Anti-Semitism',
TS 42 (1981), pp. 660-68; idem, 'The Salvation of the Jews in Luke–Acts', in
Luke–Acts: New Perspectives from the Society of Biblical Literature Seminar
(ed. C.H. Talbert; New York: Crossroad, 1984), pp. 104-28; idem, 'The
Prophetic Use of the Scriptures in Luke–Acts', in *Early Jewish and Christian
Exegesis* (W.H. Brownlee Festschrift; ed. C.A. Evans, and W.F. Stinespring;
Homage 10; Atlanta: Scholars, 1987), pp. 191-98; idem, *The Jews in Luke–
Acts* (Philadelphia: Fortress, 1987).

21. Sanders, *The Jews in Luke–Acts*: 'Luke's hostility toward Jews was not
exactly racial in the way in which we think of racial hatred today, but it was
something very close to it' (p. xvi); 'Luke thought that all Jews are perverse'
(p. 47); '[Luke believes that] the Jews are vile' (p. 237); '. . . his hatred of the
Jews. . .' (p. 310); 'I do not know what to call [Luke's] hostility if not
antisemitism' (p. xvii); 'In Luke's opinion, the world will be much better off
when "the Jews" get what they deserve and the world is rid of them'
(p. 317).

22. On one occasion Sanders ('The Salvation of the Jews in Luke–Acts',
p. 115) actually refers to Luke's 'final solution of the Jewish problem'.

23. Sanders (*The Jews in Luke–Acts*, pp. 227, 359-60, n. 159) accepts the
prayer of forgiveness as genuine; so also B.M. Metzger, *A Textual*

Commentary on the Greek New Testament (London and New York: United Bible Societies, 1971), p. 180; but see Fitzmyer, *Luke X–XXIV*, pp. 1503-504.

24. Luke regularly uses this word in reference to Christians (Lk. 22.32; Acts 1.15; 9.30; 10.23; etc.).

25. C.A. Evans, 'Is Luke's View of the Jewish Rejection of Jesus Anti-Semitic?' in *Reimaging the Death of the Lucan Jesus* (ed. D. Sylva; BBB; Bonn: Hanstein), pp. 29-56, 174-83. The role of the Jews in Luke–Acts has been assessed much more accurately in Brawley, *Luke–Acts and the Jews*.

26. Sanders, *The Jews in Luke–Acts*, pp. 298-99; idem, 'The Prophetic Use of the Scriptures in Luke–Acts', p. 198: 'Surely the Jews' rejection of and by God, as a people is here foretold'; idem, 'The Salvation of the Jews', pp. 111-12: 'There is no longer, after the time of Acts 28.28, any salvation for any Jews'. See the similar views of M. Dibelius, *Studies in the Acts of the Apostles* (London: SCM, 1956), pp. 149-50; E. Haenchen, *The Acts of The Apostles: A Commentary* (Philadelphia: Westminster, 1971), p. 724; idem, 'The Book of Acts as Source Material for the History of Early Christianity', in *Studies in Luke–Acts* (ed. L.E. Keck and J.L. Martyn; Philadelphia: Fortress, 1966), pp. 258-78, esp. p. 278; and H. Conzelmann, *Acts of the Apostles* (Hermeneia: Philadelphia: Fortress, 1987), p. 227.

27. Sanders (*The Jews in Luke–Acts*, p. 273) thinks that these people may not be converted at all, reminding the reader of his exegesis of Acts 13.43. Sanders is anxious to eliminate as many instances of Jewish conversion after the martyrdom of Stephen as possible. Acts 13.42-43, where the people beg to hear Paul again the next Sabbath and whom Paul urges to 'continue in the grace of God', therefore, is problematic for Sanders. Wishing to avoid the obvious import of the text, he argues that the Lucan Paul has rebuffed those interested in the gospel, perhaps because the apostle wanted to *prevent* their conversion (Sanders, *The Jews in Luke–Acts*, pp. 261-62, his emphasis). To support this suggestion he argues that the apostolic exhortation to 'abide in grace' means to 'remain fixed in their accustomed religious development', viz. their non-Christian faith (Sanders, *The Jews in Luke–Acts*, p. 261). However, the more natural interpretation is that these persons are to continue in the grace of the Christian gospel (cf. Acts 11.23), in which they now stand as a result of their positive response to Paul's preaching (so Haenchen, *Acts*, p. 507; C.S.C. Williams, *A Commentary on the Acts of the Apostles* [HNTC; New York: Harper, 1957], p. 166).

28. See J. Dupont, 'La conclusion des Actes et son rapport à l'ensemble de l'ouvrage de Luc', in *Les Actes des Apôtres* (BETL 48; ed. J. Kremer; Gembloux: Duculot, 1979), pp. 377-80; H.J. Hauser, *Strukturen der Abschlusserzählung der Apostelgeschichte* (AnBib 86; Rome: Pontifical Biblical Institute, 1979), pp. 108-109.

29. See Brawley, *Luke–Acts and the Jews*, pp. 76-77. What I think that

Luke believes is something like this: As long as Israel as a whole does not accept Jesus as her Messiah, the messianic kingdom will not be realized in its fullness. But the slowness of Israel to believe in the gospel does not frustrate God's plan; it only advances the Gentile mission. The Christian gospel, however, still remains 'the hope of Israel' (Acts 28.20; cf. 1.6).

30. 'Was it not necessary that the Christ should suffer. . .?' (Lk. 24.26-27, 44-47; cf. Acts 3.18; 8.32-34; 17.3; 26.23).

31. Acts 13.46-47 (quoting Isa. 49.6).

Notes to Chapter 10

1. L and other later manuscripts read ἰάσωμαι, which is an attempt to conform to the subjunctive mood.

2. 'God' is surely the understood subject, not 'Jesus' or 'Isaiah'.

3. The variant reading πεπώρωκεν (B³Δ) is due to the attempt of scribes to harmonize the tense with τετύφλωκεν, while the only other noteworthy variant, ἐπήρησεν (p⁶⁶,⁷⁵ ℵ K W), represents an attempt to find a more suitable verb; see B. Metzger, *A Textual Commentary on the Greek New Testament* (New York: UBS, 1971), p. 238.

4. C.K. Barrett, 'The Old Testament in the Fourth Gospel', *JTS* (1947), pp. 155-69, esp. p. 167, n. 2.

5. C.K. Barrett, *The Gospel according to St. John* (New York: Macmillan, 1955), p. 359, and second edn. (Philadelphia: Westminster, 1978), p. 431.

6. C. Goodwin, 'How Did John Treat His Sources?', *JBL* 73 (1954), pp. 61-75, esp. p. 71.

7. Goodwin, 'How Did John Treat His Sources?', p. 71.

8. E.C. Hoskyns, *The Fourth Gospel* (ed. F.N. Davey; London: Faber, 1961²), p. 428.

9. C.C. Torrey, *The Four Gospels: A New Translation* (New York: Harpers, 1933), p. 280.

10. C.F. Burney, *The Aramaic Origin of the Fourth Gospel* (Oxford: Clarendon, 1922), pp. 120-21.

11. E.D. Freed, *Old Testament Quotations in the Gospel of John* (NovTSup 11; Leiden: Brill, 1965), pp. 85, 87.

12. R. Schnackenburg, *The Gospel according to St John 2* (New York: Seabury, 1980), p. 416.

13. J. O'Rourke, 'John's Fulfilment Texts', *ScEccl* 19 (1967), pp. 435-36. He concedes, however, that John probably had the wording of the LXX in mind when he wrote.

14. R. Bultmann, (*The Gospel of John* [Philadelphia: Westminster, 1971] p. 453, n. 2) states: 'Whether the evangelist has taken his text from a translation that lay before him, or whether he made it himself, can hardly be

determined'. There is at least one strong contextual indication that the fourth evangelist was familiar with targumic tradition, if not the Targum itself. After the citation of Isa. 6.10 the evangelist in 12.41 comments: 'These things spoke Isaiah, because he saw his glory'. This reading is significant in the light of the readings found in the various versions of the Old Testament. The Hebrew of Isa. 6.1 reads: 'I saw the Lord'; the LXX: 'I saw the Lord'; but the Targum: 'I saw the glory of the Lord'. It is quite probable that John 12.41 reflects this targumic tradition. See Barrett, 'The Old Testament in the Fourth Gospel', p. 167.

15. It is worth noting that Tertullian cites the texts of Isa. 6.9-10 and 29.13-14 side by side on more than one occasion (cf. *Against Marcion* 3.6.5; 5.19.2).

16. E.g., Barrett, 'The Old Testament in the Fourth Gospel', p. 167; C.H. Dodd, *According to the Scriptures* (London: Nisbet, 1952), p. 39; B. Lindars, *New Testament Apologetic* (Philadelphia: Westminster, 1961), pp. 159-60. R.N. Longenecker (*Biblical Exegesis in the Apostolic Period* [Grand Rapids]: Eerdmans, 1975], p. 156) cites this quotation as an instance of 'pesher quotation'.

17. R.E. Brown, *The Gospel according to John I-XII* (AB 29; Garden City: Doubleday, 1966), p. 377.

18. S. Lieberman, *Hellenism in Jewish Palestine* (TSJTSA 18; New York: JTSA, 1962), pp. 57-62; Freed, *Old Testament in the Gospel of John*; G.J. Brooke (*Exegesis at Qumran: 4QFlorilegium in its Jewish Context* [JSOTSup 29; Sheffield: JSOT, 1985], pp. 166, 279, 294, 297-298, 306-308) has found the method practiced at Qumran.

19. Or 'when'.

20. It is likely that targumic tradition is here presupposed, for the Targum to Isa. 6.1 reads: 'I saw the glory of the Lord', while 6. 5 reads: 'my eyes have seen the glory of the shekinah of the King of Ages'.

21. Both the Lord and the Servant are described as רום ונשא (6.1; 52.13). In LXX Isa. 6.1 the Lord is ὑψηλός and full of δόξα, while in 52.13 the Servant will be ὑψοῦν and δοξάζειν.

22. Brown, *John I-XII*, pp. 486-87.

23. Perhaps in the same sense that Abraham saw Jesus' day (8.56). According to Sir. 48.24-25 Isaiah foresaw the last days. See Brown, *John I-XII*, p. 487.

24. For more on this see my study, 'Obduracy and the Lord's Servant: Some Observations on the Use of the Old Testament in the Fourth Gospel', *Early Jewish and Christian Exegesis: Studies in Memory of William Hugh Brownlee* (ed. C.A. Evans and W.F. Stinespring; Homage Series; Atlanta: Scholars, 1987), pp. 221-36.

25. For a full discussion of this theme see H. Leroy, *Rätsel und Missverständnis* (BBB 30; Bonn: Hanstein, 1968).

26. If καταλαμβάνειν in 1.5 means 'understand', then we have one more thematic announcement of misunderstanding of obduracy.

27. See Schnackenburg's excursus (*St John 2*, pp. 270-71) on the relationship of chs. 9 and 12.

28. See the recent study of D.M. Smith, 'The Setting and Shape of a Johannine Narrative Source', *JBL* 95 (1976), pp. 231-41.

29. What portion, if any, of this unit was part of a written source need not detain us here. For our purposes it is enough to assume that the material in its present form says essentially what the evangelist wishes to say.

30. The evangelist's use of the Old Testament would suggest that in Jesus' rejection and suffering scripture attains its highest level of fulfilment; see my study, 'On the Quotation Formulas in the Fourth Gospel', *BZ* 26 (1982), pp. 79-83.

31. See G.C. Nicholson, *Death as Departure: The Johannine Descent-Ascent Schema* (SBLDS 63; Chico: Scholars, 1983).

32. Smith, 'Johannine Narrative Source', pp. 236-38. Smith's thesis presupposes the earlier work of J.L. Martyn, *History and Theology in the Fourth Gospel* (New York: Harper & Row, 1968).

33. W.A. Meeks, *The Prophet-King* (NovTSup 14; Leiden: Brill, 1967).

Notes to Chapter 11

1. Portions of this chapter are taken from my study, 'Isaiah 6.9-10 in Rabbinic and Patristic Writings', *VC* 36 (1982), pp. 275-81.

2. G. Vermes, *Scripture and Tradition in Judaism* (SPB 4; Leiden: Brill, 1973²).

3. Vermes, *Scripture and Tradition*, pp. 7-10, 228-29. See also S. Sandmel, 'The Haggada within Scripture', *JBL* 80 (1961), pp. 105-22; B.S. Childs, 'Midrash and the Old Testament', in *Understanding the Sacred Text* (ed. J. Reumann; Valley Forge: Judson, 1972), pp. 48-59; M. Fishbane, 'Revelation and Tradition: Aspects of Inner-Biblical Exegesis', *JBL* 99 (1980), pp. 343-61.

4. Cf. *De Posteritate Caini* 121; *De Congressu eruditionis Causa* 160.

5. The quotation is from F.H. Colson and G.H. Whitaker (LCL 1.269).

6. His subsequent comments may bear some relationship to what Paul says about the mind in Romans 7. It must be borne in mind that there were similar non-biblical proverbial sayings with which Philo may very well have been familiar, e.g., Demosthenes, *Contra Aristogenes* 1: '... so that the proverb results, "Seeing they do not see, hearing they do not hear"'.

7. *Baḥodesh* 1 (on Exod. 19.2); for text and translation see J.Z. Lauterbach, *Mekilta de-Rabbi Ishmael* (3 vols.; Philadelphia: Jewish

Publication Society, 1933), II, pp. 196-98. *Mekilta* is the tannaitic commentary on portions of Exodus.

8. On Rephidim see Exod. 17.1-7; on Sinai see Exod. 32.1-14.

9. Lauterbach's translation at this point is misleading: '"Make the heart of these people fat', etc. (Isa. 6.10) 'lest they. . . return and. . . "' (*Mekilta* II, p. 198). The conjunction is not in *Mekilta's* citation, and its presence should not be assumed.

10. Translation from I. Epstein, ed., *The Babylonian Talmud* (London: Soncino, 1936) XIII, pp. 68-69.

11. And therefore, Jonathan's citation would be better translated: 'Make the heart of this people fat. . . unless they see with their eyes and hear with their ears. . . '

12. Translation from Epstein, *Babylonian Talmud*, XIV, p. 106. Again, the citation probably should be translated: 'Unless they, understanding with their heart, return and be healed'.

13. Translation from Epstine, *Babylonian Talmud*, XIV, p. 106.

14. Translation from W.G. Braude and I.J. Kapstein, *Tanna Debe Eliyyahu* (Philadelphia: Jewish Publication Society, 1981), pp. 221-22. There is no consensus in the dating of this rabbinic work. Some scholars have argued for a third-century date (and even accept the legend that it derives from Elijah the Tishbite who had reappeared in the guise of a rabbinic teacher), while others assign it to the ninth century. See the survey of scholarly debate in Braude and Kapstein, pp. 3-12.

15. Translation from Braude and Kapstein, *Tanna Debe Eliyyahu*, p. 222.

16. J. Jeremias, *The Parables of Jesus* (New York: Scribner's, 1963), p. 17, n. 26. See also the summarizing comments in St-B, I, p. 663.

17. H. Malter (*Saadia Gaon: His Life and Works* [New York: Hermon, 1926], pp. 141-42) defends the view that Saadia's translation is the earliest Arabic version of the Jewish Bible (i.e., the MT).

18. J. Derenbourg and H. Derenbourg (*Version Arabe d'Isaïe de R. Saadia ben Iosef al-Fayyoûmi* [Paris: Libraire de la Société Asiatique, 1896], p. 11) translate Saadia's Arabic text: 'Entendez ce que vous ne comprendez pas, regardez ce que vous ne connaîtrez pas'. Unfortunately, Saadia offers no commentary on this passage (as he usually does).

19. The following quotations of Rashi and Radak are taken from the traditional text: גדולות מקראות (New York: Pardes, 1951).

20. A. Cohen, 'השע, הכבד, השמן', *BM* 50/3 (1972), pp. 360-61. See discussion above in Ch. 1.

21. The verses from Deuteronomy are cited in reverse order.

22. Epstein, *Babylonian Talmud*, XIII, p. 22.

23. That is, who will grant Israel a heart of faith, in keeping with their promise in Deut. 5.24(27) to hear and obey God's commandments.

24. *Deut. Rab.* 7.10 (on 29.3[4]).

25. *Pesiq. R.* 41.4.

26. The inclination to evil will not finally be rooted out until the Day of salvation; cf. *Yal.* 2.981.

27. *Deut. Rab.* 7.10 (on 29.3[4]).

28. *Lev. Rab.* 27.8 (on 22.27).

29. *Pirqe R. El.* 45 (63B.1); translation from G. Friedlander, *Pirke De Rabbi Eliezer* (New York: Sepher-Hermon, 1981⁴), p. 354.

30. *Gen. Rab.* 17.5 (on 2.21).

31. *Pesiq. R.* 33.13. Translation based in part on W.G. Braude, *Pesikta Rabbati* (Yale Judaica Series 18; 2 vols.; New Haven and London: Yale University, 1968), 2.659. In the similar passage in *Lam. Rab.* 1.22 § 57, 1 Sam. 3.11 is cited to typify punishment against the ear, while Isa. 30.21 is cited as the passage of comfort.

32. *Pesiq. R.* 8.3.

33. *Gen. Rab.* 84.18 (on 37.28). Translation from H. Freedman, *Midrash Rabbah* (10 vols.; New York and London: Soncino, 1983), II, p. 783.

34. *Qoh. Rab.* 1.16 §1 (on 1.16).

35. *Lam. Rab.* 1.22 §57.

36. Isa. 6.9-10, as will be seen in the following chapter, was appealed to frequently by the fathers of the church.

Notes to Chapter 12

1. Portions of this chapter are taken from my studies, 'Isaiah 6.9-10 in Rabbinic and Patristic Writings', *VC* 36 (1982), pp. 275-81, and 'Jerome's Translation of Isaiah 6.9-10', *VC* 38 (1984), pp. 202-204.

2. ἀκοῇ ἀκούσετε καὶ οὐ μὴ συνῆτε, καὶ βλέποντες βλέψετε καὶ οὐ μὴ ἴδητε. ἐπαχύνθη γὰρ ἡ καρδία τοῦ λαοῦ τούτου, καὶ τὰ ἑξῆς.

3. ἀκοῇ ἀκούσετε καὶ οὐ μὴ συνῆτε, καὶ τὰ ἑξῆς.

4. ἐὰν μὴ πιστεύσητε, οὐ μὴ συνῆτε. See also *Commentary on John: Fragments* 92 (on John 12.39-40); *Commentary on Matthew: Fragments* 286 (on Mt. 13.13-15).

5. *Refutation of All Heresies* 5.3.3 (or 5.8.3, according to M. Marcovich, *Hippolytus Refutatio Omnium Haeresium* [PTS 25; Berlin and New York: de Gruyter, 1986], p. 155).

6. ἔτι γὰρ τὰ ὦτα ὑμῶν πέφρακται, οἱ ὀφθαλμοὶ ὑμῶν πεπήρωνται, καὶ πεπάχυται ἡ καρδία.

7. τὰ δὲ ὦτα ὑμῶν πέφρακται καὶ αἱ καρδίαι πεπώρωνται.

8. *Oration concerning Simeon and Anna* 10: ἀκοῇ... ἀκούσητε καὶ οὐ μὴ συνῆτε, καὶ βλέποντες βλέψητε καὶ οὐ μὴ ἴδητε. *Oration on the Psalms* 4: ἀκούοντες οὐκ ἀκούετε, καὶ βλέπότες οὐ βλέπετε.

9. *Against Heresies* 4.29.1: πάχυνον τὴν καρδίαν τοῦ λαοῦ τούτου καὶ τὰ

ὦτα αὐτῶν βάρυνον καὶ τοὺς ὀφθαλμοὺς αὐτῶν τύφλωσον.

10. E. Würthwein, *The Text of the Old Testament* (Grand Rapids: Eerdmans, 1979), p. 87.

11. Würthwein, *The Text of the Old Testament*, p. 87.

12. Würthwein, *The Text of the Old Testament*, p. 87.

13. Cf. 3.6.5; 5.19.2. In 4.19.2. we find the first line of the Lord's word to the prophet in v. 9, *aure. . . audietis*, while in 5.11.9 we have both lines of v. 9, in which the quotation is identical, except for the omission of the *et* preceding *oculis*. Cyprian's text (cf. *Testimonies to Quirinus* 1.3) is as follows: *aure audietis et non intellegetis et videntes videbitis et non videbitis. Incrassavit enim cor populi huius, et auribus graviter audierunt et oculos suos concluserunt, ne forte videant oculis et auribus audiant et corde intellegant et revertantur, et curem illos.* Its relationship to Tertullian's quotation and to the Greek versions will be discussed as we proceed. Part of v. 10 is quoted in Augustine, *Expositions in the Psalms* 138.8 (on Ps. 139.6): *incrassa cor populi huius, et oculos eius grava.* Portions of both verses are quoted in Caesarius of Arles: *auditu audietis, et non intellegetis; et videntes videbitis, et non videbitis (Sermons* 212.3); *incrassatum est enim cor populi huius (Sermons* 102.3). A quotation appears in Ps.-Cyprian (*On the Praise of the Martyrs* 5) as well: *oculos habent et non vident, aures habent et non audiunt. gravatum est cor insipiens eorum, ne quando convertantur et salvem illos.* The first part of the quotation has in all likelihood been influenced by Ps. 115.5b-6a: *oculos habent et non videbunt, aures habent et non audient.*

14. A. Cohen, 'השע, הכבר, ושמן', *BM* 50/3 (1972), pp. 360-61, 379. For a critical assessment of Cohen's proposal see the discussion in Ch. 1 above.

15. Cyprian adds *suos* with *oculos*, thus attesting the textual uncertainty of the corresponding αὐτῶν of the LXX.

16. See Jerome's letter (*Epistles* 18) to Pope Damascus I (381 CE), where he defends the priority of the Hebrew over the Greek.

17. Jerome's translation in *Commentary on Isaiah* 3 (on Isa. 6.9-10) differs slightly:

> 9 *Et dixit: Vade, et dices populo huic:*
>   *Auditu audite et nolite intellegere,*
>   *et videte visu et nolite cognoscere.*
> 10 *Excaeca cor populi huis,*
>   *et aures eius aggrava.*
>   *et oculos eius claude,*
>   *ne forte videat oculis suis,*
>   *et auribus audiat,*
>   *et corde intellegat,*
>   *et convertatur, et sanetur.*

18. See Ch. 10 and Evans, "Jerome's Translation of Isaiah 6.9-10', p. 203. It is probable that Jerome does have in mind John 12.41, since in *Epistles* 18

(to Pope Damascus I) he explicitly states his belief that Isaiah, at the time of his heavenly vision, saw Christ. Other aspects of his translation of Isaiah 6 may also reflect gospel traditions, see A.F.J. Klijn, 'Jérome, Isaîe 6 et l'Évangile des Nazoréens', *VC* 40 (1986), pp. 245-50.

19. Vulgate: *ceteri vero excaecati sunt*. 'To blind' is a legitimate translation of πωροῦν (see LSJ).

20. Origen, *Commentary on Romans* 8.8 (on Rom. 11.7); this portion of Origen's commentary is no longer extant in the Greek; Augustine, *Tractates on John* 53.5 (on John 12.40), where Rom. 11.7 is cited. The same variant appears in Calvin's *Commentary on Romans*.

21. See also Augustine, *On the Trinity* 2.17.31: *incrassa cor populi huius, et aures eorum oppila, et oculos eorum grava* ('Make the heart of this people fat, and make their ears heavy, and shut their eyes'): and Irenaeus, *Against Heresies* 4.29.1: πάχυνον τὴν καρδίαν τοῦ λαοῦ τούτου καὶ τὰ ὦτα αὐτῶν βάρυνον καὶ τοὺς ὀφθαλμοὺς αὐτῶν τύφλωσον ('Make the heart of this people fat, and make their ears heavy, and blind their eyes').

22. The LXX appears to lie behind the Vulgate's omission of the injunction to 'blind yourselves and be blind' in Isa. 29.9, and the use of the future tense instead of the past in 29.10. The passive of Isa. 44.18 (*lutati enim sunt. . . oculi eorum*) probably reflects the LXX (ὅτι ἀπημαυρώθησαν τοῦ βλέπειν τοῖς ὀφθαλμοῖς αὐτῶν). However, whereas Isa. 42.20 in the Vulgate is interrogative (*nonne*), both the MT and the LXX are declarative.

23. *Herm Vis.* 3.7.6: σώζονται διὰ τὴν σκληροκαρδίαν αὐτῶν. Translations are from the LCL.

24. *1 Clem.* 51.3: σκληρῦναι τὴν καρδίαν αὐτοῦ.

25. *1 Clem.* 3.1: ἔφαγεν καὶ ἔπιεν, καὶ ἐπλατύνθη, καὶ ἐπαχύνθη, καὶ ἀπελάκτισεν ὁ ἠγαπημένος.

26. *1 Clem.* 53.3, the quotation is from Deut. 9.13-14: ἑώρακα τόν λαὸν τοῦτον, καὶ ἰδού ἐστιν σκληροτράχηλος.

27. *Herm. Man.* 5.2.6: σκληρότητος.

28. *Barn.* 9.5.

29. *Herm. Man.* 12.3.4, 5; 4.4; 5.1; *Sim.* 6.2.5; 9.8.6; *Vis.* 1.4.2. Compare use of σκληρός to its usage in John 6.60.

30. *Herm. Man.* 4.2.1: ἡ καρδία μου πεπώρωται ἀπὸ τῶν προτέρον μου πράξεων.

31. *Herm. Man.* 12.4.4: οἱ δὲ ἐπὶ τοῖς χείλεσιν ἔχοντες τὸν κύριον, τὴν δὲ καρδίαν αὐτῶν πεπωρωμένην καὶ μακρὰν ὄντες ἀπὸ τοῦ κυρίου. The passage perhaps alludes to Isa. 6.10 and 29.13.

32. The translation is from J.J. Collins, 'The Sibylline Oracles', in *The Old Testament Pseudepigrapha: Volume I: Apocalyptic Literatures & Testaments* (ed. J.H. Charlesworth: Garden City: Doubleday, 1983), p. 343. Collins (pp. 331-332) dates the Christian passage between 70 and 150 CE.

33. *Dialogue with Trypho* 12.2 (cf. 33.1). The translations are in part based

on A. Roberts and J. Donaldson, eds., *The Ante-Nicene Fathers* (rev. A.C. Coxe; Grand Rapids: Eerdmans, 1950).

34. *Against Heresies* 4.29.1. Irenaeus' quotation further attests the hiphil vocalization of the MT. Moreover, he retains Mark's ἵνα. Irenaeus is content to retain the telic understanding of the passage.

35. *Against Marcion* 3.6.6.

36. *Against Marcion* 3.6.7.

37. *Against Marcion* 4.19.2-3. In *Concerning the Soul* 9.8 Tertullian explains that the soul 'has eyes and ears of its own' by which it is able to perceive spiritual things. For more on Tertullian's understanding of the purpose of parables see *On the Resurrection of the Dead* 33.2.

38. *Against Marcion* 4.31.4. Tertullian goes on to cite several judgmental passages from Jeremiah.

39. *On Modesty* 8.5.

40. *Against Marcion* 5.11.9.

41. *Apology* 21.16-17.

42. *Apology* 21.22.

43. It should be noted that in at least one place Tertullian applies Isa. 6.9-10 to non-Christian gentiles. *To the Nations* 2.1.3 reads: 'Your eyes are open, yet they see not; your ears are unstopped, yet they hear not; though your heart beats, it is yet dull, nor does your mind understand that of which it is cognizant'.

44. *Against Celsus* 2.8. The text of the LXX is followed. See also his commentary on Isaiah 6 in *Homilies on Isaiah* 6.1, 3, 9.

45. *De Principiis* 1.7; 16.1ff.

46. *Homilies on Jeremiah* 14.12 (on Jer. 15.10-19). Origen goes on to cite Isa. 3.1-3. See also 20.2 (on Jer. 20.7-12); *Homilies on Isaiah* 6.1, 3, 9 (on Isa. 6.1-13); *Commentary on Romans* 8.8.

47. *Testimonies to Quirinus* 1.3.

48. *Oration on the Psalms* 4. See also *Oration concerning Simeon and Anna* 11.

49. *Instructions* 1.38.

50. *Song of the Two Peoples* 395-402.

51. In *Didascalia Apostolorum* ('Teaching of the Apostles') 6.16 we are told that the Lord hardened the Jews' heart, as he did Pharaoh's. Isa. 6.9-10 is then quoted, followed by a paraphrase of Mt. 13.15-16. See the related passage in *Apostolic Constitutions* 5.16.4: 'Moreover, that through their exceedingly great wickedness, they would not believe in him, the scripture says: "Lord, who has believed our report? And to whom has the arm of the Lord been revealed?" [Isa. 53.1] And afterwards: "Hearing you shall hear, and shall not understand; and seeing you shall see, and shall not perceive; for the heart of this people has become fat"'. This sequence of Isaianic texts probably reflects John 12.38-40.

52. *Interpretation of the Psalms* 57 (on Ps. 58.4-5).

53. *Commentary on Isaiah* 42 (on Isa. 6.9-10).

54. 7.1. He quotes John 12.37-41. He believes that the Jews simply could not understand Christ; see *Demonstration* 2.3; 8.2; 10.16.

55. *Festal Letters* 2.3. Athanasius does not specifically mention the Jews in 2.3, but he does later in 2.6.

56. *On the Christian Faith* 2.15.130. Ambrose says that the Arians are like the Jews, who stop their ears so as not to hear the truth.

57. *Homilies on Isaiah* 2.5.

58. *Commentary on Isaiah* 3 (on Isa. 6.9-10).

59. *Commentary on Ezekiel* 3 (on Ezek. 12.1-2).

60. *Homilies on Matthew* 45.1 (on Matt. 13.10-11). In *Homilies on John* 68 (on John 12.34-41) Chrysostom argues that the evangelist has cited Isa. 53.1 and 6.10 not because the prophetic word caused blindness but because it foretold it. Jewish obduracy, Chrysostom believed, was in part demonic: 'Do you see that demons dwell in their souls?' (*Against the Jews* 1.6; see also 2.3).

61. *Homilies on Matthew* 45.2 (on Mt. 13.13-15). In *Homilies on Acts* 55 (on Acts 28.17-20), Chrysostom interprets the phrase, 'this people', to refer only to unbelievers (not to all of Israel).

62. *Conferences* 13.12.

63. *On the Gift of Perseverence* 35 (on predestination). Translations are in part based on P. Schaff, *Nicene and Post-Nicene Fathers of the Christian Church* (Grand Rapids: Eerdmans, 1956).

64. *Tractates on John* 53.4 (on John 12.38).

65. *Tractates on John* 53.5-6 (on John 12.39-40); quote from 53.6.

66. *On the Trinity* 2.16.26-17.32. God's 'passing' (*transitus*) recalls the Passover and anticipates Jesus' 'passing', via the resurrection, back to his heavenly father (citing John 13.1). The rock, behind which Moses stood, foreshadowed the rock upon which the church would be built.

67. *On the Trinity* 2.17.30-31. Moses is understood as a figure for the Jewish people.

68. *On the Trinity* 2.17.30; cf. *Expositions in the Psalms* 138.8 (on Ps. 139.6) where a similar exegesis is provided. In *Sermons* 212.3-4 Caesarius of Arles develops a similar exegesis, citing Exod. 33.14 and John 12.39-41. As in the case of Augustine's discussion, Caesarius' sermon 212 is on the trinity.

69. *Reply to Faustus* 13.11.

70. *True Religion* 5.9.

71. *Expositions on the Psalms* 17.46 (on Ps. 18.44-45). According to Cassiodorus, the Gentiles have seen and heard (citing Isa. 52.15), but the Jews are obdurate and 'sons of the devil' (citing John 8.44).

72. *Sermons* 102.3. Translation from M.M. Mueller, *Saint Caesarius of*

Arles, Sermons 81-186 (FC; Washington: Catholic University of America, 1964), p. 105. The quotation of Isa. 6.10 reads: *incrassatum est enim cor populi huius*. Sermon 102 is on the manna and the bitter water stories of Exodus 15-16.

73. In *On Fasting* 6.4 Tertullian warns the Christian that food, drink, and wealth can bring about the 'fats' that obstruct and corrupt spiritual life. Through these corrupting agents, which make the heart 'fat', the text of Isa. 6.9-10 was fulfilled with respect to the Christian. In *Refutation of All Heresies* 5.3.3 (5.8.3, Marcovich) Hippolytus (*c.* 170–*c.* 236) cites Isa. 6.9-10 in the context of explaining gnostic teaching. His reference in *Refutation* 5.12.9 (5.17.9, Marcovich) to 'those who close the eyelids' may be an allusion to Isa. 6.9-10. In *Divine Institutes* 5.1 Lactantius (*c.* 240–*c.* 320) says that those who refuse to be persuaded by the truth 'will not hear, and they cover their eyes, lest they behold the light'. In his discussion of the nature of the soul, Cyril of Jerusalem (*c.* 315-386) argues for free will. He says that before coming into the world, the soul had committed no sin (*Catechesis* 4.19). Once in the world, it has the free choice, either to sin or to be obedient. Since what is to be known of God is plainly seen (citing Rom. 1.29), the disobedient can only be understood as having 'closed their eyes' (citing part of Isa. 6.10). In *Orations* 2.94 Gregory of Nazianzus (329-389) alludes to Isa. 6.9-10, when he describes God as having opened his (Gregory's) ear to hear without heaviness. In *Confessions* 6.6.9 Augustine says that God irritates the wounded soul, so that it might 'be converted and healed'. In *Apostolic Constitutions* 3.6.5 Isa. 6.9-10 is used for an 'in-house' criticism of gossipy widows (cf. *Didascalia Apostolorum* 3.6). Cassian (*Conferences* 14.18) quotes Isa. 6.10 to explain why it is that teaching spiritual things is sometimes ineffectual, while Cassiodorus, commenting on Ps. 51.17 (*Expositions on the Psalms* 50.19), says that a hardened heart will not easily be made contrite. In the Syriac *Acts of Judas Thomas*, a talking ass, having been commissioned by the apostle Judas Thomas, says to the demons: 'To you I speak, ye enemies of mankind; to you I speak, who close your eyes to the light that ye may not see, for the nature of evil cannot be with good' (from W. Wright, *Apocryphal Acts of the Apostles* [vol. 2; London and Edinburgh: Williams and Norgate, 1871], p. 211). Finally, Ps.-Cyprian (*On the Praise of the Martyrs* 5) applies Isa. 6.9-10 (with v. 9 influenced by Ps. 115.5b-6a) to those who reject the truth of the gospel, taking pleasure, instead, in empty and worthless talk.

Isa. 6.9-10 and related obduracy passages are probably what lie behind Sura 5.71 of the Qur'an: '. . . so they [the Jews] became blind and deaf. Then Allah turned to them mercifully, but many of them became blind and deaf'.

74. Aquinas views obduracy as a divine penalty, and he cites Isa. 6.10 as scriptural evidence (*Summa Theologica* 2-2.15.2-3). However, he is careful to defend God from the charge of causing obduracy (1-2.79.3). Human malice

is the cause of spiritual blindness (he cites Sir. 2.21 and 2 Cor. 4.4). Nevertheless, because of Isa. 6.10 and Rom. 9.18, God must be viewed as involved in some way. He concludes: 'God withholds the light of grace from those in whom he finds an obstacle. In this case grace is absent not only because man has set an obstacle in its way but because God of his own accord has set it before man. In this sense God can be said to darken the mind, dull the hearing and harden the heart'; translation from J. Fearon, ed., *Summa Theologica* (vol. 24; New York: McGraw-Hill, 1969), p. 213. Throughout his discussion, Aquinas interacts with Augustine.

This solution finds expression in the reformers as well. In commenting on Isa. 6.9-10, Luther says nothing about predestination (*Lectures on Isaiah*). He thinks that the text teaches that God forsakes the obdurate. As for the Jews, they were unable to appreciate Christ's emphasis on internal (as opposed to external) righteousness. For this reason they turned a deaf ear to his teaching. To them, says Luther, apply the wise words of Solomon: 'A fool does not receive the words of prudence, unless you say those things which are in his heart' (Prov. 18.2). On Isa. 29.9 Luther says that the prophet 'speaks about that most wretched blindness of the Jews, who could not read in spite of open books, whose blindness far surpassed the dreams of the Gentiles'. These words [i.e., 'Blind yourselves and be blind'] of the prophet are fitting attributes of all apostates and hardened, ungodly people'. On Deut. 29.4 Luther says that if the Jews are obedient, God will give them 'an understanding heart, a hearing ear, and a seeing eye' (*Lectures on Deuteronomy* [on 29.1]). Translations are in part based on J. Pelikan, ed., *Luther's Works* (vols. 3–30; Saint Louis: Concordia, 1961-67).

Calvin is much more concerned with the question of predestination. He believes that the words of Isa. 6.9-10 were fulfilled in the Jewish rejection of Christ and the continuing Jewish rejection of the Christian religion. He believes that the Jews wilfully refused to hear and see and that therefore God hardened them because of this rebellion (*Commentary on Isaiah*). He also applies Isa. 29.9-10 to the Jews. They are obdurate to the message of Christ, for a veil lies over their hearts (he cites Exod. 34.10; 2 Cor. 3.16). He then cites Isa. 6.9-10 as proof that God on occasion removes the mental capacity for understanding the truth. In commenting on John 12.38 Calvin says that Isaiah's prediction of unbelief (i.e., Isa. 53.1) did not cause the Jews not to believe (*Commentary on John*). The prophet only testified to what God told him was to happen. As to Isa. 6.10 (cited in John 12.40), Calvin explains that God 'will strike the ungodly with stupidity and dizziness that he may take vengeance on their malice'; and that 'it was impossible for them to escape this punishment. For God had once determined to give them over to a reprobate mind and to change the light of his word into darkness for them' (from John Calvin, *John 11–21* [trans. T.H.L. Parker; Edinburgh & London: Oliver & Boyd, 1961], p. 46). See also his commentary on Rom. 11.7, 'the rest were blinded': 'As the elect alone are freed from destruction by the grace of God, so all, who are not elected, must necessarily remain in blindness' (from John Calvin, *Romans* [tr. F. Sibson; Philadelphia: Whetham, 1836], p. 271). For more on Calvin's exegesis and the exegesis of his time see D.C. Steinmetz, 'John Calvin on Isaiah 6: A Problem in the History of Exegesis', *Int* 36 (1982), pp. 156-70.

75. Quotations are from J.M. Robinson, ed., *The Nag Hammadi Library* (New York: Harper & Row, 1977).

76. *2 Apoc. Jas.* (NHL V, *4*) 51.15-19.

77. M. Krause and P. Labib (*Gnostische und hermetische Schriften aus Codex II und Codex VI* [Gluckstadt: Augustin, 1971], p. 146) think that Isa. 6.9-10 is alluded to.

Notes to Conclusion

1. What ultimately unites the Bible is not monotheism (as acknowledged by J.A. Sanders, *Canon and Community* [Philadelphia: Fortress, 1984] p. 43), or covenant, or salvation history, but, in the words of R. Knierim who speaks in reference to the Old Testament, it is the concern for the *'universal dominion of Yahweh in justice and righteousness'* (R. Knierim, 'The Task of Old Testament Theology', *HBT* 6 [1984] pp. 25-57, quote from p. 43 [emphasis his]).

BIBLIOGRAPHY

Aageson, J.W., 'Scripture and Structure in the Development of the Argument in Romans 9-11', *CBQ* 48 (1986), pp. 265-89.

Ackroyd, P.R., 'Isaiah I-XII: Presentation of a Prophet', *VTSup* 29 (1978), pp. 16-48.

Ahlström, G.W., 'Isaiah VI. 13', *JSS* 19 (1974), pp. 169-72.

Ambrozic. A.M., 'Mark's Concept of the Parable', *CBQ* 29 (1967), pp. 220-27.

Anderson, H., *The Gospel of Mark* (NCB), London: Marshall, Morgan & Scott, 1976.

Archer, G.L., and Chirichigno, G.C., *Old Testament Quotations in the New Testament: A Complete Survey*, Chicago: Moody, 1983.

Baars, W., *New Syro-Hexaplaric Texts: Edited, Commented upon and Compared with the Septuagint*, Leiden: Brill, 1968.

Baird, J.A., 'A Pragmatic Approach to Parable Exegesis: Some New Evidence on Mark 4:11, 33-34', *JBL* 76 (1957), pp. 201-207.

Baldwin, J., *Haggai, Zechariah, Malachi; An Introduction and Commentary*, London: Tyndale, 1972.

Barr, J., *Holy Scripture: Canon, Authority, Criticism*, Oxford: OUP; Philadelphia: Westminster, 1983.

Barrett, C.K., *A Commentary on the First Epistle to the Corinthians* (HNTC), New York: Harper & Row, 1968.

—*A Commentary on the Second Epistle to the Corinthians* (HNTC), New York: Harper & Row, 1973.

—*The Gospel of John*, New York: Macmillan, 1955; second edition, Philadelphia: Westminster, 1978.

—'The Old Testament in the Fourth Gospel', *JTS* 48 (1947), pp. 155-69.

Barthélemy, D., *Les Devanciers d'Aquila* (VTSup 10), Leiden: Brill, 1963.

—'Redécouverte d'un chaînon manquant de l'histoire de la Septante', *RB* 60 (1953), pp. 18-29.

Beale, G.K., 'An Exegetical and Theological Consideration of the Hardening of Pharaoh's Heart in Exodus 4-14', *TrinJ* 5 (1984), pp. 129-54.

Beasley-Murray, G.R., *Jesus and the Kingdom of God*, Grand Rapids: Eerdmans, 1986.

Becker, J., *Isaias-der Prophet und sein Buch* (SB 30), Stuttgart: Katholisches Bibelwerk, 1968.

Berger, K., 'Zur Diskussion über die Herkunft von I Kor. II. 9', *NTS* 24 (1977-78), pp. 270-83.

Bird, T., 'Who Is the Boy in Isa. 7:16?', *CBQ* 6 (1944), pp. 435-43.

Black, M., *An Aramaic Approach to the Gospels and Acts*, Oxford: Clarendon, 1967[3].

—*Romans* (NCB), London: Oliphants, 1973.

—'The Problem of O.T. Quotations in the Gospels', *JMUEOS* 23 (1942), p. 4.

Blank, S.H., *Prophetic Faith in Israel*, New York: Harper & Row, 1958.

—'The Current Misinterpretation of Isaiah's *She'ar Yashub*', *JBL* 67(1948), pp. 211-15.

—'Traces of Prophetic Agony in Isaiah', *HUCA* 27 (1956), pp. 81-92.

Bloch, R., 'Midrash', *DBSup* 5 (1957), cols. 1263-81.

Borgen, P., *Bread from Heaven: An Exegetical Study of the Concept of Manna in the Gospel of John and the Writings of Philo* (NovTSup 10), Leiden: Brill, 1965.

Bowker, J.W., 'Mystery and Parable: Mark iv. 1-20', *JTS* 25 (1974), pp. 300-17.

Braude, W.G., *Pesikta Rabbati* (Yale Judaica Series 18), 2 vols., New Haven and London: Yale University, 1968.

—and Kapstein, I.J., *Tanna Debe Eliyyahu*, Philadelphia: Jewish Publication Society, 1981.

Brawley, R.L., *Luke–Acts and the Jews; Conflict, Apology, and Conciliation* (SBLMS 33), Atlanta: Scholars, 1987.

Bright, J., *Jeremiah* (AB 21), Garden City: Doubleday, 1965.

Brock, S.P., *Isaiah* (Vetus Testamentum Syriace 3/1), Leiden: Brill, 1987.

Brodie, T.L., *Luke the Literary Interpreter: Luke–Acts as a Systematic Rewriting and Updating of the Elijah–Elisha Narrative in 1 and 2 Kings*, Rome: Angelicum University, 1981.

—'The Children and the Prince: The Structure, Nature and Date of Isaiah 6-12', *BTB* 9 (1979), pp. 27-31.

Brooke, G.J., *Exegesis at Qumran: 4QFlorilegium in its Jewish Context* (JSOTSup 29), Sheffield: JSOT, 1985.

Brown, R.E., *The Gospel according to John* (AB29 and 29A), 2 vols., Garden City: Doubleday, 1966, 1970.

—*The Semitic Background of the Term 'Mystery' in the New Testament*, Philadelphia: Fortress, 1968.

Brownlee, W.H., *Ezekiel 1-19* (WBC 28), Waco: Word, 1986.

—'The Habakkuk Midrash and the Targum of Jonathan', *JJS* 7 (1956), pp. 169-86.

—'The Manuscripts of Isaiah from which DSI^a was copied', *BASOR* 127 (1952), pp. 16-21.

—*The Meaning of the Qumran Scrolls for the Bible*, New York: Oxford University Press, 1964.

—'The Text of Isaiah VI 13 in the Light of DSI^a', *VT* 1 (1951), pp. 296-98.

Buber, M., *Bücher der Kündung: Das Buch Jeschaiahu*, Köln: Hegner, 1958.

Budde, K., *Jesaja's Erleben: Eine gemeinverständliche Auslegung der Denkschrift des Propheten (Kap. 6.1-9.6)*, Gotha: Klotz, 1928.

Bultmann, R., *The Gospel of John*, Philadelphia: Westminster, 1971.

—*The History of the Synoptic Tradition*, Oxford: Blackwell, 1963.

Burkill, T.A., 'Cryptology of Parables in St. Mark's Gospel', *NovT* 1 (1956), pp. 246-62.

—*Mysterious Revelation: An Examination of the Philosophy of St. Mark's Gospel*, Ithaca: Cornell, 1963.

—*New Light on the Earliest Gospel*, Ithaca: Cornell, 1972.

Burkitt, F.C., *Early Eastern Christianity*, New York: Dutton, 1904.

Burney, C.F., *The Aramaic Origin of the Fourth Gospel*, Oxford: Clarendon, 1922.

Callaway, M., *Sing, O Barren One: A Study in Comparative Midrash* (SBLDS 91), Atlanta: Scholars, 1986.

Calvin, J., *John 11-21*, trans. by T.H.L. Parker, Edinburgh and London: Oliver & Boyd, 1961.

—*Romans*, tr. by F. Sibson, Philadelphia: Whetham, 1836.

Carlston, C.E., *The Parables of the Triple Tradition*, Philadelphia: Fortress, 1975.

Carroll, R.P., 'Ancient Israelite Prophecy and Dissonance Theory', *Numen* 24 (1977), pp. 135-51.

—'Inner Tradition Shifts in Meaning in Isa 1–11', *ExpTim* 89 (1978), pp. 301-304.

—*Jeremiah* (OTL), Philadelphia: Westminster, 1986.

Cazelles, H., 'La vocation d'Isaie (ch. 6) et les rites royaux', *Homenaje à Juan Prado*, ed. by A.A. Verdes and E.J.A. Hernandez, Madri: Consejo Superior de Investigaciones Cientificos, 1975, pp. 89-108.

Ceriani, M., *Translatio Syra Pescitto Veteris Testamenti ex Codex Ambrosiano II*, Milan: Impensis Bibliothecae Ambrosianae, 1876-83.

Charlesworth, J.H., ed., *Old Testament Pseudepigrapha*, 2 vols., Garden City: Doubleday, 1983, 1985.

Childs, B.S., *Introduction to the Old Testament as Scripture*, Philadelphia: Fortress, 1979.

—*Isaiah and the Assyrian Crisis* (SBT 3, second series), London: SCM, 1967.

—'Midrash and the Old Testament', *Understanding the Sacred Text*, M. Enslin Festschrift, ed. J. Reumann, Valley Forge: Judson, 1972, pp. 47-59.

—*The Book of Exodus: A Critical, Theological Commentary* (OTL), Philadelphia: Westminster, 1974.

—*The New Testament as Canon: An Introduction*, Philadelphia: Fortress, 1985.

Chilton, B.D., *A Galilean Rabbi and His Bible: Jesus' Use of the Interpreted Scripture of His Time* (GNS 8), Wilmington: Glazier, 1984.

—*Targumic Approaches to the Gospels* (Studies in Judaism), New York: University Press of America, 1986.

—*The Glory of Israel: The Theology and Provenience of the Isaiah Targum* (JSOTSup 23), Sheffield: JSOT, 1983.

—*The Isaiah Targum* (The Aramaic Bible 11), Wilmington: Glazier, 1987.

Clements, R.E., *Isaiah 1–39* (NCB), London: Marshall, Morgan & Scott, 1980.

—*Isaiah and the Deliverance of Jerusalem* (JSOTSup 13), Sheffield: JSOT, 1980.

Cohen, A., 'השע, הכבר, השמן', *BM* 50/3 (1972), pp. 360-61.

Conzelmann, H., *1 Corinthians* (Hermeneia), Philadelphia: Fortress, 1975.

—*The Acts of the Apostles* (Hermeneia), Philadelphia: Fortress, 1987.

—*The Theology of St. Luke*, New York: Harper & Row, 1961.

Crabtree, T.T., 'The Prophetic Call—A Dialogue with God', *SWJT* 4 (1961) 33-35.

Cranfield, C.E.B., *The Epistle to the Romans* (ICC), Edinburgh: T. & T. Clark, 1979.

—*The Gospel according to Saint Mark*, Cambridge: CUP, 1963.

Daube, D., *The New Testament and Rabbinic Judaism*, London: Athlone, 1956.

Day, J., 'Shear-Jashub (Isaiah VII 3) and 'The Remnant of Wrath' (Psalm LXXVI 11)', *VT* 31 (1981), pp. 76-78.

Le Deaut, R., 'A Propos a Definition of Midrash', *Int* 25 (1971), pp. 262-82.

—'La tradition juive et l'exégèse chrétienne primitif', *RHPR* 1 (1971), pp. 31-50.

—'Un phénomène spontané de l'herméneutique juive ancienne: le 'targuisme' ', *Bib* 52 (1971), pp. 505-25.

Derenbourg, J., and Derenbourg, H., *Version Arabe d'Isaïe de R. Saadia ben Iosef al-Fayyoûmi*, Paris: Librairie de la Société Asiatique, 1896.

Dibelius, M., *Studies in the Acts of the Apostles*, London: SCM, 1956.

Diez-Macho, A., 'The Recently Discovered Palestinian Targum: Its Antiquity and Relationship with Other Targums', *Congress Volume: Papers Read at the Third*

Congress of the International Organization for the Study of the Old Testament, Oxford, 31 August to 5 September, 1959 (VTSup 7), Leiden: Brill, 1960, pp. 224-45.

Dinter, P.E., 'Paul and the Prophet Isaiah', *BTB* 13 (1983), pp. 48-52.

Dodd, C.H., *According to the Scriptures*, London: Nisbet, 1952.

—*The Parables of the Kingdom*, London: Nisbet, 1935.

Doeve, J.W., *Jewish Hermeneutics in the Synoptic Gospels and Acts*, Assen: Van Gorcum, 1954.

Driver, G.R., 'Another Little Drink'—Isaiah 28:1-22', *Words and Meanings*, D.W.Thomas Festschrift, ed. P.R. Ackroyd and B. Lindars, Cambridge: Cambridge University Press, 1968, pp. 47-67.

Duhm, B., *Das Buch Jesaia*, Göttingen: Vandenhoeck & Ruprecht, 1968.

Dumbrell, W.J., 'Worship and Isaiah 6', *RTR* 43 (1984), pp. 1-8.

Dupont, J., 'La conclusion des Actes et son rapport à l'ensemble de l'ouvrage de Luc', *Les Actes des Apôtres* (BETL 48), ed. J. Kremer, Gembloux: Duculot, 1979, pp. 359-404.

Eakin, F., 'Spiritual Obduracy and Parable Purpose', *The Use of the Old Testament in the New and Other Essays*, W.F. Stinespring Festschrift, ed. J. Efird, Durham: Duke University, 1972, pp. 87-107.

Eaton, J.H., 'The Isaiah Tradition', *Israel's Prophetic Tradition*, P. Ackroyd Festschrift, ed. R. Coggins, A. Philips, and M. Knibbe, Cambridge: Cambridge University Press, 1982, pp. 58-76.

—*Vision in Worship*, London: SPCK, 1981.

Eichrodt, W., *Der Heilige in Israel: Jesaja 1-12*, Stuttgart: Calwer, 1960.

—*Ezekiel* (OTL), Philadelphia: Westminster, 1970.

van Elderen, B., 'The Purpose of Parables according to Matthew 13:10-17', *New Dimensions in New Testament Study*, ed. R.N. Longenecker and M.C. Tenney, Grand Rapids: Eerdmans, 1974, pp. 180-90.

Ellis, E.E., 'How the New Testament Uses the Old', *New Testament Interpretation: Essays on Principles and Methods*, ed. I. H. Marshall, Grand Rapids: Eerdmans, 1977, pp. 199-219.

—'Midrash, Targum and New Testament Quotations', *Neotestamentica et Semitica: Studies in Honour of Matthew Black*, ed. E.E. Ellis and M. Wilcox, Edinburgh: T & T Clark, 1969, pp. 61-69.

—*Paul's Use of the Old Testament*, Edinburgh: T & T Clark, 1957.

Emerton, J.A., 'The Translation and Interpretation of Isaiah vi. 13', *Interpreting the Bible*, E.I.J. Rosenthal Festschrift (UCOP 32), ed. J.A. Emerton and S.C. Reif, Cambridge: Cambridge University Press, 1982, pp. 85-118.

Engnell, I., *The Call of Isaiah* (UUA 1949:4), Uppsala: Lundequistska; Leipzig: Harrassowitz, 1949.

Epstein, I., *The Babylonian Talmud*, 35 vols., London: Soncino, 1935-53.

Evans, C.A., '1QIsaiah[a] and the Absence of Prophetic Critique at Qumran', *RevQ* 11 (1984), pp. 537-42.

—'A Note on the Function of Isaiah, VI, 9-10 in Mark, IV', *RB* 88 (1981), pp. 234-35.

—'An Interpretation of Isa 8, 11-15 Unemended', *ZAW* 97 (1985), pp. 112-13.

—'Is Luke's View of the Jewish Rejection of Jesus Anti-Semitic?', *Reimaging the Death of the Lucan Jesus* (BBB), ed. D. Sylva, Bonn: Hanstein, pp. 29-56, 174-83.

—'Isaiah 6:9-10 in Rabbinic and Patristic Writings', *VC* 36 (1982), pp. 275-81.

—'Jerome's Translation of Isaiah 6:9-10', *VC* 38 (1984), pp. 202-204.

—'Obduracy and the Lord's Servant: Some Observations on the Use of the Old Testament in the Fourth Gospel', *Early Jewish and Christian Exegesis* (Homage 10), W.H. Brownlee Festschrift, ed. C.A. Evans and W.F. Stinespring, Atlanta: Scholars, 1987, pp. 221-36.

—'On Isaiah's Use of Israel's Sacred Tradition', *BZ* 30 (1986), pp. 92-99.

—'On the Quotation Formulas in the Fourth Gospel', *BZ* 26 (1982), pp. 79-83.

—'On the Unity and Parallel Structure of Isaiah', *VT* 38 (1988), pp. 129-47.

—'Paul and the Hermeneutics of "True Prophecy": A Study of Romans 9-11', *Bib* 65 (1984), pp. 560-70.

—'The Function of Isaiah 6:9-10 in Mark and John', *NovT* 24 (1982), pp. 124-38.

—'The Isaianic Background of Mark 4:1-20', *CBQ* 47 (1985), pp. 464-68.

—'The Text of Isaiah 6:9-10', *ZAW* 94 (1982), pp. 415-18.

Evans, C.F., 'The Central Section of St. Luke's Gospel', *Studies in the Gospels: Essays in Memory of R.H. Lightfoot*, ed. D.E. Nineham, Oxford: Blackwell, 1955, pp. 37-53.

Falusi, G.K., 'Jesus' Use of Parables in Mark with Special Reference to Mark 4: 10-12', *IJT* 31 (1982), pp. 35-46.

Fearon, J., ed., *Thomas Aquinas, Summa Theologica*, vol. 25, New York: McGraw-Hill, 1969.

Fee, G.D., *The First Epistle to the Corinthians* (NIC), Grand Rapids: Eerdmans, 1987.

Feuillet, A., 'L'énigme de I Cor., II, 9. Contribution à l'étude des sources de la christologie paulinienne', *RB* 70 (1963), pp. 52-74.

Field, F., *Origensis Hexapla*, 2 vols., Hildesheim: Olms, 1964.

Fishbane, M., 'Revelation and Tradition: Aspects of Inner Biblical Exegesis', *JBL* 99 (1980), pp. 343-61.

—*Biblical Interpretation in Ancient Israel*, New York: Oxford University Press, 1985.

Fitzmyer, J.A., *The Gospel According to Luke* (AB 28 and 28A), 2 vols., Garden City: Doubleday, 1981, 1985.

Fohrer, G., *Das Buch Jesaja I*, Zürich and Stuttgart: Zwingli, 1966.

—*Die Propheten des Alten Testaments*, 2 vols., Gütersloh: Mohn, 1974, 1976.

—'Die Struktur der alttestamentlichen Eschatologie', *Studien zur alttestamentlichen Prophetie (1949-65)* (BZAW 99), Berlin: Töpelmann, 1967, pp. 32-58.

—'Prophetie und Geschichte', *TLZ* 89 (1964), cols. 481-600.

—'Wandlungen Jesajas', *Festschrift für Wilhelm Eilers*, ed. by G. Wiessner, Wiesbaden: Harrassowitz, 1967, pp. 58-71.

Franklin, E., *Christ the Lord: A Study in the Purpose and Theology of Luke–Acts*, Philadelphia: Westminster, 1975.

Freed, E.D., *Old Testament Quotations in the Gospel of John* (NovTSup 11), Leiden: Brill, 1965.

Freedman, *Midrash Rabbah*, 10 vols., New York and London: Soncino, 1983.

Friedlander, G., *Pirke De Rabbi Eliezer*, New York: Sepher-Hermon, 1981.

Furnish, V.P., *II Corinthians* (AB 32A), Garden City: Doubleday, 1984.

Gaster, T.H., *The Dead Sea Scriptures*, Garden City: Doubleday, 1976.

Gaston, L., 'Anti-Judaism and the Passion in Luke and Acts', *Anti-Judaism in Early Christianity*, ed. P. Richardson, Waterloo: Wilfrid Laurier University, 1986, pp. 127-64.

Gertner, M., 'Midrashim in the NT', *JSS* 7 (1962), pp. 267-92.

Giblin, C.H., *The Destruction of Jerusalem according to Luke's Gospel* (AnBib 107), Rome: Pontifical Biblical Institute, 1985.

Gnilka, J., *Das Evangelium nach Markus* (EKKNT), 2 vols., Zürich: Benziger Verlag, 1978, 1979.

—*Die Verstockung Israels: Isaias 6, 9-10 in der Theologie der Synoptiker* (SANT 3), Munich: Kösel, 1961.

Goodwin, C., 'How Did John Treat His Sources?', *JBL* 73 (1954), pp. 61-75.

Gottwald, N.K., 'Immanuel as the Prophet's Son', *VT* 8 (1958), pp. 36-47.

Gould, E.P., *A Critical and Exegetical Commentary on the Gospel according to St. Mark* (ICC), Edinburgh: T. & T. Clark, 1896.

Grant, F.C., *The Gospel according to St. Mark*, New York: Abingdon, 1951.

Gray, J., *I & II Kings* (OTL), Philadelphia: Westminster, 1963.

Grundmann, W., *Das Evangelium nach Markus* (THKNT 2), Berlin: Evangelische Verlagsanstalt, 1959.

Gundry, R.H., *Matthew: A Commentary on His Literary and Theological Art*, Grand Rapids: Eerdmans, 1982.

—*The Use of the Old Testament in St. Matthew's Gospel* (NovTSup 18), Leiden: Brill, 1967.

Habel, N., 'The Form and Significance of the Call Narratives', *ZAW* 77 (1965), pp. 297-323.

Haenchen, E., *The Acts of the Apostles: A Commentary*, Philadelphia: Westminster, 1971.

—'The Book of Acts as Source Material for the History of Early Christianity', *Studies in Luke–Acts*, ed. by L.E. Keck and J.L. Martyn, Philadelphia: Fortress, 1966, pp. 258-78.

Hallo, W.W., 'Isaiah 28:9-13 and the Ugaritic Abecedaries', *JBL* 77 (1958), pp. 324-38.

Hammershaimb, E., 'The Immanuel Sign', *ST* 3 (1949-51), pp. 124-42.

Hardmeier, C., 'Jesajas Verkündigungsabsicht und Jahwes Verstockungsauftrag in Jes 6', *Die Botschaft und die Boten*, H.W. Wolff Festschrift, ed J. Jeremias and L. Perlitt, Neukirchen-Vluyn: Neukirchener Verlag, 1981, pp. 235-51.

Harrington, D.J., *The Hebrew Fragments of Pseudo-Philo* (Texts and Translations 3; Pseudepigrapha Series 3), Missoula: SBL, 1974.

Harrison, R.K., *Jeremiah and Lamentations: An Introduction and Commentary*, London: Tyndale, 1973.

—and Manley, G.T., 'Deuteronomy', *The New Bible Commentary: Revised*, ed. D. Guthrie, J.A. Motyer, et al., Grand Rapids: Eerdmans, 1970, pp. 201-29.

Hasel, G.F., 'Linguistic Considerations Regarding the Translation of Isaiah's "Shear-jashub"', *AUSS* 9 (1971), pp. 36-46.

—*The Remnant: The History and Theology of the Remnant Idea from Genesis to Isaiah* (AUM 5), Berrien Springs: Andrews University, 1972.

Haufe, G., 'Erwägungen zum Ursprung der sogenannten Parabeltheorie Markus 4, 11-12', *EvT* 32 (1972), pp. 413-21.

Hauser, H.J., *Strukturen der Abschlusserzählung der Apostelgeschichte* (AnBib 86), Rome: Pontifical Biblical Institute, 1979.

Hay, D.M., *Glory at the Right Hand: Psalm 110 in Early Christianity* (SBLMS 18), Nashville: Abingdon, 1973.

Herntrich, V., *Der Prophet Jesaja: Kapitel 1-12* (ATD 17), Göttingen: Vandenhoeck & Ruprecht, 1950.

Heschel, A., *The Prophets*, New York: Harper & Row, 1969.

Hesse, F., *Das Verstockungsproblem im Alten Testament* (BZAW 74), Berlin: Töpelmann, 1955.

Hoffmann, H., *Die Intention der Verkündigung Jesajas*, Berlin: de Gruyter, 1974.

Holladay, W.L., *Isaiah: Scroll of a Prophetic Heritage*, Grand Rapids: Eerdmans, 1978.

—*Jeremiah 1* (Hermeneia), Philadelphia: Fortress, 1986.

Hollenbach, B., 'Lest They Should Turn and Be Forgiven: Irony', *BT* 34 (1983), pp. 312-21.

Horgan, M.P., *Pesharim: Qumran Interpretations of Biblical Books* (CBQMS 8), Washington: Catholic Biblical Association, 1979.

Horst, F., 'Die Visionsschilderungen der alttestamentlichen Propheten', *EvT* 20 (1960), pp. 193-205.

Hoskyns, E.C., *The Fourth Gospel*, 2 vols., ed. F.N. Davey, London: Faber, 1961.

Hyatt, J.P., *Prophetic Religion*, New York: Abingdon-Cokesbury, 1947.

Iwry, S., 'Massebah and Bamah in 1QIsaiah[a] 6:13', *JBL* 76 (1957), pp. 225-32.

Jenni, E., 'Jesajas Berufung in der neueren Forschung', *TZ* 15 (1959), pp. 321-39.

Jensen, J., *The Use of Torah by Isaiah: His Debate with the Wisdom Tradition* (CBQMS 3), Washington: Catholic Biblical Association, 1973.

—'Weal and Woe in Isaiah: Consistency and Continuity', *CBQ* 43 (1981), pp. 167-87.

—'Yahweh's Plan in Isaiah and in the Rest of the Old Testament', *CBQ* 48 (1986), pp. 443-55.

Jeremias, J., *The Parables of Jesus*, New York: Scribner's, 1971.

Jervell, J., *Luke and the People of God: A New Look at Luke–Acts*, Minneapolis: Augsburg, 1972.

Kahle, P., 'Problems of the Septuagint', *Studia Patristica I* (TU 63), Berlin: Akademie, 1957, pp. 328-38.

—*Die hebräischen Handschriften aus der Höhle*, Stuttgart: Kohlhammer, 1951.

Kaiser, O., *Isaiah 1-12* (OTL), Philadelphia: Westminster, 1972, second edition, 1983.

—*Isaiah 13-39* (OTL), Philadelphia: Westminster, 1974.

Kaplan, M., 'Isaiah 6:1-11', *JBL* 45 (1926), pp. 251-59.

Käsemann, E., *Commentary on Romans*, Grand Rapids: Eerdmans, 1978.

—*Perspectives on Paul*, Philadelphia: Fortress, 1971.

Kautzsch, E., *Gesenius' Hebrew Grammar*, Oxford: Clarendon, 1910.

Kee, H.C., *Community of the New Age: Studies in Mark's Gospel*, Philadelphia: Westminster, 1977.

Kelber, W., *The Kingdom in Mark: A New Place and a New Time*, Philadelphia: Fortress, 1974.

Key, A.F., 'The Magical Background of Isaiah 6:9-13', *JBL* 86 (1967), pp. 198-204.

Kilian, R., 'Der Verstockungsauftrag Jesajas', *Bausteine biblischer Theologie*, G.J. Botterweck Festschrift (BBB 50), ed. H.-J. Fabry, Bonn: Hanstein, 1977, pp. 209-25.

Kingsbury, E.C., 'The Prophets and the Council of Yahweh', *JBL* 83 (1964), pp. 279-86.

Kirkland, J.R., 'The Earliest Understanding of Jesus' Use of Parables: Mark IV 10-12 in Context', *NovT* 19 (1977), pp. 1-21.

Kish, G., *Pseudo-Philo's Liber Antiquitatum Biblicarum*, Notre Dame: University of Notre Dame, 1949.

Kissane, E.J., *The Book of Isaiah*, vol. 1, Dublin: Browne and Nolan, 1960.

Klein, R.W., *Textual Criticism of the Old Testament: The Septuagint after Qumran* (Guides to Biblical Scholarship), Philadelphia: Fortress, 1974.

Klijn, A.F.J., 'Jérome, Isaîe 6 et l'Évangile des Nazoréens', *VC* 40 (1986), pp. 245-50.

Knierim, R., 'The Vocation of Isaiah', *VT* 18 (1968), pp. 47-68.

Koch, K., *The Prophets*, Philadelphia: Fortress, 1983.

Krause, M., and Labib, P., *Gnostische und hermetische Schriften aus Codex II und Codex VI*, Gluckstadt: Augustin, 1971.

Kuhl, C., *The Prophets of Israel*, Edinburgh: Oliver & Boyd, 1960.

Lagrange, M.-J., *Évangile selon Saint Marc*, Paris: Gabalda, 1929.

Lamsa, G.M., *The Holy Bible from Ancient Eastern Manuscripts*, Nashville: Holman, 1957.

Lane, W.L., *The Gospel according to Mark* (NIC), Grand Rapids: Eerdmans, 1974.

Lauterbach, J.Z., *Mekilta de-Rabbi Ishmael*, 3 vols., Philadelphia: Jewish Publication Society, 1933.

Leroy, H., *Rätsel und Missverständnis* (BBB 30), Bonn: Hanstein, 1968.

Lescow, T., 'Jesajas Denkschrift aus der Zeit des syrisch-ephraimitischen Krieges', *ZAW* 85 (1973), pp. 315-33.

Lieberman, S., *Hellenism in Jewish Palestine* (TSJTSA 18), New York: JTSA, 1962.

Liebreich, L.J., 'The Compilation of the Book of Isaiah', *JQR* 46 (1955-56), pp. 259-77; and 47 (1956-57), pp. 114-38.

—'The Position of Chapter Six in the Book of Isaiah', *HUCA* 25 (1954) 37-40.

Lifschitz, B., 'Greek Documents from the Cave of Horror', *IEJ* 12 (1962), pp. 201-207.

Lindars, B., *New Testament Apologetic*, Philadelphia: Westminster; London: SCM, 1961.

Lindblom, J., *A Study on the Immanuel Section in Isaiah*, Lund: Gleerup, 1958.

—*Prophecy in Ancient Israel*, Philadelphia: Fortress, 1962.

Longenecker, R.N., *Biblical Exegesis in the Apostolic Period*, Grand Rapids: Eerdmans, 1975.

Love, J.P., 'The Call of Isaiah', *Int* 11 (1957), pp. 282-96.

Malter, H., *Saadia Gaon: His Life and Works*, New York: Hermon, 1926.

Manson, T.W., *The Teaching of Jesus*, Cambridge: Cambridge University Press, 1948.

Manson, W., 'The Purpose of Parables: A Re-Examination of St. Mark iv. 10-12', *ExpTim* 68 (1957), pp. 133-34.

Mansoor, M., *The Thanksgiving Hymns*, Leiden: Brill, 1961.

Marcus, J., 'Mark 4: 10-12 and Marcan Epistemology', *JBL* 103 (1984), pp. 557-74.

—*The Mystery of the Kingdom of God* (SBLDS 90), Atlanta: Scholars, 1986.

Marshall, I.H., *The Gospel of Luke: A Commentary on the Greek Text* (NIGTC), Grand Rapids: Eerdmans, 1978.

—'Tradition and Theology in Luke (8:5-15)', *TynBul* 20 (1969), pp. 56-75.

Marti, K., *Das Buch Jesaja*, Tübingen: Mohr (Siebeck), 1900.

Martyn, J.L., *History and Theology in the Fourth Gospel*, New York: Harper & Row, 1968.

Marxsen, W., 'Redaktionsgeschichtliche Erklärung der sogenannten Parabeltheorie des Markus', *ZTK* 52 (1955), pp. 255-71.

Mays, J.L., *Amos* (OTL), Philadelphia: Westminster, 1969.

McNamara, M., *Targum and Testament: Aramaic Paraphrases of the Hebrew Bible: A Light on the New Testament*, Shannon: Irish University, 1972.

—*The New Testament and the Palestinian Targum to the Pentateuch* (AnBib 27a), Rome: Pontifical Biblical Institute, 1978.

Meeks, W.A., *The Prophet-King: Moses Traditions and the Johannine Christology* (NovTSup 14), Leiden: Brill, 1967.

Metzger, B.M., *A Textual Commentary on the Greek New Testament*, London and New York: United Bible Societies, 1971.

—'The Formulas Introducing Quotations of Scripture in the NT and the Mishnah', *JBL* 70 (1951), pp. 297-307.

Metzger, W., 'Der Horizont der Gnade in der Berufungsvision Jesajas', *ZAW* 93 (1981), pp. 281-84.

Miller, M.P., 'Midrash', *IDB Sup*, 1976, pp. 593-97.

—'Targum, Midrash and the Use of the Old Testament in the New Testament', *JSJ* 2 (1971), pp 29-82.

Moessner, D.P., 'Luke 9:1-50: Luke's Preview of the Journey of the Prophet like Moses of Deuteronomy', *JBL* 102 (1983), pp. 575-605.

Montagnini, F., 'La Vocazione di Isaia', *BeO* 6 (1964), pp. 163-72.

Montgomery, J.A., *A Critical and Exegetical Commentary on the Books of Kings* (ICC), New York: Scribner's, 1951.

Moore, C.A., 'Mark 4:12: More Like the Irony of Micaiah than Isaiah', *A Light unto My Path* (GTS 4), J.M. Myers Festschrift, ed. H.N. Bream, R.D. Heim, and C.A. Moore, Philadelphia: Temple, 1974, pp. 335-44.

Morrow, F.J., 'The Text of Isaiah at Qumran', unpublished dissertation, Washington: Catholic University of America, 1973.

Moule, C.F.D., 'Mark 4:1-20 Yet Once More', *Neotestamentica et Semitica*, M. Black Festschrift, ed. E.E. Ellis and M. Wilcox, Edinburgh: T & T Clark, 1969, pp. 95-113.

Mowinckel, S., *He that Cometh*, New York: Abingdon, 1956.

Mueller, M.M., *Saint Caesarius of Arles, Sermons 81-186* (FC), Washington: Catholic University of America, 1964.

Müller, H.-P., 'Glauben und Bleiben: Zur Denkschrift Jesajas Kapitel vi-viii 18', *VTSup* 26 (1974), pp. 25-54.

Munck, J., *Christ & Israel: An Interpretation of Romans 9-11*, Philadelphia: Fortress, 1967.

Neusner, J., *What is Midrash?* (Guides to Biblical Scholarship), Philadelphia: Fortress, 1987.

Nicholson, G.C., *Death as Departure: The Johannine Descent-Ascent Schema* (SBLDS 63), Chico: Scholars, 1983.

Nielsen, K., 'Is 6:1-8:18 as Dramatic Writing', *ST* 40 (1986), pp. 1-16.

Nolland, J., 'Impressed Unbelievers as Witnesses to Christ (Luke 4:22a)', *JBL* 98 (1979), pp. 219-29.

von Nordheim, E., 'Das Zitat des Paulus in I Kor. 2,9, und seine Beziehung zum koptischen Testament Jakobs', *ZNW* 65 (1974), pp. 112-20.

North, C.R., *The Second Isaiah: Introduction, Translation and Commentary to Chapters XL-LV*, Oxford: Clarendon, 1964.

O'Rourke, J., 'John's Fulfilment Texts', *ScEccl* 19 (1967), pp. 432-39.

Oswalt, J.N., *The Book of Isaiah: Chapters 1-39* (NIC), Grand Rapids: Eerdmans, 1986.

Patte, D., *Early Jewish Hermeneutic in Palestine* (SBLDS 22), Missoula: Scholars, 1975.

Peisker, C.H., 'Konsekutives ἵνα in Markus 4:12', *ZNW* 59 (1968), pp. 126-27.

Pelikan, J., ed., *Luther's Works*, vols. 3-30, Saint Louis: Concordia, 1961-67.

Perrin, N., *The Kingdom of God in the Teaching of Jesus*, Philadelphia: Fortress, 1963.

Pesch, R., *Das Markusevangelium*, Freiburg: Herder & Herder, 1976.

Petersen, D.L., *Haggai and Zechariah 1–8* (OTL), Philadelphia: Westminster, 1984.

Pfeiffer, R.H., *Introduction to the Old Testament*, New York: Harper & Row, 1941.

Philonenko, M., 'Quod oculus non vidit, I Cor. 2,9', *TZ* 15 (1959), pp. 51-52.

Porton, G. 'Defining Midrash', *The Study of Ancient Judaism*, 2 vols., ed. J. Neusner, New York: Ktav, 1981, vol. 1, pp. 55-92.

Prigent, P., 'Ce que l'oeil n'a pas vu, I Cor. 2,9. Histoire et préhistoire d'une citation', *TZ* 14 (1958), pp. 416-29.

von Rad, G., *Deuteronomy* (OTL), Philadelphia: Westminster, 1966.

—*The Message of the Prophets*, London: SCM, 1965.

Rahlfs, A., *Septuaginta*, Stuttgart: Württem, 1935.

Rignell, L.G., 'Das Immanuelszeichen: Einige Gesichtspunkte zu Is 7', *ST* 11 (1957), pp. 99-119.

Roberts, A., and Donaldson, J., ed., *The Ante-Nicene Fathers*, 10 vols., revised by A.C. Coxe, Grand Rapids: Eerdmans, 1950.

Roberts, J.J.M., 'Yahweh's Foundation in Zion (Isa 28:16)', JBL 106 (1987), pp. 27-45.

Robertson, A.T., and Plummer, A., *A Critical and Exegetical Commentary on the First Epistle of St Paul to the Corinthians* (ICC), Edinburgh: T. & T. Clark, 1914.

Robinson, J.M., 'Gnosticism and the New Testament', *Gnosis*, H. Jonas Festschrift, ed. B. Aland, Göttingen: Vandenhoeck & Ruprecht, 1978, pp. 129-43.

—'On the *Gattung* of Mark (and John)', *Jesus and Man's Hope*, ed. D.G. Buttrick and J.M. Bald, Pittsburgh: Pittsburgh Theological Seminary, 1970, pp. 99-129.

—'The Literary Composition of Mark', *L'Évangile selon Marc: Tradition et Rédaction*, ed. M. Sabbe, Gembloux: Louvain University, 1974, pp. 11-19.

—ed., *The Nag Hammadi Library*, San Francisco: Harper & Row, 1977.

Robinson, W.C., Jr., 'On Preaching the Word of God', *Studies in Luke–Acts*, ed. L.E. Keck and J.L. Martyn, New York: Abingdon, 1966, pp. 131-38.

Ruben, P., 'A Proposed New Method of Textual Criticism', *AJSL* 51 (1934), pp. 30-45.

Ruether, R.R., *Faith and Fraticide: The Theological Roots of anti-Semitism*, New York: Seabury, 1974.

Sanders, E.P., *Paul and Palestinian Judaism: A Comparison of Patterns of Religion*, London: SCM, 1977.

Sanders, J.A., 'Adaptable for Life: The Nature and Function of Canon', *Magnalia Dei: The Mighty Acts of God: Essays on the Bible and Archaeology in Memory of G.E. Wright*, ed. F.M. Cross, New York: Doubleday, 1976, pp. 31-60; repr. in J.A. Sanders, *From Sacred Story to Sacred Text: Canon as Paradigm*, Philadelphia: Fortress, 1987, pp. 11-39.

—*Canon and Community* (Guides to Biblical Scholarship), Philadelphia: Fortress, 1985.

—'Canonical Context and Canonical Criticism', *HBT* 2 (1980), pp. 173-97.

—'From Isaiah 61 to Luke 4', *Christianity, Judaism and Other Greco-Roman Cults*, M. Smith Festschrift, ed. J. Neusner, Leiden: Brill, 1975, pp. 75-106.

—*From Sacred Story to Sacred Text: Canon as Paradigm*, Philadelphia: Fortress, 1987.

—'Hermeneutics', *IDBSup*, 1976, pp. 402-407.

—Review of R.E. Brown, *The Birth of the Messiah: A Commentary on the Infancy Narratives in Matthew and Luke*, Garden City: Doubleday, 1977, in *USQR* 33 (1978), pp. 193-96.

—'Text and Canon: Concepts and Methods', *JBL* 98 (1979), pp. 5-29.

—'The Bible as Canon', *Christian Century* (1981), pp. 1250-55.

—'The Ethic of Election in Luke's Great Banquet Parable', *Essays in Old Testament Ethics: J. Philip Hyatt, In Memoriam*, ed. J.L. Crenshaw and J.T. Willis, New York: Ktav, 1974, pp. 247-71.

—*Torah and Canon*, Philadelphia: Fortress, 1972.

Sanders, J.T., *The Jews in Luke–Acts*, Philadelphia: Fortress, 1987.

—'The Parable of the Pounds and Lucan Anti-Semitism', *TS* 42 (1981), pp. 660-68.

—'The Prophetic Use of the Scriptures in Luke–Acts', *Early Jewish and Christian Exegesis* (Homage 10), W.H. Brownlee Festschrift, ed. C.A. Evans and W.F. Stinespring, Atlanta: Scholars, 1987, pp. 191-98.

—'The Salvation of the Jews in Luke–Acts', *Luke–Acts: New Perspectives from the Society of Biblical Literature Seminar*, ed. C.H. Talbert, New York: Crossroad, 1984, pp. 104-28.

Sandmel, S., *Anti-Semitism in the New Testament?*, Philadelphia: Fortress, 1978.

—'The Haggada within Scripture', *JBL* 80 (1961), pp. 105-22.

Sawyer, J., 'The Qumran Reading of Isaiah 6:13', *ASTI* 3 (1964), pp. 111-13.

Schaberg, J., *The Father, the Son, and the Holy Spirit: The Triadic Phrase in Matthew 28:19b* (SBLDS 61), Chico: Scholars, 1981.

Schaff, P., *Nicene and Post-Nicene Fathers of the Christian Church*, Grand Rapids: Eerdmans, 1956.

Schmidt, J.M., 'Gedanken zum Verstockungsauftrag Jesajas (Jes. 6)', *VT* 21 (1971), pp. 68-90.

Schnackenburg, R., *The Gospel according to St John*, 3 vols., New York: Seabury, 1980.

Schoeps, H.J., *Paul: The Theology of the Apostle in the Light of Jewish Religious History*, Philadelphia: Westminster, 1961.

Schoors, A., 'Isaiah, Minister of Royal Anointment', *OTS* 20 (1979), pp. 85-107.

Schreiner, J., 'Zur Textgestalt von Jes 6 und 7, 1-17', *BZ* 22 (1978) pp. 92-97.

Schweizer, E., *The Good News according to Mark*, Atlanta: John Knox, 1970.

—*The Good News according to Matthew*, Atlanta: John Know, 1975.

—'Towards a Christology of Mark?', *God's Christ and His People*, N.A. Dahl Festschrift, ed. J. Jervell and W.A. Meeks, Oslo: Universitetsforlaget, 1977, pp. 29-42.

Scullion, J., 'An Approach to the Understanding of Isa. 7:16-17', *JBL* 87 (1968), pp. 288-300.

Seeligmann, I.L., *The Septuagint Version of Isaiah: A Discussion of Its Problems*, Leiden: Brill, 1948.

Shires, H., *Finding the Old Testament in the New*, Philadelphia: Westminster, 1974.

Siegman, E.F., 'Teaching in Parables (Mk 4, 10-12; Lk. 8, 9-10; Mt. 13, 10-15)', *CBQ* 23 (1961), pp. 161-81.

Skemp, A.E., '"Immanuel" and "Suffering Servant of Yahweh", a Suggestion', *EvT* 44 (1932), pp. 44-45.

Smith, D.M., 'The Setting and Shape of a Johannine Narrative Source', *JBL* 95 (1976), pp. 231-41.

Smith, R.L., *Micah–Malachi* (WBC 32), Waco: Word, 1984.

Snodgrass, K.R., *The Parable of the Wicked Tenants: An Inquiry into Parable Interpretation* (WUNT 27), Tübingen: Mohr (Siebeck), 1983.

Sperber, A., *The Bible in Aramaic*, vol. 3, Leiden: Brill, 1962.

Steck, O.H., 'Beiträge zum Verständnis von Jesaja 7, 10-17 und 8, 1-4', *TZ* 29 (1973), pp. 161-78.

—'Bemerkungen zu Jesaja 6', *BZ* 16 (1972), pp. 18-206.

—'Rettung und Verstockung: Exegetische Bemerkungen zu Jesaja 7.3-9', *EvT* 33 (1973), pp. 77-90.

Stegner, W.R., 'Romans 9.6-29—A Midrash', *JSNT* 22 (1984), pp. 37-52.

Steinmetz, D.C., 'John Calvin on Isaiah 6: A Problem in the History of Exegesis', *Int* 36 (1982), pp. 156-70.

Stenning, J.F., *The Targum of Isaiah*, Oxford: Clarendon, 1949.

Suhl, A., *Die Funktion der alttestamentlichen Zitate und Anspielungen im Markusevengelium*, Gütersloh: Mohn, 1965.

Sundberg, A.C., *The Old Testament of the Early Church* (HTS 20), Cambridge: Harvard University, 1964.

Sweeney, M.A., *Isaiah 1-4 and the Post-Exilic Understanding of the Isaianic Tradition* (BZAW 171), Berlin and New York: de Gruyter, 1988.

Tannehill, R.C., 'Israel in Luke-Acts: A Tragic Story', *JBL* 104 (1985), pp. 69-85.

Taylor, J.B., *Ezekiel: An Introduction and Commentary*, London: Tyndale, 1969.

Taylor, V., *The Gospel according to St. Mark*, London: Macmillan, 1966.

Thackeray, H.St.J., *The Relation of St. Paul to Contemporary Jewish Thought*, London: Macmillan, 1900.

Tiede, D.L., *Prophecy and History in Luke-Acts*, Philadelphia: Fortress, 1980.

Torrey, C.C., *The Four Gospels: A New Translation*, New York: Harpers, 1933.

—*The Second Isaiah*, New York: Scribner's, 1928.

Tyson, J.B., *The Death of Jesus in Luke-Acts*, Columbia: University of South Carolina, 1986.

Vermes, G., 'Bible and Midrash: Early Old Testament Exegesis', *The Cambridge History of the Bible*, ed. P.R. Ackroyd and C.F. Evans, Cambridge: Cambridge University Press, 1970, vol. 1, pp. 199-231.

—*Scripture and Tradition in Judaism* (SPB 4), Leiden: Brill, 1973.

—*The Dead Sea Scrolls in English*, New York: Penguin, 1975.

Vermeylen, J., *Du Prophète Isaïe à l'apocalyptique: Isaïe i-xxxv, miroir d'un demi-millénaire d'expérience religieuse en Israel* (EtB), vol. 1, Paris: Gabalda, 1977.

Vischer, W., *Die Immanuel-Botschaft im Rahmen des königlichen Zionfestes* (Theologische Studien 45), Zollikon-Zürich: Evangelischer Verlag, 1955.

Vogt, E., 'Fragmenta prophetarum minorum deserti Juda', *Bib* 34 (1953), pp. 423-26.

Vriezen, Th. C., 'Essentials of the Theology of Isaiah', *Israel's Prophetic Heritage*, J. Muilenburg Festschrift, ed. B.W. Anderson and W. Harrelson, New York: Harper & Row, 1962, pp. 128-46.

—'Prophecy and Eschatology', *VTSup* 1 (1953), pp. 199-229.

Ward, J.M., *Amos & Isaiah: Prophets of the Word of God*, Nashville: Abingdon, 1969.

Watson, F., 'The Social Function of Mark's Secrecy Theme', *JSNT* 24 (1985), pp. 49-69.

Watts, J.D.W., *Isaiah 1-33* (WBC 24), Waco: Word, 1985.

Weeden, T.J., *Mark-Traditions in Conflict*, Philadelphia: Fortress, 1971.

Weiser, A., *Die Profetie des Amos* (BZAW 53), Giessen: Töpelmann, 1929.

Wenham, D., 'The Synoptic Problem Revisited: Some New Suggestions about the Composition of Mark 4:1-34', *TynBul* 23 (1972), pp. 3-38.

Westermann, C., *Isaiah 40-66* (OTL), Philadelphia: Westminster, 1969.

Whedbee, J.W., *Isaiah and Wisdom*, New York: Abingdon, 1971.

Whitley, C., 'The Call and Mission of Isaiah', *JNES* 18 (1959), pp. 38-48.

Wildberger, H., *Jesaja 1-12* (BKAT 10/1), Neukirchen -Vluyn: Neukirchener Verlag, 1972.

—*Jesaja, das Buch, der Prophet und seine Botschaft* (BKAT 10/3), Neukirchener-Vluyn: Neukirchener Verlag, 1982.

Williams, C.S.C., *A Commentary on the Acts of the Apostles* (HNTC), New York: Harper & Row, 1957.

Wilson, R.R., 'The Hardening of Pharaoh's Heart', *CBQ* 41 (1979), pp. 18-36.

Windisch, H., 'Die Verstockungsidee in Mc 4:12 und das Kausale ἵνα in der spätern Koine', *ZNW* 25 (1927), pp. 203-209.

Wolf, H., 'A Solution to the Immanuel Prophecy in Isaiah 7:14–8:22', *JBL* 91 (1972), pp. 449-56.

Worschech, U., 'The Problem of Isaiah 6:13', *AUSS* 12 (1974), pp. 126-38.

Wrede, W., *The Messianic Secret*, Cambridge: James Clarke, 1971.

Wright, A.G., *The Literary Genre Midrash*, Staten Island: Alba House, 1967.

Wright, W., *Apocryphal Acts of the Apostles*, 2 vols., London and Edinburgh: Williams & Norgate, 1871.

Würthwein, E., *The Text of the Old Testament*, Grand Rapids: Eerdmans, 1979.

York, A.D., 'The Dating of Targumic Literature', *JSJ* 5 (1974), pp. 49-62.

Young, E.J., *The Book of Isaiah* (3 vols.), Grand Rapids: Eerdmans, 1965, 1969, 1972.

Ziegler, J., *Septuaginta: Vetus Testamentum Graecum: Isaias*, vol. 14, Göttingen: Vandenhoeck & Ruprecht, 1939.

—*Untersuchungen zur LXX des Buch Isaias*, Münster: Aschendorff, 1934.

Zimmerli, W., *Ezekiel 1* (Hermeneia), Philadelphia: Fortress, 1979.

INDEXES

INDEX OF ANCIENT WRITINGS

I. OLD TESTAMENT

II. OLD TESTAMENT APOCRYPHA AND PSEUDEPIGRAPHA

III. NEW TESTAMENT

IV. QUMRAN

V. PHILO

VI. RABBINICAL LITERATURE

VII. NAG HAMMADI

VIII. PATRISTIC LITERATURE

IX. GREEK LITERATURE

X. CHURCH THEOLOGIANS

XI. OTHER ANCIENT LITERATURE

INDEX OF MODERN AUTHORS